CORRIGIBLE CORPORATIONS & UNRULY LAW

CORRIGIBLE CORPORATIONS & UNRULY LAW

John Braithwaite   John Byrne   Ton DeVos
Brent Fisse   Peter A. French   Gilbert Geis
Steven M. Hoffman   Jed S. Rakoff   Christopher D. Stone

Edited by
Brent Fisse and Peter A. French

Trinity University Press
San Antonio

Library of Congress Cataloging-in-Publication Data
Main entry under title:

Corrigible corporations and unruly law.

Bibliography: p. 217
Includes index.
1. Corporation law – United States. 2. White collar
crimes – United States. 3. Corporations – United States –
Corrupt practices. 4. Industry – Social aspects – United
States. I. Fisse, Brent. II. French, Peter A.
KF1414.C68   1985   346.73'066   85-20825
ISBN 0-939980-12-6   347.30666
ISBN 0-939980-13-4 (pbk.)

Manufactured in the United States of America

Trinity University Press • 715 Stadium Drive • San Antonio, Texas 78284

CONTENTS

PREFACE

Corrigible Corporations and Unruly Law began with "Contemporary Problems of Corporate Regulation," a conference in November 1983 sponsored by Trinity University, and later emerged from the chrysalis of San Antonio as this free-flying collection of essays.

In presenting these essays, an animating assumption has been that corporations are highly adaptive institutions which, given suitably structured and imaginatively designed laws, are capable of being persuaded or induced to choose and implement effective compliance policies. Rejected is the latter-day Spencerian notion that corporations are such complex entities that legal controls must be left to evolve and not to be created. The capacities of the modern corporation bear little resemblance to those of the Galápagos turtle: in the breeding ground of trade and commerce, a corporation that fails to undergo frequent metamorphoses soon becomes extinct.

Also rejected is the other extreme of single-minded or grand design. The law's response to corporate wrongdoing is typically regarded as primitive and unruly yet the paths of reform obscure. There is a need for much more interdisciplinary study of corporate behavior in the shadow of law, but this should not be a futile attempt to reduce the elusive phenomenon of law to some one-dimensional precept (e.g., efficiency, in the economic analysis of law; moon-phase, in horoscopic analysis of law). All of the essays to follow avoid dogma and recast much of the debate about issues which are central to the future course of corporate regulation.

We owe a number of special debts. Trinity University generously funded the conference at which a number of the papers originally were given and gave us the opportunity to work together to edit them in San Antonio during the fall semester 1983. The University of Adelaide, Australia, supplied extensive secretarial and research assistance and contributed toward the cost of a return visit to Trinity University by Brent Fisse in August 1984 when we continued our collaboration in finalizing this volume. The University of Sydney has recently hosted the final secretarial and research tasks. Beyond institutions, we warmly thank our contributors. All maintained an exemplary state of compliance throughout, so exemplary that we were soon forced to abandon our experiment with that very promising white-collar sanction, the pre-dawn trans-Pacific telephone call. We thank Virginia L. Redford for her attentive assistance in proofreading the various stages. Finally, we are greatly indebted to Lois A. Boyd, editor of Trinity University Press, for the grace and expertise with which she cracked several computer systems and converted our manuscript to public use.

Brent Fisse
Peter A. French

THE CONTRIBUTORS

JOHN BRAITHWAITE is a Senior Research Fellow, Department of Sociology, Research School of Social Sciences, Australian National University, Canberra. Formerly a Research Criminologist at the Australian Institute of Criminology, 1978-83, in 1979 he held a Fulbright Postdoctoral Fellowship at the United Nations Center on Transnational Corporations and the Program in Social Ecology, University of California, Irvine. Braithwaite is the author of six books in the fields of sociology and criminology, including *Inequality, Crime, and Public Policy, Corporate Crime in the Pharmaceutical Industry,* and *To Punish or Persuade.*

JOHN BYRNE is the director of the Center for Energy and Urban Policy Research and an assistant professor in the College of Urban Affairs and Public Policy, University of Delaware. He is the editor of *Energy Policy Studies,* an annual book series concerned with the political and economic dimensions of energy technology, production, and use. He has published articles and books on regulatory policy, cost-benefit analysis, technology policy, and urban political economy, and he coedited *Energy and Cities* and *The Solar Energy Transition: Implementation and Policy Implications.*

TON DEVOS is a professor of political science at Trinity University. His publications include *Introduction to Politics,* a textbook, and *U.S. Multinationals and Worker Participation in Management: The American Experience in the European Community.* He wrote the "Conservatism," "Political Science," and "Radicalism" entries in the new *American Academic Encyclopaedia,* and four chapters of his dissertation *(A Case Study in the Effectiveness of the United States Information Service in the Netherlands,* University of Oklahoma, 1962) have been a core component of the instruction at the Foreign Service Institute of the United States Information Agency.

BRENT FISSE is a professor of law at the University of Sydney, Australia. A Bicentennial Fellow in Criminal Law and Administration at the University of Pennsylvania Law School in 1968-69, he has held several university posts in the U.S., including that of Mitchell Visiting Distinguished Professor at Trinity University, Texas. His publications include *The Impact of Publicity on Corporate Offenders* (with John Braithwaite), and "Reconstructing Corporate Criminal Law: Deterrence, Retribution, Fault, and Sanctions," *Southern California Law Review.*

PETER A. FRENCH is Lennox Distinguished Professor of the Humanities, professor of philosophy, and chairman of the Department of Philosophy at Trinity University. He is the author of twelve books including *Shame and the Corporation, Collective and Corporate Responsibility, Ethics in Government,* and *The Scope of Morality.* He is senior editor of *Midwest Studies in Philosophy* and was general editor of the *Issues in Contemporary Ethics* series. He has published numerous articles in major philosophical journals and anthologies.

GILBERT GEIS is a professor in the Program in Social Ecology, University of California, Irvine. Formerly President of the American Society of Criminology, Geis has written numerous books on white-collar crime including *White-Collar Criminal* and *On White Collar Crime.* Recently, he coedited the Yale University Press revised, uncut edition of Edwin Sutherland's classic, *White Collar Crime.*

STEVEN HOFFMAN is a research associate in the Center for Energy and Urban Policy Research at the University of Delaware. He is also an instructor in the Department of Economics. He has published articles and research monographs in the areas of utility regulation, economic development and finance, and capital market behavior. His current research is concerned with issues of risk and uncertainty in economic theory.

JED S. RAKOFF is a partner in the Wall Street law firm of Mudge, Rose, Guthrie, Alexander & Ferdon, having formerly served as Assistant United States Attorney, Southern District of New York and chief of Business Frauds Prosecutions for that office. Rakoff is a co-author of *Business Crime,* a six-volume treatise, *Criminal Law and the Corporate Counsel,* and several other books in the area of corporate regulation.

CHRISTOPHER D. STONE is Roy P. Crocker Professor of Law at the University of Southern California. He is the author of *Law, Language & Ethics; Should Trees Have Standing?;* and *Where the Law Ends: The Social Control of Corporate Behavior.*

CORRIGIBLE CORPORATIONS & UNRULY LAW

CHAPTER 1

OVERVIEW: THE SOCIAL CONTROL OF CORPORATE BEHAVIOR

Brent Fisse and Peter A. French

Law is a curious blend of theory and practice and nowhere is the blend more curious than in the context of corporate regulation. This is largely because law is quintessentially interdisciplinary, neither art nor science, and the interdisciplinary study of corporate activities crawls in its infancy. This book provides a range of perspectives on the social control of corporate behavior, whether by means of controls aimed at the corporate entity or controls aimed at individuals acting on behalf of the corporation. Our prognosis is that only through further interdisciplinary studies is the law likely to develop in useful directions. No detailed program for legislative or administrative action is offered by the contributions, but the discussions are intended to help inform and guide policymaking among the many publics which have a stake in our corporate society.

Corporate wrongdoing (or, as some prefer to term it, "white-collar crime" committed by or on behalf of an organization) is a serious social problem.[1] The economic costs of corporate malfeasance are considerable; for instance, the Department of Justice has estimated that the annual loss is in the order of $10-20 billion, and other official estimates run as high as $174-231 billion.[2] The physical costs of corporate wrongs are also heavy. Again, the estimates vary, but it is undeniable that far more persons are killed or injured as a result of corporate offenses or violations than as a result of so-called street crime.[3] Furthermore, the speculation is rife that corporate wrongdoing erodes the moral fabric of society. As Edwin Sutherland cautioned:

> The financial cost from white collar crime, great as it is, is less important than the damage to social relations. White collar crimes violate trust and, therefore, create distrust; this lowers social morale and produces social disorganization. Many of the white collar crimes attack the fundamental principles of the American institutions.[4]

These perceptions are not elitist academic exaggerations but are shared by many in the general community. In one recent study of attitudes toward the seriousness of crimes, a national sample of 8,000 respondents rated white-collar crimes causing injury to persons, such as lethal toxic waste pollution, as extremely serious.[5] Even as long ago as 1969, another national sample taken by Louis Harris revealed antipathy, rather than neutrality, toward corporate crime. A manufacturer of unsafe automobiles was regarded as a worse culprit than a mugger by 68 percent of the respondents, only 21 percent being of contrary opinion.[6] A business person who illegally fixed prices was deemed more blameworthy than a burglar by 54 percent, while only 28 percent believed a burglar to be worse.[7] In addition to this and other survey evidence, there have been numerous public outcries over actual or alleged corporate offenses.[8] One of many examples is the Kepone case, which involved the unlawful discharge of pesticide wastes from the factories of Allied Chemical and Life Science Products.[9] The adverse publicity that ensued left no doubt that, no matter how many millions of dollars the companies might have decided to spend in order to help clean up the James and Chesapeake Rivers, there still would have been massive public resentment toward the companies because the damage done was irremediable.[10] Thus, the available evidence shows that corporate offenses not only are thought to be serious, they are sometimes passionately regarded to be so.

Expressing strong disapproval of corporate wrongdoing is one thing; providing sound well-tempered legal controls is quite another.[11] The present law employs a variety of controls, including negotiation and bargaining, civil monetary and injunctive remedies, licensing, and individual and corporate criminal liability. This array of controls has developed in largely a piecemeal fashion, and a good deal of criticism has emerged, essentially to the effect that much of the present law is inept or inefficient because it is not based on a clear and consistent policy foundation.[12] The response to this criticism has been the construction of a spectacularly wide spectrum of proposals for reform, ranging from Radical Non-Intervention (deregulation)[13] at one extreme, to Radical Intervention (state management)[14] at the other. The outcome today, put simply, is knowledge of where the present law ends, but uncertainty about exactly where a program of responsive law should begin.

One strategy for coping with this uncertainty is to abandon the idea of implementing any rationally revised policy and to resort instead to an evolutionary approach which allows the law to mature steadily in light of experience;[15] the usual title bestowed upon this strategy is Incrementalism or, in the vernacular, "muddling through."[16] Superficially attractive as this strategy may be, it is profoundly unsatisfactory. Incrementalism rests most fundamentally on the postulate that our social theories are too shaky to form the basis for policymaking, but the alternative postulate advanced is that a series of small "knee jerk" reactions is likely to work best.[17] Robert Goodin, however, has persuasively argued that there is no reason to believe that this is so.[18] On the contrary, "sleeper" and other effects beyond the scope of incremental anticipation or correction make Incrementalism foolhardy, especially in a setting where the social forces are as powerful as those of corporate action and inaction. Moreover, the suppression of theory under Incrementalism comes close to saying that social choice should depend on some cybernetic process akin to the dance of the bees;[19] tempting as it is to depict human beings as hive-bound, such a depiction is allegorical and affirms rather than denies the ideal of rational human choice.

A second possibility for coping with the uncertain future of corporate regulation is to adopt a single-minded strategy, the strategy of Monism.[20] The essence of this strategy is to reconstruct the law in accordance with the basic canons found in some other discipline; the pragmatic complexity of law is abandoned in favor of the doctrinaire simplicity of an external faith. To date, the most-favored external faith has been economics; for many commentators, including Richard Posner and other prominent lawyer-economists, reform should be governed by the economic analysis of law.[21] Attempts to reduce law to monistic order, however, are highly problematical because law is much more obviously a reflection of a multi-valued society than a projection of any ground-norm derived from a particular intellectual discipline. And why should efficiency, the ground-norm of economics, necessarily prevail over the guidance to be found in philosophy or other disciplines? Though economics may well be the queen of the social sciences, a host of other disciplines might conjunctively constitute the king.[22]

Pluralism, the strategy of rational interdisciplinary choice, if such is the case, recommends itself. Pluralism is a rather high-flown way of describing what many policymakers do if they reject Incrementalism and Monism.[23] The initial step is to assemble as much interdisciplinary material as possible on a given problem of law reform. That material is sifted carefully for clues as to defects in the present law and for insights about promising future directions. Basic criticisms and proposals for reform are then generated and, by dint of concentration, reiterative analysis, lateral thinking, comparison and weighting of alternatives, and feats of estimation and imagination, a commendable policy and program is formulated. Ultimately, after further review in light of consultation with others, the policy and program are revised and presented in expanded or contracted form as a prescription for change. This strategy hardly yields automatic or absolute answers, but it does avoid the atheoretical bias of Incrementalism as well as the tunnel vision of Monism. It is this open-ended spirit of rational inquiry which we commend, and it is the strategy which animates the presentation of this collection of interdisciplinary analyses.

The chapters to follow provide a diverse range of perspectives on the social control of corporate behavior. These perspectives do not necessarily represent the orthodox views held within any particular discipline, whether law, economics, sociology, philosophy, or political science. Certainly, they do not cover the full galaxy of the unorthodox. What we have attempted to do is to present a selective number of contributions which, in offering different interdisciplinary reflections on the corporate regulatory condition, help to further our understanding of both the limits and the possibilities of law as a means of controlling corporate wrongdoing.

The opening essay, "Corporate Regulation: The Place of Social Responsibility," is by Christopher Stone, the author of a landmark work on corporate regulation, *Where the Law Ends: The Social Control of Corporate Behavior*. In the first part of his contribution, Stone reviews the extent to which interventionist techniques of legal control should be used against corporations, the conclusion being that intervention should be the exception rather than the rule. In spelling out the prime circumstances in which the law should interfere directly with internal managerial structures or decisionmaking, Stone offers a circumspect reflection upon the limits of the bold interventionist thesis he advanced in *Where the Law Ends*. The second part of the essay is devoted to the classic unresolved issue of corporate profits vs. corporate moral responsibility. Here, Stone explores a number of interesting prudential and ethical ways in which the conflict might be reduced and, in canvassing several possible legal methods for fostering ethical decisionmaking, offers a fresh slant on the relationship between corporate law and corporate morality.

The second essay, "Taking Responsibility Seriously: Corporate Compliance Systems," is by John Braithwaite, a sociologist. Braithwaite's central thesis is that while much attention has been paid to corporate compliance policies, not nearly enough has been done to ensure that those policies are backed by effective compliance systems. The more promising avenues for strengthening compliance systems are reviewed, with particular emphasis on promoting vigilance on the part of the board of directors, open corporate governance and improved lines of internal communication, minimization of pressures conducive to irresponsibility, and identification of the key features of successful compliance systems. What makes this review especially valuable is the unique empirical experience the author brings to bear upon his subject: in recent years Braithwaite has interviewed literally hundreds of executives about compliance policies and procedures in major corporations around the world.[24]

The next chapter, "Criminological Perspectives on Corporate Regulation: A Review of Recent Research," is by Gilbert Geis, a preeminent post-Sutherland scholar in this field and the editor of the recently published "uncut" version of Sutherland's *White Collar Crime*.[25] This contribution provides a timely overview and critique of the numerous major research studies which have emerged in recent years. One facet of Geis's commentary is his reading of the divisive debate which arose over Sutherland's far-reaching definition of white collar crime, as followed by Clinard and Yeager in their sociologically oriented work, *Corporate Crime*,[26] and as often denounced by lawyers as misguided. Another facet of note is the portrayal of the deep distrust of business among many criminologists. Yet, as Geis observes, from that standpoint it is puzzling why, given the minimum risks involved, there is not a great deal more corporate crime than there seems to be. The insights offered by Geis on these and other issues underpin his conclusion that what really matters is the hidden use and abuse of corporate power and that this is the condition against which the more significant work on white-collar crime is directed.

"Toward More Effective Regulation of Corporate Behavior," by Ton DeVos, a political scientist, sets out a sober reappraisal of the regulatory and academic strategies which are most likely to win out in the struggle over corporate social responsibility. DeVos reminds us that much of what passes for regulation may be window dressing, and that a laissez-faire policy has always held widespread appeal among the American people. The "confrontational posturing" of many academic critics of business is then criticized on the ground that such a stance has inhibited productive political dialogue. DeVos also doubts the political feasibility of any extensive reform of criminal sanctions and other legal controls, largely because of the continuing influence of corporate interest groups and the surviving popular belief in the doctrine of laissez-faire. After a review of the limitations of legal liability and consumer boycotts as a means of inducing corporations to modify their behavior, DeVos suggests that the greatest promise lies in altering intracorporate motivations through noncoercive techniques. Much stress is also placed on the need for systematic research on the social costs of corporate violations and other factors specified as major items on the political agenda for corporate regulation.

Two political economists, John Byrne and Steven M. Hoffman, have written the sixth chapter, "Efficient Corporate Harm: A Chicago Metaphysic." This is an extensive critique of mainstream economic analysis of corporate liability for wrongdoing. Numerous economic analyses of corporate liability have now appeared, one seminal work being Elzinga and Breit's *The Antitrust Penalties*, but very few commentaries have challenged the assumptions on which the leading economic analyses are based.[27] Byrne and Hoffman set out clearly in jargon-free language what the pivotal economic assumptions are and then examine each of them critically. This criticism builds upon not only the contributions of Shackle and other economists who have swum against the mainstream, but also the views of Simon and others who have looked beyond the rational actor hypothesis toward the nature and implications of organizational behavior. The conclusion of Byrne and Hoffman is that any global attempt to use the canon of efficiency to govern the design and application of corporate liability is unjustified in theory and impossible in practice. The essay is thus highly provocative, and we see it as filling a major gap in the literature.

The essay by Brent Fisse, "Sanctions against Corporations: The Limitations of Fines and the Enterprise of Creating Alternatives," proceeds from a perceived need to devise more effective sanctions for the deterrence of corporate wrongdoing. Fines and monetary penalties are criticized as being often weak in impact and prone to causing unjust overspills. Four alternative possibilities – stock dilution (equity fines), probation, publicity orders, and community service orders – are canvassed with particular reference to their potential capacity for avoiding the previously identified limitations of fines. It is argued that, although fines undoubtedly have some role to play in any sentencing program, the potential advantages of the nonmonetary sanctions outlined justify their introduction as options for use where serious offenses have been committed. Many questions of design and application thereby arise, and the more important of these are mentioned by way of conclusion.

Peter A. French's "Publicity and the Control of Corporate Conduct: Hester Prynne's New Image," takes the recently revived idea of using publicity as a sanction against corporations and seeks to provide a firm philosophical foundation for it. The core of his argument is the fundamental point that publicity goes hand in hand with a shame-based system of morality. At present, a guilt-based morality system appears to underlie our criminal law, and such a system of morality is objectionable on many grounds. A shame-based approach is more commendable because it stresses forward-looking exemplary models of behavior rather than retrogressive introspection, but this and other features of a shame-based approach have been relatively neglected by philosophers in the past. French highlights the elements of a shame-based system of morality and then explains why the sanction of publicity is necessary and appropriate if shame is to be used effectively in practice. Essentially, shame is seen as a visual concept and one dependent on a sensibility to oneself. An adept penal system, it is argued, is one that can induce shame when there has been a notable incongruity with accepted models of behavior and where it is possible to use the visual and media capabilities of the society to bring out incongruity and to channel the offender's behavior in an exemplary direction.

Jed Rakoff's essay, "The Exercise of Prosecutorial Discretion in Federal Business Fraud Prosecutions," advocates retention of the broad and flexible degree of discretion that prosecutors now have in the area of white-collar crime. The exercise of prosecutorial discretion is not subject to the usual review processes of administrative law. To this extent prosecutors are exempt from the rule of law. This is an odd situation (although one by no means confined to corporate or white-collar crime), and the perceived risk of arbitrary and hence unjust prosecutions is one major obstacle in the path of any attempt to intensify the use of the criminal law against corporations and their executives.[28] Rakoff, who has been actively involved in the prosecution and, more recently, the defense of charges of corporate crime, argues that the present system of discretion works well in practice and that legal constraints upon the exercise of prosecutorial discretion are not only unnecessary but also dangerously restrictive in their potential effect. In opening up what has previously been a notorious low-visibility area of corporate crime, Rakoff's assessment heralds the need for detailed empirical studies which cover a comprehensive range of offenses and which provide a breakdown of the incidence of charges against individual and corporate defendants respectively.

The final essay, "Corporate Responses to Errant Behavior: Time's Arrow, Law's Target," pursues the implications which a reactive time frame of corporate liability has for many of the issues raised in the earlier essays. The argument is that a proactive timeframe has dominated the shape of the present law, that several major problems of corporate regulation stem from this temporal mind-set, and that the resolution of these problems might become possible if the law were reshaped in accordance with the implications of a reactive model. The particular problem areas addressed are four-fold, namely, state intervention in corporate internal affairs, standards of corporate behavior, individual accountability for corporate wrongdoing, and sanctions against corporations. Beyond these problem areas, the authors attempt ultimately to show how a reactive approach might be used to resolve the problem of making the probabilistic calculations required by an economic model of corporate liability. This leads to the conclusion that the impossibility of making such calculations in practice heads the law toward a nonprobabilistic "rules of action" approach, and that the most obvious rules of action are to be found in a reactive model of corporate liability.

It is hoped that the array of interdisciplinary material presented will prove useful in the future direction of corporate regulation. Although no fully armored programs have been attempted, and although we have raised many more questions of policy than have been resolved, our mission has been to challenge and suggest rather than to prescribe, and to live up to what we should expect from theoretical speculation; as James Q. Wilson has counselled,

> Good theory calls attention to obvious truths that were pre-
> viously overlooked, finds crucial flaws in existing theories,
> and reinterprets solid evidence in a new light. And some the-
> ories, if adopted, will make us better-off. The problem is to
> know which ones.[29]

NOTES

1. See generally Ronald C. Kramer, "Corporate Criminality: The Develop-
   ment of an Idea," in Ellen Hochstedler, ed., *Corporations as Criminals*
   (Beverly Hills: Sage Publications, 1984), 13-37; Marshall B. Clinard and
   Peter C. Yeager, *Corporate Crime* (New York: Free Press, 1980).

   By "crime" we mean misbehavior which constitutes an offense under
   existing law, whether the offense is penalized criminally or civilly (e.g.,
   an OSHA violation not causing death is penalized civilly by fine). By
   "offense" we mean to include offenses which some observers would
   describe as *mala prohibita* as well as offenses *mala in se* (as to this unsatisfactory distinction, see Note, "The Distinction between Mala Prohibita
   and Mala in Se," *Columbia Law Review* 30 [1930]: 74-86). By "corporate"
   crime we mean crime attributable to a corporate entity or any responsible individual persons acting on its behalf. For the purposes of this book
   it is unnecessary to attempt a fully armored definition of corporate
   crime. Cf. Leonard Orland, "Reflections on Corporate Crime: Law in
   Search of Theory and Scholarship," *American Criminal Law Review* 17
   (1980): 504-10. "White collar crime" is a broader term which encom-
   passes not only corporate crime in the sense indicated above, but also
   offenses committed by officers or employees *against* corporate employers. See generally Edwin H. Sutherland, *White Collar Crime: The Uncut*

Version (New Haven: Yale University Press, 1983), Ch. 1.

2. Kramer, "Corporate Criminality," 19.

3. Ibid., 19-20.

4. Edwin H. Sutherland, *White-Collar Crime* (New York: Dryden, 1949), 13.

5. M. Wolfgang, National Survey of Crime Severity Final National Level Geometric Means and Ratio Scores by Offense Stimuli Items, unpublished manuscript, Center for Studies in Criminology and Criminal Law, University of Pennsylvania, April 1980.

6. "Changing Morality: The Two Americas," *Time*, 6 June 1969: 26 (*Time*-Louis Harris Poll).

7. Ibid.

8. See e.g., Brent Fisse and John Braithwaite, *The Impact of Publicity on Corporate Offenders* (Albany: State University of New York Press, 1983); Clinard and Yeager, *Corporate Crime*, 14.

9. United States v Allied Chemical Corporation, 420 F. Supp. 122 (1976); Christopher D. Stone, "A Slap on the Wrist for the Kepone Mob," *Business and Society Review* 22 (1977): 4-11.

10. See Fisse and Braithwaite, *The Impact of Publicity on Corporate Offenders*, Ch.6.

11. See generally John C. Coffee, Jr., " 'No Soul to Damn: No Body to Kick': An Unscandalized Inquiry into the Problem of Corporate Punishment," *Michigan Law Review* 79 (1981): 386-459.

12. See e.g., M. David Ermann and Richard J. Lundman, *Corporate Deviance* (New York: Holt, Rinehart and Winston, 1982); Coffee, " 'No Soul to Damn: No Body to Kick' "; Kenneth G. Elzinga and William Breit, *The Antitrust Penalties: A Study in Law and Economics* (New Haven: Yale University Press, 1976); Christopher D. Stone, *Where the Law Ends: The Social Control of Corporate Behavior* (New York: Harper, 1975); John Braithwaite, *Corporate Crime in the Pharmaceutical Industry* (London: Routledge & Kegan Paul, 1984); John C. Coffee, Jr., "Beyond the Shut-Eyed Sentry: Towards a Theoretical View of Corporate Misconduct and an Effective Legal Response," *Virginia Law Review* 63 (1977): 1099-1278; R. Kagan and E. Bardach, *Going by the Book: The Problem of Regulatory Unreasonableness* (Philadelphia: Temple University Press, 1981).

13. See generally Milton and Rose Friedman, *Free to Choose* (New York: Harcourt, Brace Jovanovich, 1980); Ralph K. Winter, *Government and the Corporation* (Washington, D.C.: American Enterprise Institute for Public Policy Research, 1978).

14. See e.g., Stone, *Where the Law Ends*; Brent Fisse, "Responsibility, Prevention, and Corporate Crime," *New Zealand Universities Law Review* 5 (1973): 270-79.

15. See generally D. Braybrooke and C.E. Lindblom, *A Strategy of Decision* (New York: Free Press, 1963); P. Stein, *Legal Evolution* (Cambridge: Cambridge University Press, 1980).

16. Braybrooke and Lindblom, *A Strategy of Decision*.

17. Robert E. Goodin, *Political Theory and Public Policy* (Chicago: University of Chicago Press, 1982), 19-21. The discussion which follows relies heavily on Goodin's incisive analysis.

18. Ibid., 23-28.

19. See generally John Steinbruner, *The Cybernetic Theory of Decision*

(Princeton: Princeton University Press, 1974).

20. See generally Paul Edwards, *The Encyclopedia of Philosophy* 5 (1967): 363-65.

21. See e.g., Richard Posner, *Antitrust Law: An Economic Perspective* (Chicago: University of Chicago Press, 1976); *Economic Analysis of Law*, 2d ed. (Boston, Mass: Little Brown and Company, 1977); Elzinga and Breit, *The Antitrust Penalties*.

22. See generally Hugh Stretton, *The Political Sciences* (London: Routledge & Kegan Paul, 1969).

23. Consider e.g., John Braithwaite, "Enforced Self-Regulation: A New Strategy for Corporate Crime Control," *Michigan Law Review* 80 (1982): 1466-1507; Coffee, "Beyond the Shut-Eyed Sentry"; Brent Fisse, "Reconstructing Corporate Criminal Law: Deterrence, Retribution, Fault, and Sanctions," *Southern California Law Review* 56 (1983): 1141-1246; Christopher D. Stone, "The Place of Enterprise Liability in the Control of Corporate Conduct," *Yale Law Journal* 90 (1980): 1-77.

24. See e.g., John Braithwaite, *To Punish or Persuade* (Albany: State University of New York Press, 1985); *Corporate Crime in the Pharmaceutical Industry*; "Enforced Self-Regulation."

25. Edwin H. Sutherland, *White Collar Crime: The Uncut Version* (New Haven: Yale University Press, 1983).

26. Clinard and Yeager, *Corporate Crime*.

27. A notable exception is John C. Coffee, Jr., "Corporate Crime and Punishment: A Non-Chicago View of the Economics of Criminal Sanctions," *American Criminal Law Review* 17 (1980): 419-76.

28. See e.g., "Developments in the Law – Corporate Crime: Regulating Corporate Criminal Behavior Through Criminal Sanctions," *Harvard Law Review* 92 (1979): 1308-11.

29. James Q. Wilson, " 'Policy Intellectuals' and Public Policy," *Public Interest* 64 (1981): 46.

CHAPTER 2
CORPORATE REGULATION: THE PLACE OF SOCIAL RESPONSIBILITY

Christopher D. Stone

It is no wonder that conferences on corporate regulation are occurring more frequently, that more books are being written, all with, it seems, ever more urgent a tone. Our society has become a corporate society. The human birthrate may be on the wane, but the corporate "birthrate" (measured by new certificates of incorporation issued) is soaring. And it is not merely in the business sector – among the "for-profits" – that this dramatic growth is taking place. The same trend, the same proliferation of formal bureaucratic institutions, is occurring across all the governmental, charitable, and nonprofit sectors.

In this context, one does not have to buy the line that corporations are evil institutions, run by bad people, to be concerned about corporate responsibility. The fact is simply that today, when things are done, they are being done increasingly, through (and by, and to) corporations. As a consequence, when something goes wrong, whether a toxic spill or a swindle, chances are good that a corporation will be implicated. This is not to say that the law can ignore the control of ordinary persons, but that the design of social institutions, once focused almost exclusively on how to deal with individual persons acting on their own account, has to be reconsidered in the light of a society in which bureaucratic organizations have come to dominate the landscape, and when persons are accounted for, if at all, not simply as individuals, but as officeholders.

Ironically, at the same time that these organizations serve to amplify human power, they also divide and diffuse the accountability of the humans who labor within them, the officeholders who bring that amplification about. Hence, corporations present unique and often frustrating problems of control: How are we to keep them within socially approved bounds? We can fine them, oust the corporation from its charter, suspend its license to do business, enjoin it, pack its executives off to jail. We will see, throughout this anthology, a good deal about the relative strengths and weaknesses of some of those devices. I do not want to anticipate those discussions, but we all know the problem in principle. There continues to be an uneasy feeling – a rare point of agreement among practicing lawyers, judges, scholars and businesspersons – that when it comes to controlling corporations, there is a need for something other than conventional legal mechanisms: Call it "corporate social responsibility." What I will discuss is this: How can all the vague and lofty talk about this "something other" – whatever of it, at least, that has merit – be transformed into tangible and workable institutional design?

Let me first explain how I use the term corporate social responsibility. For me, if the term is to have any real significance, it has to denote a way of modifying corporate conduct that contrasts with, and is defined against the backdrop of, the generally prevailing techniques employed for modifying corporate behavior.

The conventional approach is three-tiered. First and fundamentally, the firm is subject to the discipline of its various markets. A company that saves money by producing shoddy goods, or cutting corners on employee safety, tends to get a bad reputation, so as to risk some offsetting losses when it comes to hiring, selling, and borrowing. If the disincentives the market attaches to misconduct are too weak, we can superimpose the discipline of law. In some circumstances, this takes the form of adding to the ordinary commercial risks of misconduct the risks of the market-measured damages the firm may cause, ordinarily through civil liability, but possibly also through some surrogate, such as a pollution tax. If the specter of these ordinary damages inadequately deters, we can superimpose the third tier of discipline: Penalties, punitive damages, and fines. The point to notice about all three tiers is that while they differ in degree, they share a common assumption about how corporations are best controlled: That the way to deter undesired behavior is through threats against enterprise profits.[1] In this, the conventional approach, it is left entirely to the enterprise participants (the managers, ordinarily) to decide how best to avoid the prospective penalties of the law, just as it is left to them to avoid the penalties of the market.

It is against this background that one must consider what those who, like myself, are advocating when we speak of corporate misconduct. Quite simply: We have considerable misgivings about the efficacy of this conventional strategy for controlling corporate misconduct. The proposals for institutionalizing corporate social responsibility – divided into two categories – are each a response to a distinguishable misgiving. One set of challenges generates what I shall call Interventionism; a second, Voluntarism. In roughest outline, the Interventionist wants to amend the law; in particular, to nudge the corporation into a more responsible posture (in effect, to make it mimic the behavior of a responsible person) by directly ordering certain alterations in enterprise variables that are presently affected only indirectly through the contingent threat against profits. The Voluntarist challenge is more thoroughgoing. It questions the adequacy not only of the market, but of the law, as well – even of the law as it might emerge after the Interventionist had reformed it. Thus, the Voluntarist wing of the Responsibility Movement is not satisfied merely to amend, as would the Interventionist, the company's bureaucratic and organizational structure; the Voluntarist would go on to amend, if need be, the very goals and constraints of the corporation, to substitute some other table of values for what is (law-corrected) profitable.

I will examine, in turn, these two challenges to the prevailing system, these two wings, as I would call them, of the Corporate Social Responsibility movement.

Interventionism

The conventional legal approach to control corporate misconduct, already alluded to, relies predominantly on what I have called Harm-Based Enterprise Liability Rules (HBELRs).[2] The rules are harm-based in that the law stays its hand unless and until the enterprise engages in the unwanted conduct or causes the unwanted outcome. The rules are enterprise-based in that they target the enterprise as an inpenetrable atom, leaving its participants free, so far as the "outside world" is concerned, to reach whatever internal arrangements they may bargain for as how best to avoid the law's judgments and how to allocate the burdens of those judgments it fails to escape. If the firm is convicted of a crime, "it," ordinarily, pays the judgment either directly or indirectly; thereafter, the shareholders may replace the managers, the managers may hire new subordinates, the subordinates may redesign a plant layout – or they may do nothing at all.

One line of the Interventionists' criticism goes to the first part, the harm-based, and, hence, after-the-fact character of the current system. More directly preventative measures, aimed specifically at organizational policies and procedures, can be supported in many circumstances, such as where there is a deep societal aversion to a particular sort of catastrophe (a nuclear explosion, for example); where the injuries that are envisioned may be inadequately compensable (genetic damage); and where the complexity and costs of after-the-fact litigation may deprive the injured party of compensation and put undue strains on the dispute-resolving institutions (such as where the injurious agent, e.g., asbestos, may have originated from many sources over many years, making it hard to sort out who was to blame).

A second criticism takes issue with current emphasis on making the enterprise the law's quarry and, in particular, questions the underlying economic and managerial assumptions on which that approach is based. Specifically, the conventional wisdom presumes that, in the face of the law's threats against firm profits, the enterprise participants will modify their behavior in the correct (socially ideal) way. For one thing, this strategy is almost certainly at its *best* (whatever its weaknesses) as applied to the for-profit corporations. As applied to public corporations, charities, associations, and many other forms of non-profit corporations, even more problematical is how effective the threat of monetary penalties will be. Even if we limit ourselves to companies that are, ostensibly, profit-seeking, many reasons remain to question the capacity of the law to modify adequately their behavior.

The enterprise-targeting strategy is undermined, for example, by bars to judgment – limited liability and bankruptcy – by virtue of which the investors may never have to settle up the liabilities that their enterprise incurs. What real teeth are there in the threat of damages against an asbestos manufacturer if it can simply declare bankruptcy when the liability prospects look too grim? Bars to judgment aside, there is the possibility that the managers, over some interval (presumably when profits are sufficient to retain them in power), may trade off the maximization of share values for the maximization of some competing value, such as prestige, expansion, or sales volume, making the firm less responsive to the profit-threats whose effectiveness the law is presuming. The enterprise may be "irrational" in the sense of employing an abnormally high discount rate, which will dilute the present force of anticipated penalties. Or the managers may underestimate the legal risks; that is, in their enthusiasm for their own undertaking, attach too low a probability to the hazards they are raising. Or they may find that some risks that the law has made unacceptable to the investors are not dissuasive to them: Profit-sharing arrangements may be so skewed that the managers stand to capture a goodly share of a dramatic immediate success (such as if their new drug becomes a commercial triumph), while being shielded, relatively speaking, from severe, but possibly remote, risks on the downside (such as if the drug becomes another Thalidomide). There is the further possibility that even if the law does motivate the managers properly, they may not be able to exercise the requisite control over the far-flung operating divisions and lower-level employees – the bowels of the firm, where much of the trouble brews.[3]

These criticisms are telling even if we lack evidence that such deviations from the classical, profit-maximizing behavior of the textbooks are in fact widespread. In designing legal strategies we cannot pass over as lightly as can the macroeconomist the significance of even scattered incidents of nonrational firm activity. The macroeconomist aims to portray the whole economy in its broad contours, a task which demands no close attention to the fine lines of individual deviations from the norm; statistically, these tend to cancel one another out, particularly over time, as persistently deviant firms fall by the wayside. But when our concern shifts to the restraint of misconduct, we cannot so easily disregard the "irrational" actors, for many of the same reasons that the laws designed to constrain ordinary persons have to be written, not so much with the model citizen in mind, but with the aberrant – the demented killer, the sociopathic thief. Hence, so far as the law presumes that corporations are simply the Economic Man of the textbooks writ large, it has not adequately prepared to deal with the risks they present.

What the Interventionist Would Do About It

In light of these misgivings about such conventional strategies, the Interventionist favors the law taking an approach that is at once more preventative and more intrusive. Instead of trying to daunt the managers into taking appropriate precautions indirectly, through threat of a future profit loss, the Interventionist would require a present precaution directly, even to the point of displacing managerial discretion over how the very management system itself is designed. In effect, the law shifts its emphasis from penalizing outcomes to mandating process.

The connection with responsibility can be appreciated if we model what being responsible involves in the case of an ordinary person and then ask how those patterns of conduct can be institutionalized into an organization. To begin with, responsible persons are ones who, at the least, think before they act, not only about the benefits to themselves, but about the effects their actions are likely to have on others. They gather and take into account information bearing on distant consequences, on how their choices will impact neighbors and neighborhood. They weigh alternatives with reference to certain socially sensitive categories, e.g., "right," "wrong," "harm."

It is useful to think of the Interventionist reforms in this light, as aiming to impinge the firm's bureaucratic structure in such a way that the corporate decision process mimics the decision process of the responsible individual. If a responsible individual is one who looks before s/he acts, who traces out consequences, the responsible corporation is one whose bureaucratic structure, information-gathering protocols, etc., are similarly oriented. The Interventionist approach is to force these alterations: To make the corporation "responsible," ironically, through law.

This sort of requirement – sensitizing corporate conduct through mandatory organizational arrangements – is not unknown to the law. The typical corporation code requires that the company establish certain offices (there must be a board of directors, a sort of corporate superego) and imposes certain powers and obligations of office (to declare dividends, not to self-deal). But such familiar incursions have been designed to advance the interests of the investors principally and typically touch the highest level corporate offices only. Only recently have there begun to appear, on scattered fronts across the law, requirements that go beyond these two conventional constraints: Interventions made on noninvestor behalf, and which tamper deep within the organization to achieve their aims. For example, the Food and Drug Administration requires pharmaceutical companies to establish internal procedures that assure that "responsible corporate officials" be notified, in writing, of FDA actions affecting their products.[4] In other instances, corporations have been required to establish certain new positions,[5] or to add specified powers, obligations, or duties to existing posts.[6] In a few areas, the law has taken steps to affect the qualifications for holding certain corporate offices.[7]

Several of these control tactics are illustrated in the regulations of the U.S. Nuclear Regulatory Commission. Licensees (companies constructing and operating nuclear facilities) are required to develop and submit for approval elaborate plans for the protection of fuel shipments, including how they intend to go about the selection, qualification, and training of escorts.[8] The company must adopt procedures whereby "responsible officers" are informed of failings or defects.[9] The development of a Quality Assurance Program is not a matter left solely to managerial discretion (subject to ordinary market and legal penalties), but is made an express requirement of law. And the law lays down its prescriptions in considerable detail, even constraining, for example, who shall conduct the audits (appropriately trained personnel not having direct responsibilities in the area being audited).[10]

None of this strikes me as untoward. But it does stand in sharp contrast with the notion that has prevailed in the United States, that so far as the "outside world" is concerned, the company's managerial design is a "black box," immune from public reach, or even gaze.

It has to be emphasized that such interventions on noninvestor behalf as I have been illustrating, while a growing practice, remain, and probably ought to remain, the exception. For one thing, the defects of the HBELR technique, on which the Interventionist's case is rested, can often be responded to by alternative measures; for example, by insisting that the firm insure, by increasing the level of the penalty that the enterprise can expect (as by raising fines and increasing the rate of convictions), or by extending the personal liability of agents.[11] Moreover, we cannot disregard the peculiar drawbacks of the Interventionist techniques themselves: Whenever we on the outside displace managerial choice, we are meddling in a delicate process about which we ordinarily know considerably less than do the participants. The Interventionist "remedy" may cost society more than the harm it was seeking to avert.

A comparison of the strengths and weaknesses of all these various alternatives – both practical and theoretical – is a complex subject, and I will have to refer anyone interested to some examinations I have made of these problems elsewhere.[12] My position, in summary, has been that the more intrusive the Intervention, the more it should be reserved for a relatively narrow class of situations in which the warrant for doing so appears especially strong, at least until we have had more experiences with them to evaluate. For example, the proponents of an intervention might have the burden of showing that the hazard to be guarded against is of such a character, e.g., a nuclear or toxic catastrophe, that society is committed to prevent it even if doing so entails paying a high "social risk premium"[13] in terms of the wealth that the intervention, with its vexing and potentially costly strictures, may cause society to forego. Moreover, the class of enterprises affected by the intervention should be narrow enough, so that the costs of strait-jacketing potentially innovative and compliant companies is outweighed by the benefit of controlling their more intransigent competitors.

Interventionism and High Level Managers

I will close this examination of Interventionism by turning to the area that draws the most publicity: How might directors be enlisted into these reforms aimed at making the firm more "responsible"?

Keeping in mind that even where the circumstances may warrant an intervention of some sort, the requirement need not, and often ought not, directly involve the highest levels of the corporate hierarchy. For one thing, there are the opportunity costs to consider. What the Board as an institution is uniquely well suited to provide is general business guidance and a monitoring of the company's financial health. Each additional chore imposed on the directors is purchased with a diversion from these principal missions, from which, particularly during a period of worldwide financial instability, we should be most chary of dividing their attention. Moreover, even looked at from the perspective of the noninvestor whose interests we might be seeking to advance, we should not be quick to suppose that a seat in the board-room is the best strategy. Consider, for example, the protection of workers from unsuspected workplace hazards. From the workers' point of view, representation on the board is probably less valuable than participation at middle and lower levels of the company's bureau-cratic structure, such as by representation on worker health and safety committees, a practice that I gather is sanctioned by law in some of the European countries and mimicked in the United States in some indus-tries through collective bargaining agreements.

With these considerations in mind, the narrow, and I believe cor-rect, question to ask is this: In what special circumstances ought Inter-ventionist techniques affect the directors and highest level managers directly, either by grafting additional tasks onto existing offices, or, more radically, by requiring a firm to add to its bureaucratic structure a new high-level post or committee that did not exist before? It seems to me that two sorts of situations merit consideration for high-level intervention, even in the face of the many problems such devices will raise. I call these the *demonstrated delinquency situation* and the *generic industry problem.*

The Demonstrated Delinquency Situation

The first situation warranting top-level intervention would involve a company that has run afoul of the law so repeatedly that one can regard the presumption in favor of the conventional control tech-niques as rebutted. As a last resort, a court or other agency, as part of a probation order and subject to a hearing,[14] might either impose special compliance chores on some designated high-level officer, or even mandate the appointment of a "special public director" to monitor the company's compliance efforts.[15] Such a thing is not unheard of. In the past fifteen years or so, a number of securities law cases have been set-tled on terms requiring the defendant company to establish special committees of the board with designated tasks (compliance commit-tees, litigation committees), to hire investigative counsel, and even, in some cases, to add to the board a new director subject to the approval of the Securities and Exchange Commission and court. Such disposi-tions are generally unfamiliar outside the securities area, where they function to advance, or at least their rationale is to advance, traditional investor interests.[16]

On the other hand, a few cases have been settled on terms aimed at providing comparable relief for noninvestors. The government's case against the American Telephone & Telegraph Company, alleging employment discrimination against women, blacks, and other minorities, was ultimately settled with a consent decree that added new offices to the management structure (compliance officers in each operating company) and grafted additional tasks onto existing managers.[17] For example, the Vice-President of Personnel was required to review and take action on specified information regarding the firm's hiring and advancement of minorities.[18]

It seems to me that cases of this sort, wherein the company subject to the order will already have shown itself to be a recidivist, should indicate that its personnel would be readier to accept the intervention as legitimate and therefore be less inclined than otherwise to subvert and co-opt those responsible for implementing compliance responsibilities.

Generic Industry Problems

The second situation that might warrant managerial-level interventions involves matters of serious public concern that can be associated with a particular industry. Asbestos workers, we know, have high risks of asbestosis. Plastic workers are susceptible to certain forms of liver cancer. Various other industries produce waste whose hazards will hang as a sword over future generations. In contrast with the demonstrated delinquency situation, the companies to be dealt with will not necessarily be in violation of any law. Indeed, the problem may be a problem precisely because no existing rules or regulations can deal with it satisfactorily. For example, the government may be aware that a hazardous situation exists, yet have only the skimpiest information as to its exact source, gravity, or remedy. Abatement technology may be in early stages of development. Thus, absolutely eliminating the hazard through traditional measures, e.g., fines set at punitive levels, or injunctions, or an industry-wide requirement to install state of the art abatement devices, may either shut down the entire industry or prescribe the wrong solution, while impeding the development of the right one.

In these circumstances, it may be preferable for the agencies involved to defer promulgating sweeping substantive rules until they have developed more information; but as a quid pro quo for temporizing, and to provide the public assurances that something positive is being done, the government might be warranted to impose high-level interventions specially designed to support its lawmaking efforts. For example, each company in the industry might be required to establish an executive committee assigned to gather in-house data, assess the hazard, and relay findings to the appropriate authorities. In fact, there is already a gesture in this direction in the regulations of the Nuclear Regulatory Commission, referred to earlier. Each company in the industry is not only required to adopt procedures whereby "responsible officers" are informed of serious problems, but those officers are also obligated, under penalty of law, to relay certain information regarding hazards to the NRC.

Finally, I want to emphasize that in none of these situations (of either the demonstrated delinquency or generic industry variety) would anyone be assigned to advance "the public interest." Anyone working under so foggy a mandate can barely know where to begin. Instead, wherever the powers, qualifications, duties, etc., of an executive were to be affected, the details would be specially tailored to fit the particular exigency at hand. Take for example a company with a history of repeated toxic waste violations. A court that responded by appointing a special director as part of a probation order would be expected to designate not some well-meaning generalist, but a sanitary engineer or epidemiologist. Such an appointee,[19] by virtue of having recognized relevant expertise, gains credibility throughout the firm. Moreover, the terms of the probation order would be expected to focus the appointee's efforts, spelling out, for example: (1) the problem for his or her concentration; (2) the resources the company would have to make available, in terms of records, staff, and budget constraints; (3) the character of the appointee's linkage to outside bureaus, e.g., the requirements of divulsion and privilege in communications with the court itself, the Environmental Protection Agency, and various state pollution bureaus.

In addition to the tangible services, such as gathering data relevant for lawmakers and enforcers, that this appointee might serve are symbolic values. On the one hand, viewed as a sanctioning alternative (and not merely as a rehabilitative aid), there is much to be said for the device. To a delinquent organization, the threat of a well-publicized invasion of its autonomy may be less lightly dismissed than a million dollar fine. And viewed as a rehabilitative measure, the appointment might give a useful "lift" to those employees throughout the organization who can identify with the appointee professionally. For example, instating a Vice-President for Environmental Affairs (with significant resources and badges of prestige) could signal to the entire organization a commitment that environmental despoliation was to be taken seriously.

Voluntarism

As a means of "sensitizing" the corporation, the Interventionist techniques described above would enlist relatively innovative legal measures: Direct impingements of managerial autonomy. But while the *measures* may be nonconventional, their underlying *orientation* is not quite as radical. By-and-large, interventionism leaves unchallenged the assumption that the business of business is to make profits, but simply expands the arsenal of behavior-modifying – because profit-threatening – contingencies. For example, there is no reason why an interventionist requirement such as a mandatory internal information system, or a mandatory Vice-President for Environmental Affairs, cannot simply be girded onto the existing liability rules.[20] A company that failed to abide such a requirement, and consequently caused injury, could be made liable to punitive damages and penalties on top of any ordinary civil damages it might incur. Conversely, we could legislate that good faith abidance, even if not precluding ordinary damages, would rule out any penalties for related injurious incidents. Indeed, abidance with such interventionist requirements can even be made a condition for doing business, or for a license or permit.

I am not saying, and I am surely not hoping, that the success of interventionist techniques would turn exclusively on the implicit threats that back them up. Laws have effect because they help recognize what is widely considered *right*, and people will often do what is right without calculation of advantage. A company forced to install an environmental officer may better discern its long-term self-interest, penalties aside, because the officer may better help them avoid ordinary liabilities, anticipate changes in regulatory environment, stay abreast of relevant technology, etc. But as long as profitability remains the exclusive constraint, there is a question whether the Interventionist techniques are competent to modify corporate behavior to an extent that social welfare warrants.

Suppose, for example, that a company does install (whether under legal compulsion or not) a Vice-President for Environmental Affairs. And suppose that the vice-president's office – liberally staffed and earnestly diligent – discovers that one of the company's water effluents poses more dangers than have been appreciated in the literature or reflected in the law. Suppose the staff fairly assigns to the foreseeable injuries, say, a present value of $12 million. It also identifies a preventative device – a settling pond of some sort – which, if the firm is willing to expend $10 million, can absolutely eliminate the hazard. But suppose that the members also report that for a number of reasons (including the lapse of time before others identify and appreciate the damages the firm is causing, the problems of proof that will face future litigants, e.g., dealing with proximate cause, joint causality, assumption of risk, and various other transactions costs), the discounted present value of the prospective liabilities under existing law is not the full $12 million, but only $8 million. On these assumptions, while one can well argue that the preventative device appears warranted socially ($12 million social saving, $10 million social cost) it appears unwarranted from the perspective of firm profits ($10 million versus $8 million).

If, in these circumstances, the intuition of the reformer, the advocate of "corporate social responsibility," is for the company to install the device (or take some alternate remedial action), the problems shade away from the implementation of nonconventional legal *strategies* into an even more tangled area, that of implementing nonconventional *goals* and *constraints.*[21] Here we reach the idea, long if often fuzzily debated in the literature, that we should "liberate" the managers from a singleminded pursuit of (law-corrected) profit in favor of broader, and, it is urged, nobler motives.[22]

Any reformer who takes this position, who thinks the company ought to install the $10 million device in the face of a conflicting profit message, faces, at the outset, a whole battery of counterarguments.

First, the opponent of "corporate social responsibility" will point out that the discretion of the firm's managers to divert funds to noneconomic uses is limited by the pressures of competition. If the managers ignore these constraints in any nontrivial way, the company, it will be said, cannot survive.

Second, the managers have obligations to others to consider — investors, creditors, employees — obligations which have a moral as well as a legal basis. If competition in the industry is imperfect enough that the managers are retaining discretionary funds, the shareholders, it will be said, have a prior claim on them. For that matter, why should a risk be transferred from the firm's neighbors to its lenders?

Third, there is the presumptive capacity of the market to allocate resources correctly. And the opponents of social responsibility need not stand upon any exaggerated virtues of "the market system" per se. If a disapproved course of conduct emerges profitable under prevailing market constraints, then, as we have observed, society can "correct" the company's course by superimposing legal constraints — if need be, through some of the nonconventional interventionist techniques examined above. The law-corrected profit signal can thus be portrayed as presumptively the most accurate proxy for the social welfare.

From this last point, one could argue, finally, that any deviation by the managers involves an unwarranted arrogation of political power. To illustrate, suppose the factory managers in our illustration do try to weigh, independent of profitability, "What increment of benefit to downstream land-owners offsets what incremental burdens to the consumers of our products, our workers, our lenders, etc.?" Reflective reasoning about such questions will often, if not ordinarily, yield a range of vague and even conflicting solutions, particularly in areas where the social consensus is not strong enough to have produced a firm rule of law. Indeed, even if, following Kenneth Arrow,[23] we refuse to accept any law as a token of perfectly expressed collective choice, what warrant have the managers to assume their own judgment as to society's best interests would be *less* indefensible than our present "democratic" arrangements? Thus, even if we regard the law-corrected market signal as an imperfect proxy for the social welfare, it nonetheless carries a strong presumption of being superior to any other guide available.

The conclusion to be drawn is this: If the society wants to amend the laws in such a way as to render the existing mode of operation unprofitable, let it; but unless and until the law is changed, the managers should continue with business as usual.

It is impossible, in this limited space, to undertake a point by point analysis of each leg of argument on which that conclusion rests. Let me just say that even as an advocate of (some forms of) corporate social responsibility, I concede the general strength: Overall, corporate managers *should* orient themselves to law-corrected profits as the best proxy for the social welfare. But this does not dispose of the question that the Voluntarist wants to put: Are there no circumstances in which noncompliance with the law is warranted?

To approach this question, the starting point is that the various arguments against corporate social responsibility prove, I think, too much. In the form in which they are usually put, almost all of them could be raised as arguments against ordinary (noncorporate) mortals acting unselfishly. Yet, while we acknowledge the undoubted legal *right* of persons to do whatever they please within the bounds of law, no society that we know of has regarded the law as the only constraint on what people morally ought to do. Instead, societies everywhere encourage their members to abide by moral codes, to engage in ethical reasoning, even simply to practice good manners and mores (not to push to the front of the line) rather than to give vent to their first impulse within the bounds of law. The virtue of these nonlaw conventions is to coordinate life, and keep it pleasant, without incurring the various "costs" of achieving the same level of ordering through law.

The reasons why we should want corporations to internalize some analogous rules of conduct and decisionmaking are much the same (putting aside for a moment how the internalization might be achievable). We know that it is futile to expect lawmakers to anticipate and sensibly provide for all forms of socially undesirable behavior as the society evolves. We know, too, that to order and control society through law entails various sacrifices, and that beyond some margin, the incremental benefit of enforcing social desiderate by law exceeds those marginal costs. Indeed, it is possible that by relying on law as a control device, and therefore laying down a relatively precise "bright line" standard of impermissible conduct, we may tempt actors to press their conduct to the outer bounds of what they can get away with. As a consequence, reliance on clear legal rules may induce more unwanted activity than if we trust in the looser and less authoritative prohibitions of moral codes.

Indeed, I think that all the "anti-responsibility" literature I have read is based upon implicit assumptions about morality that contemporary philosophy would regard as controversial, at least. Essentially, the "anti" position is invariably consequentialist (that is, one judges the rightness of conduct by reference to its consequences) and invariably utilitarian (the consequences are evaluated and ranked by reference to some sort of welfare-maximizing metric). On both counts, the writers have ignored a significant body of mainstream philosophy. Specifically, between the neo-Kantians and the "rights" advocates, there are sturdy challenges to the antis' suppositions (1) that rightness is determined solely by consequences, rather than by conformity to consequence-detachable duties and (2) that so far as consequences do count, social welfare overrides all other consequences.

As abstract as these debates sound, they have strong implications, too long slighted, for corporate social responsibility. For example, building on the Kantianism, the reformer may maintain that a change in process (say, placing nurses on the board of a hospital) is a moral good that deserves an accounting independent of its social welfare consequences.[24] Similarly, under a "rights" analysis, if the worker has a "right" not to be exposed to undisclosed health hazards, that "right" is not (by definition of a "right"),[25] to be straightforwardly trumped by the general welfare.

With these considerations and possibilities in mind, it seems reasonable to suppose some legitimate space exists for the internalization of corporate social responsibility; that is, for encouraging the development of constraints as boundary conditions upon, even as substitutes for, the law-corrected market signals. Or the relationship could be lexicographic: The managers might be encouraged to maximize profits up to a certain point, but when that point is reached, the other constraints would come into play.

The blending in of "other" constraints might best be argued for in two types of situation. The first involves social responsibility in the face of profit-indeterminate alternatives; I call it (for want of any better heading) *The space for cooperative egoism*. The second involves social responsibility in the face of profit-conflicting alternatives: I call this *The space for corporate altruism*.

Corporate Responsibility in Profit-undifferentiable Situations: The Space for Cooperative Egoism

At many times in the life of the enterprise, the array of alternatives that present themselves for choice will not be rankable on the basis of profit-maximization; across some range, the managers will face possibilities that are softly differentiable on that basis, at best.

This indeterminacy is inevitable, first, because the definition of "profit-maximizing" is too vague to allow an unambiguous identification of what is most profitable in all cases. The managerial strategy that maximizes short-term share performance will not (except in the most perfect market conditions) maximize performance over longer time; the decisions best for the preferred shares is not that which is best for the common. Even if we dispel this particular ambiguity by settling on the present value of the common shares as the touchstone, some range of alternatives will remain profit-unrankable by reason of imperfect information. As Simon has pointed out, corporations, in actual practice, must eschew the "global rationality" of the classic textbooks – that is, abandon the ephemeral search for the unique profit-maximizing solution to every problem – and impose on themselves a "bounded rationality" in which any of several "satisficing" alternatives is acceptable.[26] In this view, profitability can serve to eliminate from further consideration a host of possibilities – those clearly unprofitable. But some range of profit-undifferentiable alternatives will remain.

One may suppose that, as long as we are in the range where all choices under consideration are *consistent with* long-run benefit to the shareholders, no one really questions the managers doing what they conceive to be the moral thing: What more needs be said? The question is not, however, merely rhetorical,[27] the issue to contend with being one that calls for close assessment of our expectations of director performance. If the firm has not developed and legitimated any conflicting vocabulary of motive – no other principles other than profits and losses on which firm decisions can be justified – there will be temptation to underestimate this range of profit-indeterminate outcomes. The alternatives may be forced into a profit-ranking, even if the supposed distinctions cannot be supported by the quality of the information at hand, so that the ultimate selection is no better than random with respect to expected value across some range. Such a disposition is particularly likely in view of the fact that profit calculations (and, at operating levels, the targets and goals generated by reference to them) form a stabilizing influence on the enterprise, so that frankly to introduce any constraints other than the most apparent medium- (even short-) term profit-maximization is a hazard for the organization, best handled only at the highest levels. As a consequence, if there is to be any expansion of the perceived range of profit-undifferentiable choices, and, thus, development of the space and style for moral differentiation, it would seem to be uniquely a board function deserving of conscious effort.

Moreover, "acting responsibly" often involves discovering a roundabout path to one's own self-interest, through varieties of cooperative egoism. Particularly where the profit-rankings are soft, top-level executives, duly encouraged to look for them, may discern opportunities that entail no loss (possibly even long-term benefit) for the firm, and certainly gains for society. In the terms of the pollution illustration used previously, if the firm discloses the hazard and installs the device without the whip of the law, it may encourage other companies to mimic its good behavior. This would lessen the competitive disadvantages of unilateral action and perhaps operate to the mutual advantage of all companies in the industry by averting the enactment of more repressive measures, if enforcers should be left to uncover the hazard, belatedly, on their own. To put the example in more general terms, as in any form of "gaming," a person who plays at business strategically can control the responses of other players to advantage. For example, law-enforcers (against whom, in this metaphor, the regulated businessman is playing) have limited resources – limited "chips" to play – and, other things being equal, will incline to concentrate surveillance and prosecution upon those firms that have displayed the worst conduct. A company that makes a record of "coming forward" will, although suffering some losses in the circumstances, have helped the enforcers; it may stand therefore to divide with the enforcers some of their gains.[28] I am assuming here that across some range of such "gaming" solutions there will be some "plays," the *profitability* of which is frankly indeterminate but whose *rightness* will be relatively clear.

No one knows how much space exists for such behavior, for the cooperative egoism, the strategizing, and so on. Roland McKean has examined the conditions under which cooperative egoistic considerations might be expected to operate and concludes, rather pessimistically, that they are not likely to be as significant in affecting the modern corporation in its complex commercial dealings as, say, the ordinary townsperson in his/her relations with his neighbors.[29] One reason is that moral rules of conduct tend to be too vague to provide direction in the situations that arise; any single firm's abidance by them does not assure reciprocal gains to all actors; the cheaters will "free ride" on the abiders; and the sanction of social pressure is less strongly operative in the national, even worldwide business context. Much of this is true. But these objections go to the reasonableness of *expecting* compliance. They do not mean that we should not *encourage* corporations to identify and consider the actual extent of choices that, not "dictated" by profits, leave room for moral reflection consistent with mutual advantage.

At the least, we might improve the likelihood of such a development – of expanding the perceived space for cooperative egoistic discussion and enhancing the social quality of that discussion – by making some changes in the present atmosphere and expectations surrounding board performance. One reform often voiced involves change in board composition, ranging from constituency directors, such as consumer and labor representatives, to more generally "public" directors, such as are seated on the boards of a few federally chartered corporations, including Comsat.[30] There is much to be said about such proposals, but overall the complications are undeniably worrisome. With the constituency directors, there are the risks of special interest wrangling; with the general public directors, those of a futilely overbroad focus.[31] We may take some heart in the thought that at least for the present purposes – to discern and realize the potential benefits of the profit-undifferentiable region – there seems no clear need to get entangled with appointments of either character. For reforming board composition, we can probably realize whatever benefits there are to be gained by requiring nothing more than that the firm select some percentage of independent directors of its choosing.[32] After all, the circumstances of present concern raise no hard collision with profit; we are merely after a more circumspect consideration of what profit truly *dictates* in the light of alternative values.

Even more than making some such shift in the rules for board composition, it might serve society's interest to alter the exposure of the directors to legal liability. To begin with, the present rules are ordinarily, in the last analysis, toothless. Derivative suits against directors for having negligently allowed the company to, for example, price-fix or bribe, are rarely if ever pressed to a successful conclusion. And in various cases when a judgment or settlement may be won, the director (or other top officer) is not necessarily fated to bear the brunt of it. The settlement may provide for the corporation to pick up the tab; if not, there is increasingly liberal indemnification as well as officers and directors liability insurance.[33]

In fact, considered as a body, the present rules are probably worse than toothless. They may be positively counterproductive of bringing about an internal information and authority system that is ideal from society's point of view. In trying to protect directors even from the "hassle" of litigation, management inclines to shield them from the very predicaments we would most want to reach the board's attention – and have them do something about. This is so because, unfortunately, the directors may be more in jeopardy (even if it is ultimately a theoretical, but nonetheless vexing jeopardy) for what they know than for what they never heard of.

Several reforms merit consideration. We might productively narrow the range of circumstances in which a director could be held liable, particularly in the area of corporate losses arising from ordinary negligence (want of due care). In turn, we might do well to expand statutory liabilities for nonperformance of more narrowly tailored requirements, that is, for failure to perform those chores the society feels it should and realistically can impose on the board (perhaps industry to industry). To substantiate *those* liabilities, it would serve to require by law that the directors receive relevant information, backing up the requirement with effective sanctions, both as to the directors (for failing to obtain it) and underlings (for failure to provide it). This would restrict pleas, after some catastrophe, that those at the top "never heard a word about it." Well worth considering, too, is the establishment of more realistic and therefore less problematical sanctions, such as disqualification from holding comparable corporate office, or, as Alfred Conard has suggested (in connection with negligence liability) placing ceilings on the magnitude of exposure, to make the law's threats that much more credible.[34]

Corporate Responsibility in the Profit-conflicting Situations: The Space for Corporate Altruism

But finally, however "profit-maximizing" be defined, and however liberally the firm allows for the possibility of recapturing some benefits of its "nice" conduct through, e.g., corporate good will and indirect and long-term strategic advantage, there will remain a class of situations in which the "socially responsible" action being urged squarely and irreducibly conflicts with profits. At that point, the question is one of pure corporate altruism: Under what circumstances should the managers subordinate the normal profit-defined interests for some competing value?

Considering all that has been said on behalf of profit as the presumptively preferred signal for transmitting social values, one can argue that, when alternatives can be clearly profit-ranked, only in the most limited circumstances should the profitable course be vetoed, and even then that only the most broadly shared and strongly held principle should qualify as a displacer. The other problem is that in any concrete circumstance it will be difficult to identify some governing principle that so qualifies to override profits. After all, if some alternate principle is so broadly shared and strongly held, why – by virtue of what legislative failure – was it not accounted for in the enactments of law?

This sort of criticism can cast doubt on the most plausible maxims for altruistic behavior. Take, for example, a possible profit-constraining maxim, "under no circumstances should anyone commit a crime (even if it is profitable to do so)." The skeptic[35] can rejoin that only few crimes (fewer still of a sort corporations ordinarily commit)[36] are so heinous as to be unacceptable under *any* circumstances; many fines are popularly regarded as a sort of unpleasant business expense. From this it could be argued that the managers, if they eschewed a crime that was on net profitable, would be wrongly arrogating legislative power. To illustrate, suppose the legislature has set a fine for some type of conduct involving pollution at $1 million in addition to the ordinary liabilities. The fine may be interpreted as a collective judgment that the legislature deems the social costs of the misconduct not captured by the expected civil damages to be something on the order of, say, $250,000 (supposing that the legislature, in fixing the penalty at $1 million, assumed that the chances of a violator being caught and convicted were 1 in 4). Under these assumptions, if, by violating the law the firm could make $1 million, for the managers *not* to violate the law would be to withhold goods or services that the society values at $1 million in exchange for avoiding a social cost of $250,000 – a course of conduct which, if presented in those terms, would command no clear social consensus.[37]

I believe that most people will feel uncomfortable enough with that line of analysis – so to dismiss the fine – to suspect that it constitutes a *reductio ad absurdum* of the position of the "antis." Without dwelling on that point, let us add a few details that make the managers' nondeviation from profits appear even more indefensible. Suppose (1) that the hazard posed by the pollution includes some irreversible injury to human genetic material, so that the harm posed may not be satisfactorily monetizable in damages. Or, assume (2) that the legislature does not appreciate, and the firm does appreciate (or could most cheaply appreciate), the hazard, thereby eroding the presumption that the laws represent the choices of a well-informed populus, and with it the presumption that the prospective liabilities to the firm have been equated with society's aversion to the conduct. Or (3) assume, per contra, that the legislature is informed and has set penalties which, together with the expected damages, pose a potential liability to the firm that substantially exceeds its expected benefit; but assume also that only because the investors are protected from the severe downside risks of a mass calamity (by bars to judgment, e.g., limited liability, bankruptcy) does the jeopardous activity emerge as the most profitable course of conduct.[38]

At least on these assumptions, I think that most people would *want* the managers to engage in some moral analysis that is not constrained to stop short of sacrificing investor profits for the good of others. I grant that what such an analysis involves is a question that has produced many books and no few answers. But the dominant thread, running through the Golden Rule, Kant, Sidgwick, Hare, Rawls, and other writers in various ways, is an exhortation to place ourselves in the position of others whom we will affect and to consider whether we can universalize our contemplated action into a general rule of conduct. The notion may come clothed in a form something like "if you can, at relatively small cost to yourself, significantly advance the welfare of others, you should do so."[39] As with any general rule, such a maxim (or one of its more familiar predecessors) entails no unique solution but may be consistent with several outcomes, only one of which can be effectuated. For example, the managers, submitting the previously illustrated dilemma to ethical analysis, might find it appropriate:

(1) to install the $10 million device;
(2) to eliminate production at the plant pending further (nondisclosed) investigation of the hazard and alternative ways to abate it;
(3) to inform the lawmaking bodies of everything they presently know about the hazard (at least not to lobby, profitably, for more lenient laws!); or
(4) to inform the lawmaking bodies (as above), deferring production for a reasonable period of time in order for the lawmakers to respond; after a reasonable period, if no such response is forthcoming, to resume production as before.

The point I want to emphasize is this. The fact that we may not be able to wring from moral analysis the "one right answer" is not a sufficient reason for disregarding moral analysis — as long as we believe that *any* of solutions (1)-(4) (or others) is preferable to the company simply proceeding with business as usual.

Of course, it is one thing to identify situations in which we might *want* other constraints to override profits. It is quite another to *be able* to influence the institution in such a way that we may expect correct profit-colliding decisions to be made at the right times. In regard to the profit-undifferentiable cases above, I proposed that we might be able to achieve an appropriate decisional environment by requiring some mix of unaffiliated directors and striking some new balance in the liability rules. In this second region, however, more thoroughgoing (and therefore, more problematical) reforms would almost certainly be required if one hoped to achieve any appreciable differences in firm conduct.

In particular, if we are seriously committed to extracting any gains that may be realized in this region, it might be necessary to give the government a stronger, more direct hand in the director selection process. Elsewhere I have suggested that we might see the day where the very largest corporations would be required to seat, say, for every million dollars of sales, one general public director nominated by a public agency, the nominees being subject to company veto.[40] As I presently envision the prospect, such public directors would always be in a minority and therefore outvotable. Nonetheless, they would be able to inject to the discussion considerations now being ignored; and characteristic of many of the issues of concern is that if someone on the board, preferably one of the public directors, has the "bad manners" to raise them, the board's other members may not feel they can, with decency,[41] brush them aside. Assuming a strong moral basis for the proposed sacrificing action, I suspect that in many cases when we would collectively want the sacrifice, the board as a whole would do the right thing.

To institute such a system would require definition of duties and liabilities. I have suggested such general public directors might, for example, be assigned special functions such as

(1) assuring that the company is complying with the law;
(2) serving as liaison in the lawmaking process;
(3) filling a "hotline" function (that is, being available to receive information that employees or outsiders want brought to company attention in a limited, nonpublic way); and
(4) overseeing the preparation of impact studies.

On the other hand, the various costs of such far-reaching reforms are large, from the direct expenses of the directors and their staffs (which public directors would almost certainly require to be effective) to the less calculable costs of the dysfunction they might cause. Some may feel that the benefits to various noninvestors are too slender to hazard upsetting the system. My guess is that the first gestures toward public directors endowed with broad powers and obligations[42] will come in connection with government bail-out loans or loan guarantees.[43] In those circumstances, the government will find itself with an independent investment stake which, if combined in the circumstances with special reasons to protect noninvestors, might be seen to justify some such experiment. Considering the present state of the economy, the clamor for government assistance, and the dissatisfaction with present institutions, the prospect is not unlikely.[44]

Conclusion

Will any of this—the Interventionist techniques, the Voluntarist's exhortations to search out opportunities for cooperative egoism and even altruism—make a difference, a positive contribution in modifying corporate behavior? Obviously, the likelihood of any real benefit will vary from case to case, from firm to firm, and industry to industry. Despite the drawbacks, I am persuaded that among the notions I have presented, there are some that will come to be accepted, and even prove successful, precisely because corporate managers will come to recognize that, as a way of dealing with a significant range of problems, these approaches have something in it for them as well as for the public.

This may sound odd. But what is most evidently missing in our corporate/social relations today, and needs to be restored, is a measure of mutual trust and respect. As things stand, we are settling into a self-defeating cycle in which the anticorporate sentiment is increasingly shrill and ill-informed, and the corporate response is too often self-defensive, unheeding, and unconstructive. When the evidence suggests a potential problem such as work-related cancer, governmental agencies, distrustful of what is going on within the corporation's walls, are under pressure to slap together a battery of regulations without adequate information, if only to protect themselves from criticism. For their part, the corporations incline to deny, delay, cover-up, and counterattack.

In these circumstances, some systematic integration of the "inside" with the "outside," some further exhortation of corporate social responsibility, could lead—and may be the only way to lead—to new, more productive patterns of cooperation and growth.

NOTES

1. To achieve economy in this essay, I am disregarding sanctions aimed at key executives personally. The advantages and limitations of sanctions aimed at corporate executives is a complex part of the picture, which I have examined in some detail elsewhere. See Christopher D. Stone, "The Place of Enterprise Liability in the Control of Corporate Conduct," *Yale Law Journal* 90 (1980): 28-35.
2. See ibid., 11-28. The analysis in the text could be extended to certain kinds of risk-based liability rules which also leave corporate management free to devise their own policies and procedures for the prevention of corporate harmdoing. An example would be an offense of recklessly engaging in activities likely to cause death or bodily injury: A risk-based liability rule of this kind leaves managers considerable freedom to choose what preventive action, if any, should be taken by their company.
3. See Christopher D. Stone, *Where the Law Ends: The Social Control of Corporate Behavior* (New York: Harper Colophon, 1976), 40-46.
4. Current Good Manufacturing Practice for Finished Pharmaceuticals, 21 C.F.R. §§211.1-.208 (1980) (FDA regulation requiring pharmaceutical firms to establish procedures to bring certain FDA regulatory activities to attention of executives).
5. See AT&T Discrimination Settlement, 8 *Labor Relations Reporter* (-BNA-) (431 Fair Empl. Prac. Man.) 73, at 87 (AT&T consent decree requiring each major subdivision to establish "Equal Employment Opportunity Coordinator" to assist in preparation of local affirmative action programs, to receive and investigate employee complaints, and to report to Assistant Vice-President-Personnel if corrective action necessary); 10 C.F.R. §-73.50(a)(3) (1980) (Nuclear Regulatory Commission regulation requiring licensee to establish security organization that "shall establish, maintain, and follow written security procedures").
6. See AT&T Discrimination Settlement, at 86-88 (affirmative action duties added to corporate personnel management); 10 C.F.R. §21.21(B)(1)-(4) (1980) (regulations of the Nuclear Regulatory Commission (NRC) require that directors and responsible officers of subject companies report to the NRC any information concerning certain failures, hazards, or defects).
7. See e.g., 21 C.F.R. §211.25 (1980) (FDA requires broad qualifications for personnel engaged in manufacture of drug products).
8. See 10 C.F.R. §73.30(d) (1980) (Nuclear Regulatory Commission Licensee required to submit plan for selection and qualifications of escorts for nuclear materials).
9. See 10 C.F.R. §21.21(a) (1980) (Nuclear Regulatory Commission regulation requires subject firms to adopt procedures to inform responsible officers of failings or defects in construction or operation of facilities or activities).
10. See 10 C.F.R. at 50 App.B, III (1981) (design control) (Nuclear Regulatory Commission licensees required to delegate verification and monitoring of design measures to individuals other than those who performed original designs). See also ibid., XVIII (audits) (requiring periodic audits to be performed by personnel independent of areas being audited).

11. See Stone, "The Place of Enterprise Liability," 28-35.
12. See Stone, "Law and the Culture of the Corporation," *Business and Society Review* 15 (1975): 5-17; Stone, *Where the Law Ends.*
13. That is to say, just as individuals will pay a premium – some amount over and above the expected value – to protect against certain outcomes toward which they are risk-averse, so the whole society, as I see it, is prepared to pay a sort of social risk premium to avoid calamities of a sort described in the text.
14. See Christopher D. Stone, "Stalking the Wild Corporation," *Working Papers for a New Society* 4 (Spring 1976): 17-21, 87-93, 90-91.
15. See Christopher D. Stone, "Public Directors Merit a Try," *Harvard Business Review* 54 (2) (1976): 20-34, 156; Stone, *Where the Law Ends*, 174-83.
16. Although the rationale may be to advance traditional investor interests, the FCC may also settle cases in ways that affect, and are probably intended to affect, noninvestor interests. For example, Occidental Petroleum Corporation's headquarters-level efforts to develop corporate-wide environmental programs received much of its impetus not from any environmental litigation, but from the settlement of a Securities and Exchange Commission's action which arose from another company's take-over tactics to avoid being acquired by Occidental in 1978. To avoid the shaky securities law objections, Occidental agreed to designate a director, an environmental official, and an independent consulting firm to prepare a report that would recommend procedures relating to environmental matters. See *In the Matter of Occidental Petroleum Corporation,* Exchange Act Release No. 16950, July 2, 1980. The firm's response to the order is reviewed in Frank B. Friedman, "Organizing and Managing Effective Corporate Environmental Protection Programs," *The Environmental Forum* (May 1984): 40-45.
17. See text and references to Notes 5-6 above.
18. Ibid.
19. In my view, the "appointment" would best be subject to the approval of the company involved in order to avoid unnecessary friction.
20. This does not amount to a merger of the interventionist techniques with what I have called HBELRs; the HBELRs operate after the fact, that is, they are triggered by improper company *output*, such as so many units of pollutant per hour. Connecting liabilities to interventionist measures means triggering the law to flaws in company *process.*
21. Of course, one response of the reformer is to request interventionist measures; but if interventionist measures are not in place or inadequate, then the response will be voluntarist.
22. Principally because my contribution is oriented towards the for-profit corporation, in the text I identify Voluntarism with the introduction of constraints other than profits. But the analysis is equally interesting to apply to corporations whose "own" self-interests are not profit-maximization, ranging from charitable corporations to business corporations that are supposed already to have assimilated nonprofit constraints – prestige, expansion, community service, and so on. Much of the analysis would still be of interest in regard to such institutions: Could we not just substitute for subordination of profits, subordination of some other dominant interests? Consider as a "corporate social

responsibility" case the charity that, in order to realize its aims—say, to deliver food to the needy in Southeast Asia—must bribe local officials.

23. Kenneth J. Arrow, *Social Choice and Individual Values*, 2d ed. (New Haven: Yale University Press, 1963).
24. For example, democratic process can be defended on grounds other than that it provides more beneficial *results*.
25. Ronald Dworkin, *Taking Rights Seriously* (London: Duckworth, 1977).
26. Herbert A. Simon, "Rational Decision Making in Business Organizations," *American Economic Review* 69 (1979): 493-513.
27. Actually, I suppose that some skepticism could be developed. For one thing, encouraging a search for profit-undifferentiable alternatives as a regular practice may encourage the managers to overextend that range, overlooking data which, conscientiously analyzed, would indicate differences in profitability that ought not to be smoothed over. Even worse, managers could use the practice as a shield for advancing their own private gain. For a possible example, the managers of one major American corporation not long ago persuaded their shareholders to adopt an article instructing the board that, when evaluating tender offers and acquisition proposals, it should give consideration to the impact on a variety of noninvestor interests. Cynical spectators generally suppose that such propositions are put forward in an effort to give incumbent management an additional safeguard against unwanted, and often legitimate tender offers.
28. John T. Scholz, "Voluntary Compliance, Legalism, and the Regulatory Dilemma," paper presented at the Law & Society Annual Meeting, Toronto, Canada, June 4, 1982.
29. Roland N. McKean, "Economics of Trust, Altruism, and Corporate Responsibility," in E. Phelps, ed., *Altruism, Morality, and Economic Theory* (New York: Russell Sage Foundation, 1975), 29-44.
30. Herman Schwartz, "Governmentally Appointed Directors in a Private Corporation—The Communications Satellite Act of 1962," *79 Harvard Law Review* 79 (1965): 351-57.
31. Phillip Blumberg, "Reflections on Proposals for Corporate Reform Through Change in the Composition of the Board of Directors: Special Interest or Public Directors," *Boston University Law Review* 53 (1973): 547-73; Alfred F. Conard, "Reflections on Public Interest Directors," *Michigan Law Review* 75 (1977): 941-61.
32. See generally, Lewis D. Solomon, "Restructuring the Corporate Board of Directors: Fond Hope—Faint Promise?" *Michigan Law Review* 76 (1978): 581-610.
33. See Auerbach v Bennett, 47 N.Y.2d 619, 419 N.Y.S.2d 920, 393 N.E.2d 994 (1979) (shareholders' derivative action against defendant corporate directors).
34. Alfred F. Conard, "A Behavioral Analysis of Directors' Liability for Negligence," *Duke Law Journal* (1972): 895-919.
35. The argument that follows in the text is, in essence, one of those made by David L. Engel, "An Approach to Corporate Social Responsibility," *Stanford Law Review* 32 (1979): 37-55. In my view, Engel's article contains some of the literature's most thoughtful criticisms of the corporate social responsibility proponents (including myself).

36. Corporations are more likely to be involved in regulatory than in *malum in se* offenses.
37. Engel, "Corporate Social Responsibility," examines several variations of the illustration in the text. Assuming that the flouting of law demoralizes and sets a bad example, society suffers some generalized welfare loss through law-breaking, over and above the losses directly attributable to the pollution per se. Those supplemental costs could, however, be accounted for in the level of fine; whether or not they were included in any particular instance would be one of the matters for the directors to consider in weighing the negative legislative signals against positive private benefits.
38. J. Simon, C. Powers and J. Gunnemann, *The Ethical Investor: Universities and Corporate Responsibility* (New Haven and London: Yale University Press, 1972), 171, develop something like this under the name of the "Kew Gardens principle," which is discussed in Engel, "Corporate Social Responsibility," 60-70.
39. One response to this last point is to reform the rules of limited liability; see Stone, "The Place of Enterprise Liability," 65-76. Another is to draw from the long-standing acceptance of limited liability the same conclusions one can draw from the fine level itself – that it reflects the considered, presumptively correct social judgment and ought not be specially accounted for by the private sector managers; see Engel, "Corporate Social Responsibility."
40. Stone, *Where the Law Ends*, 158-73.
41. Conscience and peer-group pressures need not be the only motivators. A well-designed system of directors and officers liability of a sort outlined in the text above might hold the directors personally liable for some egregious outcomes of which they had provable prior notice. The public directors, by injecting discussion of the problem at the board meeting, would pierce the information shield referred to earlier, and, by tainting the directors with knowledge, intensify the prospect of their personal liability. Query: Under what circumstances might we want to make some course of conduct unprofitable for the directors (and other agents) even if it might remain profitable for the company?
42. As opposed to the special public directors described in the text above.
43. There already exists authorization for some broad review of the borrower's management as a condition of federal bond guarantees: Emergency Loan Guarantee Act §6(b), 85 Stat. 178 (1971).
44. Consider the election to the Chrysler board of a high-level labor executive, a development of considerable note in the United States. While not required by the government, can anyone believe it was unrelated to that company's need for federal assistance and public goodwill and credibility?

CHAPTER 3
TAKING RESPONSIBILITY SERIOUSLY: CORPORATE COMPLIANCE SYSTEMS

John Braithwaite

Corporate social responsibility means two things. First, it implies corporate policies which demand organizational performance beyond the minimum required by law in areas such as consumer protection, environmental stewardship, occupational health and safety, discrimination and other labor-relations practices. Second, it requires internal compliance systems to ensure that such policies are put into practice. This chapter is concerned only with the second dimension of corporate responsibility.

This dimension has been relatively neglected by scholars, while libraries are filled with corporate ethics books concerning what the policies of responsible companies should be.[1] The imbalance is perverse because a company with voluminous and ethically sound policies to promote social responsibility but no mechanisms to enforce them is a greater danger to the community than a company with no corporate responsibility policies at all but adequate mechanisms for at least assuring compliance with the law. What companies do and how they are structured to channel behavior in prescribed directions is ultimately more important than what they say they should do.

The discussion of the systems that companies can put in place to improve prospects of legal compliance will be equally relevant to compliance with corporate values which go beyond the legal minimum. We will commence with a consideration of the role the board of directors can play. Then the role of openness and disclosure in corporate governance will be considered, followed by ways of dealing with structural pressures for unethical conduct, and finally the place of systems within the company designed specifically for the purpose of assuring compliance.

While it is all very well to identify the things which companies might do to improve compliance with their own ethical standards, there might not be grounds for optimism that companies will find such an investment worthwhile. Thus, the final section of the chapter explores the potential of mandatory internal compliance systems.

A Vigilant Board

The board of directors has an important role to play in ensuring compliance with ethical policies, but it is a mistake to exaggerate its importance. In the United States there is a large literature on the prospects of outside directors acting as superegos for the erratic ids of insiders.[2] Reflective of this concern is the fact that nonexecutive directors are more prevalent than in any other country.[3]

The corporate crime literature offers little hope of outside directors becoming effective superegos. With the hundreds of companies from many industries which disclosed foreign bribery to the Securities and Exchange Commission in the mid-1970s, in not one case was it discovered that an outside director had been apprised of the problem.[4] In contrast, in more than 40 percent of the SEC foreign payment disclosures, it was revealed that senior management was aware of the payments and the surrounding circumstances.[5] While most law schools educate their students about directors' duties and the decisionmaking power of the board, observers of corporate behavior continue to conclude that the board's influence is feeble.[6]

Coffee[7] has posited an analogy which captures the irrelevance of the board to preventing most corporate misconduct. Conventionally, the board is viewed as the corporation's "crow's nest." As such, it can spot impending problems on the horizon, but can hardly discover or correct troubles in the ship's boiler room below. Corporate crime and breaches of ethical standards occur in the boiler room and would rarely be noticed by directors whose job it is to scout the horizon looking for new investment opportunities, sources of finance, possible mergers, joint ventures, and the like.

The point about Coffee's analogy is that communications from both the crow's nest and the boiler room run to the bridge, where top management holds the helm. Strategic reforms will therefore sheet responsibility home to the bridge and ensure that communication channels to the bridge from the boiler room are free. There is certainly more hope for progress in this direction than by attempting to establish radical new communication channels from the boiler room to the crow's nest. Even if these new channels can be made to work, all the crow's nest can do is shout, while the bridge can take corrective action.

It follows that it is more important for reports from corporate compliance groups to be read and acted upon by the chief executive officer than by some social responsibility committee of the board. Undoubtedly, both would be desirable. But since both board and chief executive suffer from an information overload, choices must be made. Since the chief executive currently already has the greater ability to know about and correct law-breaking, measures to impose assurances that those on top will know, and measures to define responsibilities to act, should also concentrate on the chief executive.

Obviously, there are exceptions. It is surely preferable for the board, or an audit committee composed of outside directors, to review matters which touch on the personal financial interests of the chief executive,[8] such as loans to companies in which the latter has an interest.

A practical constraint upon corporate compliance groups reporting to a subcommittee of the board rather than to top management is that for most board members the monthly meeting is as much time as they are prepared to invest in their responsibilities. One also suspects that such a reporting relationship would encourage the chief executive to filter what went up to the board. Instead of a frank and efficient reporting system which guarantees that *someone* at the top is formally put on notice of wrongdoing, we increase the risk that no one will be formally notified. The chief executive may be informally notified (in his/her secret role as censor), but will rarely be held formally accountable where the company rules allocate responsibility to the board.

Outside directors have little interest in challenging the chief executive officer to stop interfering with the flow of information to them. Most of them are on the board because the chief executive put them there. Some might have the chief executive on their own board. Tacit understandings that "you keep your nose out of my internal affairs and I'll keep my nose out of yours" flourish.

The initiative which has been suggested by Ralph Nader, Christopher Stone, and others to cut through this cronyism is the government-appointed public-interest director. If the public-interest director is to get a meaningful picture of what is going on in the corporation s/he will need an investigative staff to dig out the facts. Management experts are generally apprehensive about tensions threatened by "shadow staffs" which are not answerable to the chief executive. Eisenberg[9] believes that such staffs would have an "institutionalized obligation to second-guess the management, but very limited responsibility for results." Their advice is frequently oriented towards placating the powerful barons they serve, and hence the result is to promote confusion in managerial environments which demand decisiveness.

These efficiency debits of the public-interest director concept are not fully answered by supporters such as Stone.[10] Stone suggests that public-interest directors and their staffs should be part of the corporate team in most normal respects. The public-interest director should also be a director for the corporation in the sense of assisting with general corporate goals such as profit and growth. Although the public-interest director is appointed to government, no one should be appointed who is not acceptable to the board. Stone suggests that public-interest directors should not turn over information uncovered in the course of their investigations to public authorities. Only if the company indicates an unwillingness to rectify a problem identified by the public-interest director should s/he go public or notify the government.

Certainly there is a difficult choice to be made. Consumers can have a director representing their interests who is no longer accountable to the public, sufficiently tame to be acceptable to management, and therefore in considerable danger of co-optation. Or they can have an aggressive public-interest director who is consequently frozen out of internal decisionmaking and who impairs managerial efficiency. The latter two deficiencies are related. If staff of the mistrusted public-interest director insist on attending a scheduled meeting, then a second (discreet) gathering will have to be convened to cover the same ground.

One wonders whether the public interest would be better served if consumerists, unionists, and environmentalists resisted co-optation and fought corporate abuses unmuzzled from outside the corporate walls. Naturally, corporate compliance groups which are under chief executive control are more likely to have their recommendations ignored than if a representative of the public interest were to know of the recommendations. The former kind of compliance group, however, is more likely to get the cooperation necessary to give it something worthwhile to report.

It might be better to have a compliance group which is "in the know" and which taints the chief executive with knowledge of illegalities by placing written reports on his or her desk. Public interest movements could then concentrate on enticing insiders to leak stories of chief executive officers ignoring compliance group reports. They can make allegations and call on the company to deny them. They can encourage whistle blowing. Constructing an artificial consensus between business and consumer groups by having public-interest directors as dedicated members of the company team may be less productive of corporate responsibility than outright conflict.

Critics of public-interest directorships have often likened the idea to having virgins run brothels.[11] Since the board is never really in charge of the modern corporation, a more appropriate analogy might be appointing a pacifist as an advisor to the general on how the troops are performing. While it does appear in some ways to be a structurally naive solution, it is one which should be piloted in a few companies and evaluated.[12] The armchair evaluation indulged in above is no substitute for empirical observation of what happens in a company when the public-interest director intervenes. The reform has not been tried

and found wanting, but found wanting for lack of having been sufficiently tried.

Open Corporate Governance

An alternative to putting independent outsiders onto a board which
conducts its affairs secretively is to chip away at this secretiveness so
that all outsiders will have a clearer view of what is going on. As
Joseph Pulitzer argued: "There is not a crime, there is not a dodge,
there is not a trick, there is not a swindle, there is not a vice which
does not live by secrecy."[13]

Over the past two decades the consumer movement has played an
important role in lifting the veil of corporate secrecy by encouraging
and supporting whistle blowers from within the corporation who
expose wrongdoing to the public.[14] A growing number of jurisdictions
have statutory provisions which protect whistle blowers against unfair
dismissal and other abuses.

Another employee right which should be legally guaranteed is a
right of research scientists to publish their findings even though the
employer might object to such publication. This is a difficult area since
it obviously would be undesirable to give scientists carte blanche to
reveal trade secrets. Nevertheless, the very fact that some companies
give their scientists a contractual right to publish so long as secrets are
not revealed demonstrates that such difficulties are surmountable.[15]

In addition to laws guaranteeing rights to blow the whistle, an argument can be made for a duty to blow the whistle in certain extreme
circumstances. This was the reasoning behind amendments to the
Federal Criminal Code introduced in Congress in 1979. These amendments sought to make it an offense for "an appropriate manager" who
"discovers in the course of business as such manager a serious danger
associated with" a product and fails to inform each appropriate federal
regulatory agency of the danger within thirty days.[16] The value of such
a law would not be that it would punish guilty people, but that it
would help lift the lid on dangerous products before they did any
harm. It is conceivable that the existence of such a law in Germany
could have prevented the thalidomide disaster, remembering that it
takes only one person to blow the whistle.[17]

It would be foolish to put too much faith in whistle blowing of either
the mandated or voluntary varieties. The informal social pressures
against betraying the company or colleagues at work cannot be under-
estimated. Informers are often regarded with disdain even by the side
to which they defect and frequently are viewed as misfits with low
public credibility. From a company's point of view, whistle blowing is

something to be prevented, because it undermines trust and confidence, and therefore open communications, within an organization. As Powers and Vogel have argued:

> The task of *ethical management* is to have anticipated the pressures which would give rise to the concealed and harmful practice, and to have helped create patterns of communication within the organization so that whistle-blowing would not be necessary.[18]

A fundamental requirement of effective internal compliance systems is that there be provision to ensure that "bad news" gets to the top of the corporation. There are two reasons for this. First, when top management gets to know about a crime which achieves certain subunit goals, but which is not in the overall interests of the corporation, top management will stop the crime. Second, when top management is forced to know about activities which it would rather not know about, it will often be forced to "cover its ass" by putting a stop to it. Gross has explained how criminogenic organizations frequently build in assurances that the taint of knowledge does not touch those at the top:

> A job of the lawyers is often to prevent such information from reaching the top officers so as to protect them from the taint of knowledge should the company later end up in court. One of the reasons former President Nixon got into such trouble was that those near him did not feel such solicitude but, from self-protective motives presumably, made sure he did know every detail of the illegal activities that were going on.[19]

There are many reasons why bad news does not get to the top. Stone[20] points out that it would be no surprise if environmental problems were not dealt with by the board of a major public utility company which proudly told him that it had hired an environmental engineer: The touted environmentalist reported to the vice-president for public relations! More frequently, the problem is that people lower down have an interest in keeping the lid on their failures. Consider how a "cover-up" of bad news about the safety and efficacy of a pharmaceutical product can occur.

At first, perhaps, the laboratory scientists believe that their failure can be turned into success. Time is lost. Further investigation reveals that their miscalculation was even more extensive than they had imagined. The hierarchy will not be pleased. More time is wasted drafting memoranda which communicate that there is a problem, but in a gentle fashion so that the shock to middle management is not too severe. Middle managers who had waxed eloquent to their supervisors about the great breakthrough are reluctant to accept the sugarcoated bad news. They tell the scientists to "really check" their gloomy predictions. Once that is done, they must attempt to design corrective strategies. Perhaps the problem can be covered by modifying the contraindications or the dosage level? Further delay. If the bad news must go up, it should be accompanied by optimistic action alternatives.

Finally persuaded that the situation is irretrievable, middle managers send up some of the adverse findings. But they want to dip their toes in the water on this. Accordingly, they first send up some unfavorable results which the middle managers earlier predicted could materialize and then gradually reveal more bad news for which they are not so well covered. If the shockwaves are too big, too sudden, they'll just have to go back and have another try at patching things up. The result is that busy top management get a fragmented picture which they never find time to put together. This picture plays down the problem and overstates the corrective measures being taken below. Consequently, they have little reason but to continue extolling the virtues of the product. Otherwise, the board might pull the plug on their financial backing, and the sales force might lose faith in the product which is imperative for commercial success.

In addition, there is the more conspiratorial type of communication blockage orchestrated from above. Here, more senior managers intentionally rupture line reporting actively to prevent low-level employees from passing up their concern over illegalities. The classic illustration was the heavy electrical equipment price-fixing conspiracy of the late 1950s:

> Even when subordinates had sought to protest orders they considered questionable, they found themselves checked by the linear structure of authority, which effectively denied them any means by which to appeal. For example, one almost Kafkaesque ploy utilized to prevent an appeal by a subordinate was to have a person substantially above the level of his immediate superior ask him to engage in the questionable practice. The immediate superior would then be told not to supervise the activities of the subordinate in the given area. Thus, both the subordinate and the supervi-

sor would be left in the dark regarding the level of authority from which the order had come, to whom an appeal might lie, and whether they would violate company policy by even discussing the matter between themselves. By in effect removing the subject employee from the normal organizational terrain, this stratagem effectively structured an information blockage into the corporate communication system. Interestingly, there are striking similarities between such an organizational pattern and the manner in which control over corporate slush funds (in the 1970s foreign bribery scandals) deliberately was given to low-level employees, whose activities then were carefully exempted from the supervision of their immediate superiors.[21]

The solution to this problem is a free route to the top. The lowly disillusioned scientist who can see that people could be dying while middle managers equivocate about what sort of memo will go up should be able to bypass line management and send the information to an ombudsman, answerable only to the board or chief executive, whose job it is to receive bad news. General Electric, Dow Chemical, and American Airlines all have such short-circuiting mechanisms to allow employees anonymously to get their message about a middle management cover-up to the top.

The ombudsman solution is simply a specific example of the general proposition that if there are two lines to the top, adverse information will rise up much more often than if there is only one. For example, if an independent compliance group answering to a senior vice-president periodically audits a laboratory, scientists in the laboratory have another channel up the organization through the audit group. Naturally, the middle managers responsible for the laboratory would prefer that they, rather than the compliance group, give senior management the bad news.

There are also ways of creating *de facto* alternative channels up the organization. Exxon has a requirement that employees who spot activities which cause them to suspect illegality must report these suspicions to the Law Department. Say a financial auditor notices in the course of his or her work a memo which suggests an antitrust offense. In most companies, auditors would ignore such evidence because it is not their responsibility and because of the reasonable presumption that they are not expected to be experts in antitrust law. Exxon internal auditors, however, would be in hot water if they did not report their grounds for suspicion to the Law Department.

Once a violation is reported, there is an obligation on the part of the recipient of the report to send back a determination as to whether a violation has occurred, and if it has, what remedial or disciplinary action is to be taken. Thus, the junior auditor who reports an offense and hears nothing back about it knows that the report has been blocked somewhere. He or she must then report the unresolved allegation direct to the audit committee of the board in New York. To date this free channel to the top has never been used by a junior auditor. The fact that it exists, however, and that everybody is reminded annually that it does, makes it less likely that it will have to be used. The most effective control system is one incorporating such strong situational incentives to compliance that it never has to be used.[22]

In reaching the conclusion that procedures to get bad news to the top of the corporation are more important than unrealistic aspirations about widespread blowing of whistles to the outside world, it is important not to stray from our purpose of assessing openness of corporate life to outside scrutiny as a route to social control. The most influential type of openness strategy beyond whistle blowing is the social audit.[23]

In its extreme manifestation, social audit means placing dollar values on the social benefits and costs the corporation's activities impose on the wider community during a given year. Thus, for example, the wealth generated by the company must be discounted for any harm to the environment caused in generating the wealth. The idea is quaint and impractical, not to mention its ensnarement by the economist's propensity to allow the more measurable to drive out the more important.

Nevertheless, enhanced disclosure of pertinent facts about the corporation's social performance is an important route to sharpened social responsibility. Responsible companies should be willing to enter into social contracts with unions, consumer, environmental, and other public-interest groups to disclose on a comparable basis from year to year key social performance indicators which would enable the groups to monitor corporate performance. Companies concerned about affirmative action should negotiate with womens' groups the terms of disclosure in annual reports of appointments, promotions, and pay increases for women. Environmental groups might be involved in framing public disclosure guidelines for effluent levels and investment in clean-up, unions in guidelines for reporting accident rates and average exposure levels for ambient hazards, and consumer groups in guidelines for disclosure of product recalls and statistics on consumer complaints.

Why should any company voluntarily expose itself to the risk of public criticism for deteriorating performance under these kinds of public-interest criteria? One reason might be that it is so committed to improving performance on such criteria that it is willing to make the investment to ensure that performance in fact improves. It is prepared to put itself under pressure of risking criticism from outsiders to do so. It is keen to make sure before the event that public-interest groups will be convinced when performance does improve that this is not a statistical fiddle concocted by the public relations department. If performance really changes for the better, and the improvement is accepted as such by the corporation's critics, then self-respect and morale might be enhanced within the corporation and respect for the corporation and its values by external publics might also be nurtured. Certainly, there are many corporations and executives who crave neither self-respect nor respect from the community, but for those who do, voluntary disclosure as part of a social contract negotiated with the relevant publics of the corporation is part of taking corporate responsibility seriously.

Watching Pressures for Irresponsibility

The corporate world is littered with irresponsible companies which have responsible policies. One reason for this is that performance pressures often force middle managers to act irresponsibly if they are to achieve corporate goals.[24] This was illustrated in my research on corporate crime in the pharmaceutical industry:

> Take the situation of Riker, a pharmaceutical subsidiary of the 3M corporation. In order to foster innovation, 3M imposes on Riker a goal that each year 25 percent of gross sales should be of products introduced in the last five years. Now if Riker's research division were to have a long dry spell through no fault of its own, but because all of its compounds had turned out to have toxic effects, the organisation would be under pressure to churn something out to meet the goal imposed by headquarters. Riker would not have to yield to this pressure. It could presumably go to 3M and explain the reasons for its run of bad luck. The fact that such goal requirements do put research directors under pressure was well illustrated by one American executive who explained that research directors often forestall criticism of long dry spells by spreading out discoveries— scheduling the programme so that something new is always on the horizon.
>
> Sometimes the goal performance criterion which creates

pressure for fraud/bias is not for the production of a certain number of winners but simply for completing a predetermined number of evaluations in a given year. One medical director told me that one of his staff had run 10 trials which showed a drug to be clear on a certain test, then fabricated data on the remaining 90 trials to show the same result. The fraud had been perpetrated by a scientist who was falling behind in his workload and who had an obligation to complete a certain number of evaluations for the year.[25]

One might say that this is an inevitable problem for any company that is serious about setting its people performance goals. But there are great differences in the degrees of seriousness of the problem. At one extreme are companies that calculatedly set managers goals that they know can only be achieved by breaking the law. Thus, the pharmaceutical chief executive may tell the regional medical director to do whatever has to be done to get a product approved for marketing in a Latin American country, when he or she knows this will mean paying a bribe. Likewise, the coal mining executive may tell the mine manager to cut costs knowing this will mean cutting corners on safety.

The mentality of "Do what you have to do but don't tell me how you do it" is widespread in business. Eliminating it is easy for executives who are prepared to set targets which are achievable in a responsible way. It is a question of top management attitudes, to which we will return later. IBM is one example of a company which Brent Fisse and I found to have the approach to target setting which I have in mind.[26] IBM representatives do have a sales quota to meet. There is what is called a "100 Percent Club" of representatives who have achieved 100 percent or more of their quota. A majority of representatives make the 100 Percent Club, so the quotas are achievable by ethical sales practices. IBM in fact has a policy and program for ensuring that targets are attainable by legal means. Accordingly, quotas are adjusted downwards when times are bad.

As Clinard found,[27] unreasonable pressure on middle managers comes from the top, and most top managers have a fairly clear idea of how hard they can squeeze without creating a criminogenic organization. In the words of C. F. Luce, Chairman of Consolidated Edison: "The top manager has a duty not to push so hard that middle managers are pushed to unethical compromises."[28]

Specialized Compliance Functions

In a recent research project, I identified the five American coal mining companies with the lowest accident rates in the industry for the early 1980s (U.S. Steel, Bethlehem Steel, Consolidation Coal Company, Island Creek Coal Company, and Old Ben Coal Company) and set out to discover what it was about their safety compliance systems which made them so successful.[29]

"You can't cookbook safety," Bethlehem Steel's Director of Safety said to me during one interview. He was becoming a trifle annoyed with my constant questions about the place of safety within the organization—who answers to whom and the like. The Senior Vice-President for Operations, Coal, also felt my questions were misguided. He pointed out that even though Bethlehem was a leader in safety performance, there might be very little that other companies could learn from Bethlehem in terms of formal structures because each company has a unique history, a unique set of personalities in senior positions, and different organization charts; consequently, each must find a unique solution to the problem of the place of safety within its structure.

The criticism was apt. In these interviews I suppose I was in search of some magic formula that would be evident in all of the companies with the very best safety records. Then perhaps it would be possible to enact laws to require other companies to adopt this same formula.

One hunch was that the safety leaders would be companies which granted their inspectors independence by having them answer to a safety department rather than to the mine superintendent. The theory here was that safety would less likely be compromised when the inspector could only be overruled by another safety professional rather than by a line manager whose primary concern was production. In fact, it was found that at U.S. Steel and Island Creek, inspectors at the mine, chief inspectors at the district level, and the senior safety person at the corporate level, all reported directly to the line manager at their level. At Island Creek only a dotted line connected safety staff at different levels of the organization to each other. At the other extreme Old Ben showed only a dotted line from inspector to mine superintendent while solid lines connected the inspector to the director of safety and the director of safety to the Manager, Corporate Safety. Consol had an unusual compromise with one set of safety staff reporting to line managers and another set reporting through staff channels to the Vice-President, Safety. Bethlehem had yet another sort of compromise, namely, mine inspectors having a solid line to the divisional manager of Safety and Health and only a dotted line to their mine superintendent, while the divisional manager of Safety and Health answered not to a corporate safety person, but to his or her divisional general manager.

In other words, there were five companies, all safety leaders, among which existed the whole range of conceivable reporting relationships for safety staff within the organizational power structure.

The companies also had quite different approaches to enforcing compliance with their safety rules. U.S. Steel's approach was quite punitive, with employees frequently being dismissed or given days off without pay for failing to comply with safety standards. Consol also not infrequently adopted this punitive stance, while the other three positively rejected such punitiveness in building motivation for safe practices among employees. Island Creek was different from the others in the way they used financial carrots rather than disciplinary sticks to encourage safety. While none of the other companies made explicit payments to employees for achieving improved safety, they did to varying degrees incorporate safety performance into the overall evaluation of managers for promotion or bonus.

The size of safety staffs was another variable on which the five companies were quite different. At one extreme was Consol with a safety staff which peaked at 300; at the other, U.S. Steel with a staff of 35. On the one hand, Consol achieved a striking improvement in accident rates after trebling its safety staff; on the other, Old Ben achieved an even more remarkable improvement by reducing and rationalizing its inspectorial force.

In summary, the place of safety in the formal power structure of the organization, the human resources dedicated to safety, the punitiveness with which safety was enforced, and the use of tangible rewards for safety performance varied radically among the five safety leaders.

What then did the five companies have in common?

Even though the place of safety departments in the formal organizational structure was quite varied, for all of the companies it was clear that safety personnel had considerable informal clout. Moreover, in all cases this derived from a corporate philosophy of commitment to safety and communication of the message that top management did not perceive cutting corners on safety to achieve production goals as in the interests of the corporation. When a company inspector recommended that a section of a mine be closed down because it was unsafe, in all of these companies it was considered inadvisable for line managers to ignore the recommendation because of the substantial risk that top management would back the safety staff rather than themselves.

In all of the companies the line manager, not the safety staff, was held accountable for the safety of his work force. A universal feature was also the clear definition of the level of the hierarchy which would be held responsible for different types of safety breakdowns. They were all companies that avoided the problem of diffused accountability: People knew where the buck stopped for different kinds of failures.

Control over safety programs was also relatively decentralized in all five companies. This came as a surprise because some of these are renowned as highly centralized corporations. Pointing out how ironical it was that control over safety was so decentralized, one Bethlehem Steel executive said: "Bethlehem is probably close to the most centralized corporation in the United States."

However, while the companies had decentralized control over safety, they also had centralized assessment of the safety performance of line managers. All companies carefully monitored each mine and each district to ascertain whether their accident and fatality rates were improving or worsening compared to the performance of other mines and districts. Again, different companies achieved this centralized monitoring of performance in different ways. Monthly criticism and self-criticism sessions were held at U.S. Steel whereas Bethlehem relied on routine daily telephone calls from the Senior Vice-President, Operations, while safety targets for Old Ben executives were set by head office. But in all companies the sense that the head office was intensively monitoring their safety performance was pervasive.

Four of the five corporations had a set of programs which built-in guarantees that safety training/supervision and communication and rectification of safety problems were working as they should. These included formal requirements for writing safe job procedures, basic training, individual safety contacts between supervisors and subordinates, detailed employee safety records, and accident investigation and audit (Island Creek being an exception in the last-mentioned area).

The company which did not have all of these formal safety programs was the smallest one, Old Ben. It may be that smaller companies can have great success at minimizing accidents simply by having a charismatic manager of corporate safety who enjoys the backing of top management (this is certainly true in the case of Old Ben), while larger companies must depend on more formal organizational guarantees. In Weberian terms, larger corporations cannot rely on charismatic leadership to achieve their goals, at least not in the long term, and must opt for some sort of routinization of charisma.[30]

In the final analysis, the conclusions about what these five companies had in common could be regarded as mundane. They were companies which: (1) gave a lot of informal clout and top management backing to their safety inspectors; (2) made sure that clearly defined accountability for safety performance was imposed on line managers; (3) monitored that performance carefully and let managers know when it was not up to standard; and (4) had mostly formal (informal in the case of Old Ben) programs for ensuring: (a) that safety training and supervision (by foremen in particular) was never neglected; (b) that safety problems were quickly communicated to those who could act on them; and (c) that a plan of attack existed for dealing with all identified hazards.

It remains to be seen whether empirical work on internal compliance systems in other industries would confirm my findings from coal mining. The importance of the attitude of top management for the ethical climate of companies is not without support in other industries, however. It was the most repeated theme which emerged from my 131 interviews with pharmaceutical executives:

> He [the chief executive] sets the tone and the rest of management fall in line. The ethical standards of anyone other than him don't matter so much. Well, unless you have one of those companies where an old guy at the helm has a right hand man making all the real decisions [American executive].[31]

Baumart[32] found that executives ranked the behavior of their superiors in the company as the principal determinant of unethical decisions. In a fifteen-year follow-up of Baumart's work, Brenner and Molander[33] found that superiors still ranked as the primary influence on unethical decisionmaking. Half of the 1977 sample of executives believed that superiors often do not want to know how results are obtained, so long as the desired outcome is achieved. Clinard's middle managers also repeatedly argued that it was "top management, and in particular the chief executive officer (CEO) who sets the ethical tone."[34]

Governmentally Mandated Internal Compliance Guarantees

If it is the case that "you can't cookbook compliance," that compliance systems will only be effective to the extent that they are consonant with the culture of the corporation concerned, then scope for government intervention to mandate effective compliance systems is limited. Let us assume that future research confirms my findings that what matters is a top management commitment to back up the judgment of compliance staff against line managers, to impose clearly defined accountability for compliance on line managers (as opposed to compliance staff), to take a personal interest in monitoring compliance performance, and to insist on programs to guarantee training with respect to compliance, plus unblocked communication concerning compliance breakdowns. What can governments really do to foster these things?

Governments can require companies to have a compliance staff, but the critical element of the success of such compliance groups seems to be not its size or its location in the formal structure of the organization, but how much informal backing it has from top management. Governments find it difficult to influence the latter. Nevertheless, as Hagan and Scholtz point out:

> By requiring pharmaceutical companies to hire certified personnel to direct premarket clearance experiments for new drugs, the FDA has strengthened the professionalization and intracorporate power of company researchers . . . [35]

Governments can require companies to lodge with enforcement agencies a clearly defined set of accountability principles to indicate who will be held responsible for different specified types of noncompliance. This possibility is the topic of another paper.[36]

We have seen that governments can legislate for a more open window on corporate misfeasance by protecting whistle blowers and mandating whistle blowing on life-threatening corporate misconduct. Disclosure of selected social performance indicators (pollution levels, accident rates, minority hiring rates, consumer complaints, etc.) can also be required.

Governments can also insist that training take place in certain areas (e.g., compliance with industrial safety rules). While this can be worthwhile, there is little to prevent an irresponsible company from carrying out the training in a perfunctory fashion.

Internal procedures can be mandated to stop blockages of bad news from reaching the top. Such mandatory internal procedures could be modelled on those of Exxon, discussed earlier. But it is difficult for the government to guarantee that employees will all be told of their rights and duties to report blockages direct to the board audit committee or of their duty to insist on a written reply from their superior on what has been done with a reported breach of legal or ethical standards.

Governments can require that companies have plans to deal with breakdowns in compliance. For example, the Environmental Protection Agency requires oil companies to have Spill Prevention Control or Countermeasure Plans.[37] But governments cannot do a great deal to guarantee that the plans are sufficiently well thought out to deal with the contingencies a particular company is likely to face or to ensure that the company will not try to cover up a minor spill rather than put their plan into action.

In most of these areas governmental requirements that internal compliance systems be effective can never be as important as top management commitment to making the systems effective. This has two implications—a conservative one and a punitive one.

The conservative implication is that regulatory agencies should engage in maximum consultation with top management of companies in the industry to build commitment to agency goals, be they environmental improvement, combatting discrimination in employment, or improving occupational health and safety. This is indeed a strange proposition to be advanced by an author who for the past few years as a consumer activist has faced the frustration of bureaucrats being responsive to the concerns of business about new laws or standards, while neglecting those of consumer groups. Undoubtedly, more consultation with industry implies a very real risk of more regulatory capture. Probably, though, the benefit of enhanced top management commitment to the regulatory outcome desired is worth that risk. In any case, an addition to the already considerable consultation with business could be matched by a quantum increase in consultation with public interest groups (in some cases from a base of zero consultation).

More important than the amount of dialogue with business by regulators is the question of who will be the business representatives targeted for dialogue. We have concluded that it is the chief executive and other top management of companies whose commitment is crucial. Yet throughout the world the trend has been for intermediaries— outside lobbying firms, in-house "directors of regulatory affairs," or trade associations—to deal with government on behalf of business. The trouble with these intermediaries is that they have an economic interest in confrontation. As Robert Reich has persuasively argued, conflict between a client and a regulatory agency means money for the lobbyist, and the more prolonged and bitter the conflict, the greater the monetary reward.[38] Bitter, drawn-out confrontations with regulators erode the commitment of business to regulatory goals. Lobbyists are reluctant to nip disagreement in the bud by working with regulatory agencies on compromises which would leave all parties happy with and committed to the rules. On the contrary, as Reich has observed, "they can do far better by waiting until regulatory action has begun (or even by quietly encouraging it) and then going into battle with guns blazing."[39]

Regulatory agencies can deal with this problem by making clear their reluctance to consult with lobbying professionals and their desire

to have direct discussions with the top management of companies subject to the regulations imposed. After the Hawke Labor government
was elected in Australia in 1983, it adopted a package of measures to
discourage lobbyists. This included a cabinet decision that "Ministers
should as far as possible . . . ensure that lobbyists who make personal
representations to them are accompanied by the principals they represent."[40] The government's attitude has tended to be that if industry
wants to persuade us, then let the captains of industry put their case
directly to us. The result has been a Labor government, at least for its
first two years, with a better rapport with business and a superior
capacity to lock business into accepting its policies than previous conservative governments. Professional purveyors of conflict have lost a
good deal of their significance in business-government negotiations in
Canberra.

In addition to the suggestion that top management commitment to
regulatory goals ought to be strengthened by maximum government
dialogue directly with chief executives, commitment at the top also
can be enhanced by sheeting home the consequences of corporate
wrongdoing personally to the chief executive. Virtue arises from both
belief in the value of being virtuous and fear of the consequences of
being sinful. Unfortunately, the latter consequences are rarely felt by
chief executives of large corporations. Penalties for corporate violations of the law are typically imposed on the corporation, often in the
form of fleabite fines which might ultimately be paid for by consumers; and when individuals are punished as well, they are normally
more junior employees.

The employees who perpetrate crimes on behalf of the corporation
frequently are responding to performance pressures that only the
chief executive is able to change. Often it is only the chief executive,
after opening his shut eye, to see that unreasonable performance
expectations are being obtained by flouting the law, who can insist
that the law be obeyed. In these circumstances, chief executives
should be indicted on the basis of wilful blindness, a form of fault
accepted as equivalent to knowledge.[41] Additionally, a more stringent
basis of responsibility should be introduced. An important step toward
rendering chief executives more vulnerable in this way was taken in
Park,[42] a decision of the U.S. Supreme Court in 1975.

John Park was the chief executive officer of Acme Markets, a
national food retailer with 36,000 employees. He was charged with
violating the Food, Drug and Cosmetic Act by allowing food to be
stored in a rodent-infested Baltimore warehouse. The crucial question
was whether Park could be held responsible for a rodent problem in

Baltimore when his office was in Philadelphia. In 1972 Park had received a letter from the Food and Drug Administration (FDA) complaining of conditions in the Baltimore warehouse. Park called in his vice-president for legal affairs who informed him that the Baltimore division vice-president "was investigating the situation immediately and would be taking corrective action and would be preparing a summary of the corrective action to reply to the letter." Hence, the defendant claimed he had done all that could reasonably be expected of a chief executive officer to rectify the problem. Nevertheless, when the FDA reinspected the warehouse and found that the problem had not been rectified, Park was charged.

The FDA contention was that Park had failed to ensure that his company had adequate procedures for guaranteeing hygienic warehouse conditions. The Supreme Court upheld Park's conviction and the fine of $50 on each of five counts. In doing so the court reaffirmed the view in *Dotterweich*[43] that where dangers to public health are involved, "The accused, if he does not will the violation, usually is in a position to prevent it with no more care than society might reasonably expect and no more exertion than it might reasonably exact from one who assumed his responsibilities." So the *Park* decision interpreted the Food, Drug and Cosmetic Act as imposing on the chief executive of a large corporation a duty of foresight and vigilance and an obligation to ensure that measures to prevent or correct violations are implemented. The *Park* decision falls just short of imposing a standard of strict liability on the chief executive officer. In effect, *Park* recognizes a defense of impossibility: If the defendant can show that he or she exercised extraordinary care, liability is avoided on the basis of "powerlessness."[44] Thus, on facts such as those which arose in *Park*, absolute reliance on any single individual, no matter how trustworthy, is insufficient to satisfy the standard of care required; the chief executive officer is expected to ensure compliance personally.[45]

The *Park* decision was controversial because it highlighted the question whether statutory offenses should be defined so as to depart from the common law principle that individual criminal responsibility requires proof of personal *mens rea*. For an offense which is the subject of only a relatively small fine, such a departure can be justified for the sake of protecting human health. But there is provision for imprisonment under the Food, Drug and Cosmetic Act. So the *Park* decision could lead to jail for an executive in similar circumstances though, as yet, it has not produced this result. The imprisonment of people who lack blameworthy intent seems counterproductive because of the real risk of undermining public commitment to the moral force of the criminal law. At the other extreme, when ordinary citizens see unemployed people going to prison for minor theft and the chiefs of large corporations go unpunished for recklessly endangering the public health, this also undermines respect for the law.

The *Park* decision is objectionable because it permits the imprisonment of individuals for acts of which they had no knowledge or reckless suspicion. However, a criminal standard of extraordinary care is much less objectionable if the sanctions that can be imposed on individuals do not run to incarceration.[46] Merely to fine a corporate officer may not be effective (companies have many ways of indemnifying employees for fines or monetary penalties) but there are other possibilities short of imprisonment, notably a sentence of community service.

The strength of the *Park* decision is that it shifts responsibility to the people who can make a difference. This is not to belittle the importance of continuing to punish more junior employees and corporate entities for offenses committed by them. It is simply to say that if we wish to maximize the compliance impact of additional investment in enforcement, the most productive targets will be chief executives.

It is the chief executive who usually manages to get his or her photograph in the business magazines when record earnings are announced. Accordingly, perhaps the best contribution that could be made to strengthening corporate compliance systems would be regular appearances in the business magazines of pictures of chief executives charged with corporate offenses.[47] What president would not give full backing to an environmental affairs director against intransigent factory managers if it will reduce the risk of a presidential mug shot in *Fortune*? Even a mug shot in the *Funeral Directors' Gazette* might be the ultimate in mortification if one's reference group is funeral directors.

NOTES

1. E.g., Tom L. Beauchamp and Norman E. Bowie, eds., *Ethical Theory and Business* (Englewood Cliffs, N.J.: Prentice-Hall, 1979); Richard T. De-George and Joseph A. Pichler, eds., *Ethics, Free Enterprise, and Public Policy: Original Essays on Moral Issues in Business* (New York: Oxford University Press, 1978); Leonard Silk and David Vogel, *Ethics and Profits: The Crisis of Confidence in American Business* (New York: Simon and Schuster, 1976).
2. See the reviews by A. A. Sommer, Jr., "The Impact of the SEC on Corporate Governance," *Law and Contemporary Problems* 41 (1977): 115-45; Noyes E. Leech and Robert H. Mundheim, "The Outside Director of the Publicly Held Corporation," *Business Lawyer* 31 (1976): 1799-1838.
3. W. Van Dusen Wishard, "Corporate Response to a New Environment,"

Law and Contemporary Problems 41 (1977): 222-44.

4. U.S. Senate, *Report of the Securities and Exchange Commission on Questionable and Illegal Corporate Payments and Practices; Hearings of Banking, Housing and Urban Affairs Committee*, 94th Cong., 2d Sess., 1976. See also De Mott's account of how the government-appointed Emergency Loan Guarantee Board failed to become aware of Lockheed's foreign bribery escapades: Deborah A. De Mott, "Reweaving the Corporate Veil: Management Structure and the Control of Corporate Information," *Law and Contemporary Problems* 41 (1977): 182-221.

5. Marshall B. Clinard and Peter C. Yeager, *Corporate Crime* (New York: Free Press, 1980), 279-80; John Collins Coffee, Jr., "Beyond the Shut-Eyed Sentry: Towards a Theoretical View of Corporate Misconduct and an Effective Legal Response," *Virginia Law Review* 63 (1977): 1105.

6. Melvin Aron Eisenberg, "Legal Models of Management Structure in the Modern Corporation: Officers, Directors and Accountants," *California Law Review* 63 (1975): 375-439; Myles L. Mace, *Directors: Myth and Reality* (Boston: Harvard Business School Division of Research, 1971); S. Prakash Sethi, Bernard Cunningham, and Carl Swanson, "The Catch-22 in Reform Proposals for Restructuring Corporate Boards," *Management Review* (January 1979): 27-41.

7. Coffee, "Beyond the Shut-Eyed Sentry," 1140.

8. Noyes E. Leech and Robert H. Mundheim, "The Outside Director of the Publicly Held Corporation," *Business Lawyer* 31 (1976): 1823-26.

9. Eisenberg, "Legal Models of Management Structure," 390.

10. Christopher D. Stone, *Where the Law Ends: The Social Control of Corporate Behavior* (New York: Harper, 1975).

11. E.g., James Q. Wilson, quoted in Ovid Demaris, *Dirty Business: The Corporate-Political-Money-Power Game* (New York: Avon Books, 1974), 442.

12. Sommer, "The Impact of the SEC on Corporate Governance," has made a start by an evaluation of such minor examples of "public-interest directors" as have already existed. The most famous instance is the court-mandated appointment of outside directors to the board of Mattel, Inc.

13. Quoted in David Boulton, *The Grease Machine* (New York: Harper & Row, 1978), 253.

14. See generally Ralph Nader, Peter J. Petkas, and Kate Blackwell, eds., *Whistle Blowing* (New York: Grossman, 1972); Alan F. Westin, ed., *Whistle Blowing! Loyalty and Dissent in the Corporation* (New York: McGraw-Hill, 1981).

15. John Braithwaite, *Corporate Crime in the Pharmaceutical Industry* (London: Routledge & Kegan Paul, 1984), 107.

16. See e.g., S.1722, 96th Cong., 2d Sess., 1617 (1979).

17. See Phillip Knightley, Harold Evans, Elaine Potter, and Marjorie Wallace, *Suffer the Children: The Story of Thalidomide* (New York: Viking Press, 1979).

18. Quoted in Norman Bowie, *Business Ethics* (Englewood Cliffs, N.J.: Prentice-Hall, 1982), 144. Italics in original.

19. Edward Gross, "Organizations as Criminal Actors," in P. R. Wilson and J. Braithwaite, eds., *Two Faces of Deviance: Crimes of the Powerless and Powerful* (Brisbane: University of Queensland Press, 1978), 203.

20. Stone, *Where the Law Ends*, 190.

21. Coffee, "Beyond the Shut-Eyed Sentry," 1133.

22. For a more detailed account of this system at Exxon, see Brent Fisse and John Braithwaite, *The Impact of Publicity on Corporate Offenders* (Albany: State University of New York Press, 1983), 171-81.

23. See e.g., Frederick D. Sturdivant and Larry M. Robinson, *The Corporate Social Challenge: Cases and Commentaries*, rev. ed. (Homewood, Ill.: Irwin, 1981), 145-50; Clark C. Abt, *The Social Audit for Management* (New York: Amacom, 1977); David Imberg and Peter McMahon, "Company Law Reform," *Social Audit* 1 (2) (1973): 3-17; Lee J. Seidler and Lynn L. Siedler, *Social Accounting: Theory, Issues and Cases* (Los Angeles: Melville, 1975); Douglas M. Branson, "Progress in the Art of Social Accounting and Other Arguments for Disclosure on Corporate Social Responsibility," *Vanderbilt Law Review* 29 (1976): 539-683; Robert W. Ackerman, *The Social Challenge to Business* (Cambridge: Harvard University Press, 1976), Ch. 2.

24. For the leading exposition of the role of middle managers in corporate crime, see Marshall Clinard, *Corporate Ethics and Crime: The Role of Middle Management* (Beverly Hills: Sage, 1983). See also Donald R. Cressey and Charles A. Moore, *Corporation Codes of Ethical Conduct* (Santa Barbara: Dept. of Sociology, University of California, Santa Barbara, 1980), 48.

25. Braithwaite, *Corporate Crime in the Pharmaceutical Industry*, 94.

26. Fisse and Braithwaite, *Impact of Publicity on Corporate Offenders*, 209.

27. Clinard, *Corporate Ethics and Crime*, pp. 91-102, 140-44. Cressey and Moore, *Corporation Codes of Ethical Conduct*, also found that all 25 auditors they interviewed felt that the example of top management was a critical factor in ethical conduct.

28. Quoted in Clinard, *Corporate Ethics and Crime*, 142.

29. John Braithwaite, *To Punish or Persuade: Enforcement of Coal Mine Safety* (Albany: State University of New York Press, 1985).

30. See Max Weber, *The Theory of Social and Economic Organization*, ed. T. Parsons (New York: Free Press, 1964), 64-71, 363-73.

31. Braithwaite, *Corporate Crime in the Pharmaceutical Industry*, 351.

32. R. C. Baumart, "How Ethical are Businessmen?" in Gilbert Geis, ed., *White-Collar Criminal* (New York: Atherton, 1968).

33. S. N. Brenner and E. A. Molander, "Is the Ethics of Business Changing?" *Harvard Business Review* 55 (1) (1977): 59-70.

34. Clinard, *Corporate Ethics and Crime*, 132.

35. Robert A. Hagan and John T. Scholtz, "The 'Criminology of the Corporation' and Regulatory Enforcement Strategies," in Keith Hawkins and John M. Thomas, eds., *Enforcing Regulation* (Boston: Kluwer-Nijhoff, 1984): 67-95.

36. John Braithwaite and Brent Fisse, "Varieties of Responsibility and Organizational Crime," *Law and Policy* 7 (1985): 315-43.

37. The oil companies must follow EPA guidelines in preparing their Spill Prevention Control or Countermeasure Plan, but the plan is reviewed by the agency only if a spill occurs. In normal circumstances, the plan need only be certified by a professional engineer, who must attest that the plan accords with good engineering practices. See 40 C.F.R. § 112.3(d) (1981). The guidelines can be found in 40 C.F.R. § 112.7 (1981). For some

other examples of government-mandated plans to deal with breakdowns in compliance, see John Braithwaite, "Enforced Self-Regulation: A New Strategy for Corporate Crime Control," *Michigan Law Review* 80 (1982): 1483-90.
38. Robert B. Reich, "Regulation by Confrontation or Negotiation?" *Harvard Business Review* 59(3) (1981): 82-93.
39. Ibid., 88.
40. *Government Decisions About the Establishment of a General Register of Lobbyists, A Register of Lobbyists Who Act on Behalf of Foreign Governments and Their Agencies, and Guidelines for Ministers Regarding Their Dealings With Lobbyists,* Australia, Senate, *Hansard,* 6 December 1983, 3297-98.
41. See Larry C. Wilson, "The Doctrine of Wilful Blindness," *University of New Brunswick Law Journal* 28 (1979): 175-94; Brent Fisse, "Responsibility, Prevention, and Corporate Crime," *New Zealand Universities Law Review* 5 (1973): 255-57.
42. United States v Park, 421 U.S. 685 (1975).
43. United States v Dotterweich, 320 U.S. 277 (1943).
44. United States v Park, 421 U.S. 660, 673 (1975).
45. United States v Park, 421 U.S. 660, 678 (1975).
46. Colin Howard, *Strict Responsibility* (London: Sweet & Maxwell, 1963), Ch. 2.
47. For more detailed discussion of the role of adverse publicity directed at both chief executives and other targets in improving corporate compliance, see Brent Fisse, "The Use of Publicity as a Criminal Sanction Against Business Corporations," *Melbourne University Law Review* 8 (1971): 107-50; Fisse and Braithwaite, *Impact of Publicity on Corporate Offenders;* Clinard and Yeager, *Corporate Crime,* 318-22; Francis E. Rourke, *Secrecy and Publicity: Dilemmas of Democracy* (Baltimore: John Hopkins Press, 1961), Ch. 6.

CHAPTER 4
CRIMINOLOGICAL PERSPECTIVES ON CORPORATE REGULATION: A REVIEW OF RECENT RESEARCH

Gilbert Geis

- "White-collar criminality in business is similar to what Al Capone called 'the legitimate rackets.' "
- "White-collar criminals are relatively immune because of the class bias of the courts and the power of their class to influence the implementation and administration of the law."
- "White-collar criminality flourishes at points where powerful business and professional men come into contact with persons who are weak. In this respect, it is similar to stealing candy from a baby."
- "Political graft almost always involves collusion between politicians and businessmen, but prosecutions are generally limited to the politicians."

These are among some of the more pointed and pungent observations that Edwin H. Sutherland offered in his presidential address to the American Sociological Society on December 27, 1939, in Philadelphia.[1] Sutherland, a fifty-six-year-old Nebraska native and a professor of sociology at Indiana University, had titled his talk "White-Collar Criminality," and he thereby introduced into the English language a new and extraordinarily evocative term and into criminology a topic that until then had been virtually ignored by its academic practitioners. As had Sutherland in his earlier years, criminologists had concentrated almost exclusively on malefactors in residence in the nation's jails and prisons, and on juvenile delinquents, whose return to righteousness was seen as a particularly important challenge.[2]

The ferocity of Sutherland's attack on the business world was notable. "White-collar criminality is found in every occupation," he insisted. All you had to do to discover this ubiquitous lawbreaking was to ask any person: "What crooked practices are found in your occupation?"[3] The intensity of Sutherland's attack and its uncompromising tone seem surprising from a man who uniformly is described by those who knew him with terms such as "imbued with sincerity and objectivity," "soft-spoken," and "never given to sarcasm, ridicule, or abuse."[4] Jerome Hall, a preeminent legal scholar, wrote on Sutherland's death that he had been "distinguished by an attitude of extraordinary objectivity and thorough inquiry maintained at a high level" and that he was an individual "who knew how to keep his feelings and personality from intruding into the discussion."[5] This sounds like the description of another man than the Sutherland who wrote of the public utility companies that "[p]erhaps no group except the Nazis have paid so much attention to indoctrinating the youth of the land with ideas favorable to a special interest, and it is doubtful whether even the Nazis were less bound by considerations of honesty in their propaganda."[6]

Sociologists of Sutherland's time held tightly to the conviction that they primarily were scientists, performing value-free and sophisticated assessments of human activity that would enable enlightened political leaders to make the world a better place. Sutherland echoed this belief. But his populist feelings, bred into him on the Nebraska frontier during the heyday of William Jennings Bryan's campaigns for the presidency, erupted in his work on white-collar crime. Rather lamely, Sutherland insisted that he was not concerned in his work with reforming business, but only with redeeming criminological theory by demonstrating that broken homes, Oedipal fixations, and similar alleged causes of crime had little, if any, relevance to white-collar offenses – and, therefore, that they were not adequate as fundamental explanations of criminal behavior.

The hostility toward business in Sutherland's pioneering polemic on white-collar crime has ever after permeated criminological studies and statements on the subject. It reflects a deeply held belief among most social scientists that the conduct of business is an endemically corrupt enterprise. Any endeavor whose basic goal is profit maximization, it is felt, will be tainted and twisted. Most social scientists undoubtedly would reflexively endorse the stark judgment rendered by Micah of Moresheth, a prophet of the biblical period, regarding commercial activity: "A merchant shall hardly keep himself from doing wrong and a huckster shall not be freed from sin . . . As a nail sticketh between the joinings of the stone, so doth sin stick close to buying and selling."[7] Illegal acts are particularly likely to occur, the formula goes, when the profit-seeker is powerful, and the agents of control and the means at their disposal are weak. Perhaps the most puzzling phenomenon from the viewpoint of the social scientists is that there is not a great deal more corporate crime than there seems to be, given the minimum risks involved.

I would be less than forthright if I did not admit that I share in the lore of my academic discipline regarding corporate misconduct. I truly appreciate that my views may be naive, at least in some respects, though perhaps no more so than those involved in the common businessworld image of scholarly existence and its insufficiencies when compared to life in that place grandiloquently said to be "the real world." I raise this matter only to make clear that by far the most pervasive underlying emphasis in criminological work on white-collar crime through the years has been an irrefragable bias—even an anger—regarding business conduct. Robert Heilbroner, a notably perceptive commentator on the social aspects of economic life, after posing the issue rhetorically, offers the following explanation of attitudes toward corporations:

> What . . . explains the fury with which we turn on the corporation for despoiling the air and water, and for vending shoddy or dangerous wares? I suspect that the answer lies more in our resentment of the kind of presence the corporation represents than in the particular crimes it commits (which . . . I have no wish to condone or minimize). What fuels the public protest against corporate misbehavior is the same animus that fuels the protest against the Teamsters Union or against "Welfare." It is an aspect of a widely shared frustration with respect to all bastions of power that are immense, anonymous and impregnable, and yet inextricably bound up with the industrial society that few of us wish to abandon.[8]

I leave it to others to adjudicate the accuracy of this interpretation. What is essential is that it be recognized as a particularly significant ingredient pervading the research and writing that constitutes the core contemporary criminological work on white-collar crime.

Briefing Background

A few quick brush strokes are necessary to review research on white-collar crime from the time when Sutherland's work burst upon the sociological scene until the present period. Such work can roughly be divided into three time periods. The first ran from 1939 to 1963 and saw a considerable spate of pioneering work. During the 1964-1975 span there took place a sharp decline in concern with corporate crimes. Since about 1975, however, there has been a dramatic revival of interest in the subject.

The 1939-1963 Period

There was considerable outpouring of work on white-collar crime in the wake of Sutherland's vivifying contribution. Much of it involved rather sterile joustings about the proper definition and embrace of the term itself, including charges (significantly mostly from sociologists who also possessed law degrees) that criminologists were branding "innocent" businessmen as crooks merely because they did not approve of them.[9] In a rather odd outburst, Ernest W. Burgess, one of the renowned sociologists of the period, argued that there was something inherently wrong with labelling persons "criminals" who did not so regard themselves.[10] This was perhaps the low point intellectually in the semantic sorties. Paul W. Tappan exemplified the debate when he objected to labelling as white-collar criminals businessmen who had not been convicted in the criminal courts, but only sanctioned by administrative bodies.[11] Sutherland fought back by pointing out that common criminals such as murderers and burglars need not be captured or convicted to be reasonably regarded as criminals, and he thought that the same logic ought to apply to corporate wrongdoers who patently had violated a criminal law, regardless of what procedural options (if any) the authorities chose to apply against them.[12]

There also emerged during this period a rich lode of field research on white-collar crime, virtually all of it carried out by persons with academic ties to Sutherland or his students, indicating that the concept had not truly entered into the mainstream of the criminological enterprise.

Representative of such work was Marshall B. Clinard's study of wartime black market operations. Clinard suggested that the most useful explanation of such white-collar crime might be established in terms of the personalities of the particular offenders.[13] Such a suggestion has rarely found favor with later scholars, who tend to seek structural explanations. Additional studies during the period were contributed by Richard Quinney on pharmacists,[14] Donald Newman on public attitudes regarding pure food and drug laws,[15] and Frank Hartung on rationing violations in the meat industry.[16] Quinney found that pharmacists whose orientation is more businesslike than professional are most apt to violate the laws regulating their trade. Newman discovered that the general public felt that persons breaking pure food and drug laws should be punished more severely than they were, but not as harshly as the law permitted. Hartung established that price violations at one point in the retail process were duplicated throughout the sales chain until ultimately the consumer was forced to pay the illegally high cost of the product.

It is notable that none of the major studies dealt with *corporate* crime. Robert Lane had conducted research that indicated that New England shoe manufacturing companies which were in financial difficulty were more apt to violate the regulatory laws than those with a healthier balance sheet.[17] Except for this inquiry, conducted by a political scientist interested in organizational behavior, the corporate world remained untouched by social scientists concerned about white-collar crime. In large measure, this was because access was strictly limited — or thought to be. "Private enterprise remains extraordinarily private," Roy Lewis and Rosemary Stewart wrote. "We know more about the motives, habits, and most intimate arcana of primitive peoples in New Guinea . . . than we do of the denizens of executive suites in Unilever, Citroen, or General Electric."[18]

The 1964-1975 Period

By 1964 it appeared that the study of white-collar crime was well established. During the next decade, however, work on the subject came to a virtual standstill. A case study of the General Electric heavy equipment antitrust case represented the only major academic contribution to emerge.[19] That study was made possible largely because of extensive Congressional investigations prompted by the celebrity of the case and by Senator Estes Kefauver's political ambitions.[20]

The abrupt disappearance of social science interest in white-collar crime is not easily explained. Economic conditions were both good and poor during the period. It seems likely that the dearth of scholarly work on the subject represented an aftermath of earlier times, when challenges to established centers of power could prove hazardous, especially during the reign of Senator Joseph McCarthy. The cold war standoff between the United States and the Soviet Union also had produced an uneasy acceptance of the status quo. Academic work, it seems, requires an incubation period: It had been stifled during the cold war years in regard to iconoclastic ventures. It would be reborn with the turmoil of Vietnam and Watergate and bear fruit in a later time.

The Contemporary Scene

It was then the phenomena of social unrest that reached their peak in the early 1970s that apparently contributed to the revival of interest in the study by criminologists of white-collar crime. Students at universities turned militant, daring the power of the authorities. The Vietnam involvement fueled beliefs that elected officials were deceitful. Underdog groups, such as blacks, women, and homosexuals, demanded fair and equal treatment. Poor persons demanded that wealth should be equitably shared, and criminal offenders became politicized, insisting that social injustice, not personal pathologies, lay at the root of their lawbreaking. The uncovering of the Watergate scandals and the subsequent resignation of President Richard M. Nixon further undermined public confidence in leaders. The widely publicized work of Ralph Nader and his colleagues indicated that bureaucracies were penetrable, and that rot, real or perceived, could be found upon close scrutiny.[21] The government, responding to President Jimmy Carter's own populism, began to allocate sizeable amounts of money for research on white-collar crime, and the priorities of the federal Department of Justice reflected his turn of focus.[22] Finally, the incursion into criminological thinking of Marxist doctrine carried with it a strong condemnation of upper-class privilege and a categoric assumption that such privilege was being abused.[23]

A large amount of empirical and theoretical work has been produced during this period. I will select for further discussion recent contributions that I regard as of particular importance either as representative of a point of view or for their substantive contribution.

Overseas Opinions

The term "white-collar crime" has only occasionally been adopted by European and Asian scholars, though the subject matter is increasingly being addressed overseas, generally as "economic crime," or, in the phrase preferred by the United Nations, as "abuse of power."[24] Corporate violations remain largely an untouched issue: The focus rather is on offenses against employers or those against the state. There is a vast literature on corruption, particularly in regard to Third World countries,[25] and much discussion about whether such corruption proves beneficial by allowing a creaky system to operate at all, or dysfunctional because of its consequences and the attitudes it fosters.[26]

For the Soviet Union and Eastern European bloc nations, corporate crime is a nonsubject, though periodic outbursts of official moral indignation and regular bursts of firing squad activity indicate that marketplace crimes are not uncommon and can be punished very severely in the communist world.[27] Absent private corporations though, Soviet criminologists can—and often do—adopt a tone of superiority based on the fact that no corporate crime exists within their countries.

The focus of much overseas criminology on white-collar offenses tends to be on marginal enterprises and activities, carried out by persons with underworld identifications, such as counterfeiters and smugglers. Two particularly notable recent English inquiries in the mainstream of study of white-collar crime are Michael Levi's investigation of long-firm fraud[28] (what Americans call "bankruptcy scams") and W. G. Carson's examination of occupational safety violations in the course of North Sea oil drilling.[29] Carson suggests that the frantic rush to meet high oil production quotas invited neglect of mandated safety regulations, sometimes with disastrous results.

A recent report of the Council of Europe on economic offenses illustrates overseas concerns and conclusions.[30] The Council noted that considerations of justice demand that more attention be paid to economic offenses, and it recommended the formation of special police units to deal with such behavior. Agreement could not be reached on a proper embracive definition of the subject matter; instead the Council decided to list sixteen specific kinds of offenses it regarded as matters concerning it. That list is worth noting: It includes (1) cartel offenses; (2) fraudulent practices by multinational companies; (3) fraudulent procurement or abuse of state or international organizations' grants; (4) computer crime (e.g., theft of data, violation of secrets, manipulation of computerized data); (5) bogus firms; (6) bookkeeping offenses and stealing of balance sheets; (7) fraud concerning the economic position and capital of corporations; (8) violation by a company of safety and health standards; (9) fraud to the detriment of creditors (e.g., bankruptcy); (10) consumer fraud – in particular misleading statements on goods, offenses against public health, abuse of consumers' weakness or inexperience; (11) unfair competition (including bribery of an employee of a competing company) and misleading advertising; (12) fiscal offenses and evasion of social costs by enterprises; (13) customs offenses (e.g., evasion of duties, breach of quota restrictions); (14) offenses concerning currency; (15) stock exchange and bank offenses; and (16) offenses against the environment.[31]

This is a smorgasbord inventory, concocted by a body that must accommodate to diverse viewpoints. It blends corporate offenses and corporate victimizations as well as crimes by individuals. What is also notable is that the Council's findings on economic crime do not bear much relationship to the stipulated subject matter. The Council advocated, for instance, that victims be associated with the prosecution of white-collar cases so that they could recover their losses more expeditiously, a procedure not uncommon in other forms of Continental court procedure. Among the Council's reported findings are these: (1) economic offenses increase in affluent times as citizens are tempted by the richness around them; (2) tax evasion goes up in direct proportion to tax assessment rises; (3) economic offenders increasingly resort to legal stratagems to avoid criminal responsibility; tradespeople, for example, are incorporating themselves in order to limit or deflect their liability; and (4) economic crimes seem to occur particularly in businesses that begin with inadequate capitalization.[32] These conclusions are rather far afield from the world of powerful corporations whose activities form a significant portion of the definitional territory staked out by the Council.

Absence of a focus on corporations in the Council of Europe's findings may be the result of the fact that there has been rather little work among its member countries on "respectable" corporate bodies. Perhaps they are inviolable and inaccessible, or perhaps it is only that criminologists have not turned their attention to them; or perhaps they truly are respectable and law-abiding and fall beyond criminology's ken.

Braithwaite on Bromides

Nobody doubts that the multinationals, the subject of the Council's second definitional category, sometimes fly high and handsome in regard to the letter of the law and most assuredly with regard to its spirit. By far, the most prominent contribution on the subject is now John Braithwaite's study of the multinational pharmaceutical companies, recently published in England.[33]

Braithwaite's book provides extensive documentation of "abominable harm" caused by the pharmaceutical industry. It includes a thorough case study of the blatant falsification by Richardson of tests on MER/29 (triparanol), a drug designed to reduce blood cholesterol. The company was fined $80,000 for flagrant deceptive practices; had its reports not been controverted, Richardson stood to gain more than four million dollars annually on the product.

Braithwaite examines bribery and extortion, said to be "routine and widespread," and drug dumping onto Third World countries. He notes that the multinationals use lower quality standards overseas than at home, though in Third World countries their standards tend to be higher than those of indigenous companies. Portions of the study are devoted to cartels, tax evasion, unsafe manufacturing, and safety testing. The multinationals are said to engage primarily in "law evasion rather than blatant law breaking. The corporation exploits differences in national law to find the line of least resistance to achieving its ends."[34]

A sizeable segment of Braithwaite's monograph deals with suggested remedies. He strongly endorses corporate self-regulation, superintended by alert and powerful government forces which can exercise unremitting control. Thus:

> Often consumers will be better protected by a deal whereby the company agrees to dismiss certain responsible employees, immediately recall certain products from the market, institute restitutive measures and rehabilitate its organizational processes to insure that the offense will not be repeated. Legalists who opt for an absolutist principle of even handed enforcement of the law would cause the

deaths of consumers while some cases slowly dragged through the courts.[35]

Government control of corporations would be kept from becoming abusive or too indulgent by being carried out openly and through vigilance by media, consumers, and union watchdogs. Besides, corporations have never been shy about seeing to it that their views are widely broadcast. Braithwaite is intrigued by John Coffee's suggestion of "equity fines," under which new stock of a convicted corporation would be issued as a penalty and deposited with the crime victims compensation fund for its reparative work.[36] But he believes more experience would be needed to evaluate the proposal satisfactorily. He finds the use of the criminal sanction of imprisonment for law-breaking corporate executives not notably practical. This view is held despite the observation that corporate executives have "an irrational fear of prosecution"; and that during his interviews several identified themselves, only half-jokingly, as "the vice-president in charge of going to jail." Braithwaite believes that equity between lower-class and corporate criminals can most decently be achieved not by imprisoning more of the latter, but rather by incarcerating fewer of the former.

Clinard's Contributions

Typically, criminological scholars in the past have written their doctoral dissertation or a monograph on some aspect of white-collar crime, published a few articles on the subject, and then moved to other topics. This was essentially the path that Marshall Clinard took, but after a distinguished career that focused largely on international criminological issues, he decided to return to the subject of white-collar crime, producing in recent years two significant books.

Corporate Ethics and Crime: The Role of Middle Management, Clinard's recent book, in some respects is an old-fashioned piece of sociological work.[37] It relies heavily on interviews and questionnaires rather than on the manipulation ("massaging" is the in-group term) of massive mounds of data; and it was carried out with a $60,000 grant from the National Institute of Justice, a miniscule amount compared to most research awards.

The study's importance is in providing empirical testimony on a key issue: How law-abiding is the corporate world? Benign interpretations insist that corporations mean well (after all, their leaders are decent citizens, like the rest of us), and that they will conform to the law if they are counseled or, if necessary, cajoled. Clinard found much evidence supporting a contrary conclusion. He interviewed 64 middle

managers who had retired within the past ten years from 51 companies on the Fortune 500 list. He located by far the largest number (87.5
percent) of study participants in retirement communities near Phoenix
and Tucson. The respondents had been employed with their organization for an average of 31.8 years. About three out of four believed that
top management knew of corporate law violations either in advance
or shortly after they occurred. The retired middle managers were
strongly in favor of reporting to the government authorities serious
worker safety violations in their plants, but just as strongly opposed to
reporting price fixing, illegal rebates and kickbacks, and illegal payments to foreign officials. "Price fixing involves money," said one,
apparently providing the rationale that underlay the majority viewpoint. "Not people's safety or the national interest." Other responses
included: "It is not my responsibility since it is a problem of top government. Anyway, price fixing is not a clearcut violation," and "Am I
God that I should go to the government on a top management pricefix-
ing agreement and sacrifice myself?" Another person noted, "I was not
hired to protect prices for consumers," with a fourth observing: "If top
management does not want to do anything about it, why should I?"[38]

The middle managers felt that many violations of the law were the
result of "extensive and serious" pressures placed upon them by top
management – time pressures and production and sales quotas, in particular. They did not believe that industry self-regulation could work.
Clinard summarizes their views this way:

> In their opinions, the unethical behavior of certain top
> management personnel within an industry, plus the greed
> and unethical practices of some corporations, have made
> government regulation necessary. Moreover, they could
> visualize no way in which industry rules might be effec-
> tively enforced.[39]

An interesting finding was that a considerable number of respondents indicated that the ethics of the founders of their company
seemed to have played a vital role in setting standards that remained
pervasive generations after the founders were no longer around. The
middle managers also tended to believe that outsiders brought in to
manage a company were much more likely to foster a climate of dis-
honesty than insiders promoted from within the corporate ranks. The
outsiders were seen as hustlers, intent on further mobility, and anx-
ious to show quick profit improvement at any price in order to facilitate their own advancement.

Clinard's earlier study was a replication of the analysis that constituted the core of Sutherland's pioneering 1949 book on white-collar crime. In collaboration with Peter Yeager, Clinard utilized statistical techniques and methodological refinements not yet introduced into sociology in Sutherland's era to examine the records of the nation's leading corporations. The titling of the two publications of his findings is instructive: The Government Printing Office report was called *Illegal Corporate Behavior;*[40] the commercial printing was titled *Corporate Crime.*[41] For Clinard the latter heading was perfectly appropriate; as he notes, "[I]t is generally impossible to determine the seriousness of a corporate offense by the nature of the action taken . . . [E]ven serious violations generally receive only administrative sanctions."[42]

In support of this position, Clinard and Yeager note that two-thirds of the cases that they defined as serious and four-fifths of those they regarded as moderately serious were handled administratively by government officials.

These are some of Clinard and Yeager's findings: A total of 1,553 federal cases were begun against the 562 companies whose records were examined for two years, for an average of 2.7 violations for each company. About 60 percent of the companies had at least one case against them; for those companies, the average was 4.4 cases. Violations were far more likely to be committed by the larger rather than the smaller companies, perhaps because of their exposure to a greater number of regulations. The oil, pharmaceutical, and motor vehicle industries were the most likely to be proceeded against for law violations.

Clinard and Yeager clearly endorse tougher penalties for corporate wrongdoing. "Knowledgeable persons generally concede that penalties for corporate offenses are far too lenient," they observe, and they proceed to offer a roster of changes that might be adopted: (1) The strengthening of consent agreements and decrees to provide substantial remedy and to include follow-ups to ascertain compliance. Tougher penalties are advocated for failure to abide by such decrees. (2) Increases in fine ceilings, and, even more suitably, fines assessed according to the nature of the violation and in proportion to the company's annual sales. (3) Stiff criminal penalties for violations of health and safety or environmental regulations that "recklessly endanger" the public or employees. (4) Stronger statutes to prohibit corporations that previously have violated federal laws from receiving federal contracts. (5) Mandatory publicity for corporate civil and criminal violations, with the cost to be borne by the offender. (6) More extensive use of imprisonment with longer sentences. Community service in place of incarceration should be prohibited by law, except for unusual circumstances. (7) Convicted corporate offenders should be prevented by law from being indemnified by their companies. (8) Management officials convicted of criminally violating corporate responsibilities should be prohibited for three years from assuming similar management positions in their company or in others. (9) Directors would be liable, but not criminally, for being derelict in their duty to prevent illegal corporate actions. (10) A new commercial bribery statute should be enacted to help prosecute corporate executives who receive kickbacks from their customers or suppliers.[43]

Law-Sociology Disputation

Renewal of the debate about the proper characterization and investigation of white-collar crime was a by-product of Clinard and Yeager's book. The rule seems to be that when sociologists also have legal training they find irresistible the impulse to hector other sociologists about the grave importance and intricate imperatives of the law as it relates to definition and control of corporate conduct. Their tone often tends to blend anger and condescension. The anger focuses on what they see as the high-handed and irresponsible manner in which sociological criminologists condemn behaviors which the law writers regard as "morally neutral,"[44] things such as patent violations and false advertising. Little attention is paid to public harms from such acts, and even less mention is made of corporate offenses which produce maiming and death. Lawyers who operate exclusively from within their own domain (rather than crossing into social science) seem more able to view the law as one of the arguable aspects of discussion of white-collar crime, rather than as ordained wisdom inadequately appreciated.[45] But for many lawyers in this field, nothing seems quite as simple as they believe social scientists are apt to make it.

Social scientists, for their part, tend to adopt appalled attitudes regarding the partisan for-sale pursuits of most lawyers and, in particular, to be condescending about the low level of methodological sophistication and inept data analysis that is found in much legal thinking and writing. Social scientists also believe that they have a firmer idea (or at least that they can meticulously determine) what is acceptable and not acceptable to the public sense than do lawyers, whose skill lies in redefining the meretricious more benevolently. But social scientists can be dismissive and high-handed about details of legal concerns and legal definitions and insensitive to important jurisprudential distinctions that stand at the core of fundamental human rights and civil liberties.

The several law review examinations of Clinard and Yeager's work hold true to form. One commented slurringly on the book's "apparent

attempt to preserve at least a semblance of objectivity,"[46] an odd observation from a vocation dedicated to client interest, often at the
expense of objectivity. Another critique was more sweeping. Leonard
Orland found that "the nonlegal literature [on white-collar crime] is
hopelessly misguided," and that a new generation of scholars was not
only perpetrating, but also extending, Sutherland's errors. To prove
this latter point, Orland cites only a 1978 doctoral dissertation that has
had no impact whatsoever. In all, Orland found Clinard and Yeager to
have engaged in "a startling example of a Sutherlandian exercise in
misconceived empiricism."[47]

The legal and social science sides sometimes are not clearly aligned
in terms of professional training, of course. Ralph Nader, legally educated, is in a far corner of the social science camp. But that the debate
continues is an important consideration in contemporary white-collar
crime research and writing.

Herbert Edelhertz, a lawyer and former federal prosecutor, who has
worked assiduously in the scholary realm of white-collar crime, suggests that Sutherland's original formulation may have much to do with
the distancing between lawyers and social scientists. He notes, for
instance, that "no prosecutor could accept, as a basis for a criminal
charge, that embezzlement by a bank president was white-collar
crime, and that the same act by a low-paid bank teller was not."[48] The
interests of social scientists, in short, tend to focus on class distinctions
and their relationship to human behavior; those of lawyers involved in
enforcement stress equal justice for all, and the absence of distinctions. Neither, of course, is "right" – people are not equal in their access
to criminal opportunity or in terms of the implications of their crimes,
but there is also a good deal to be said for pretending that they are, and
treating them as if they were.[49]

Hopefully, time may produce a rapprochement between law and
social science regarding white-collar crime, annealed by the strengths
of the different viewpoints. The recently published study by Brent
Fisse, a lawyer, and John Braithwaite, a social scientist, on corporate
responses to publicity about their derelictions represents the kind of
high-caliber collaborative effort that can be carried out when both perspectives together are brought to bear on the subject.[50]

Sentencing Schedules

Two major studies on the sentencing of white-collar offenders illustrate the overdue movement of the subject matter into the mainstream
of academic criminology. They represent the first publications of work
on white-collar crime in the profession's leading journal, the *American*

Sociological Review, since Sutherland's time.

Both studies indicate that, contrary to Sutherland's intuitive belief, and that of his followers, white-collar offenders appear to be sentenced more harshly than other persons convicted of felonies. Neither study, however, is without methodological difficulty that renders its conclusion suspect, despite (or perhaps because of) the employment of carefully considered operationalizations of key concepts and highly sophisticated statistical methods of analysis.

Both studies confined themselves to the sentencing practices in selected federal district courts, largely because these courts deal with considerable numbers of white-collar offenders and because they had available centralized tabulations of necessary information. Hagan, Nagel, and Albonetti define white-collar criminals as persons with a college education or more who committed specified offenses.[51] They compared the sentencing of members of this group with that of persons of less education who commit the same offenses, those with less education who commit nonwhite-collar crimes, and those with college education who commit nonwhite-collar offenses. Wheeler and his collaborators analyzed only white-collar crimes and, holding constant other variables (such as age, harm inflicted, possible sentence available to the court, and previous offenses), they examined the length of sentence imposed in terms of the offender's social status.[52] Hagan and his co-workers found that sentences generally are tougher for college-educated offenders than for persons in other categories, while Wheeler's study found that possibility of imprisonment rose with an increase in the occupational status of the offender. Wheeler's inquiry concluded that the two conditions associated with a white-collar offense that are most closely tied to imprisonment are: (1) the allowed maximum sentence, with more than three-quarters of those who could have done 15 years or more going to prison in contrast to less than one-third of persons with an offense carrying a penalty of one year or less; and (2) the financial impact of the crime, with those who take under $500 less likely to go to prison than those whose offenses create losses in the millions.

Both studies are careful to call attention to their possible flaws and shortcomings. Most notable, of course, is the fact that certain offenses and offenders may have been siphoned off much earlier in the judicial process. Judges may only get the most awful white-collar offenses and may be responding to these.[53] Also nonwhite-collar federal offenses, such as auto theft, may provide an idiosyncratic representation of the universe of street crimes to which the white-collar cases were compared. Nonetheless, these studies are landmark inquiries, both as challenges to further, even more refined work and as indications of the return to social science importance and "the scientification" of the subject of white-collar crime.

Shapiro on the SEC

The considerable concern expressed during the Carter administration about white-collar crime was translated into funding priorities at the National Institute of Justice. By far, the largest sum was awarded to Yale University's Law School. Some first-rate articles have now seen print based on the Yale projects, and an array of books is being published, beginning with Susan Shapiro's work on the Securities and Exchange Commission.[54]

Shapiro's research, with its focus on a particular enforcement agency, may represent the direction of future criminological inquiry. Such work, however, requires access; it is likely that such entre will not continue to prove available if criminologists adopt their traditionally critical attitude toward bureaucracies.

Shapiro was housed in the Securities and Exchange Commission during 1967-1977 while carrying out her Ph.D. research, and she was permitted to go through regular agency training. Her task became the analysis of more than 500 investigations the agency had done from 1948 to 1972, a quarter of a century's work. The SEC, she found, largely focused on small fry and not, as might have been expected, on the giants of the corporate world:

> Sensitized by post-Watergate scandals, we expect to find New York Stock Exchange listed securities, Fortune 500 corporations, Wall Street brokerage firms, and slick sophisticated Harvard Business School types among the ranks of the wayward capitalists. Instead, we find itinerant preachers, a part-time rabbi-insurance salesman, buddies forming an investment club, "Mom and Pop" operations, foundering brokerage firms, and the like.

Major emphasis in the study is on the manner in which the Commission goes about locating cases. Shapiro finds its acquisition of information "haphazard and fortuitous." It relies, she says, "upon the curiosity or imagination of SEC investigators with perhaps extra time on their hands or the anger, vengeance, good citizenship, conscientiousness, and persistence of agency outsiders." Her basic recommendation is that the SEC rationalize its information-gathering system so that desired consequences are maximized, though she offers no particular guidelines regarding how the agency should prioritize its goals. She found that "what is distinctive about the SEC is not its overreliance on prosecution to discharge its regulatory responsibilities, but rather its prosecutorial restraint," though again no standard is provided by which a reader might be able to judge what reasonably constitutes "restraint" and what might be said to be absence of that attitude. This conclusion seems to contradict in some ways a later observation that SEC enforcers "are so preoccupied with the power and drama of their investigative and 'prosecutorial' responsibilities that they have abdicated creative responsibility for detecting and selecting the violations they will subsequently 'enforce.' "

Focus on enforcement groups, such as Shapiro's, is of course but one way into the world of white-collar crime. The research can be done as well from the perspective of the offending organization, that of victims, and that of offenders, among others. Selection of the approach inevitably colors the kinds of material gathered and the conclusions reached.

Organizational Emphases

Studies in the past few years have begun to insist that white-collar crime can more satisfactorily be understood if the unit of analysis is the organizational entity rather than the behavior of any particular individuals. They ask about a company's hierarchical arrangements, its competitive position, reward systems, informal and formal communications patterns, and similar conditions in their attempt to understand why a corporation violated the law and a competitor did not, or why one type of industry seems to have so different a law-abiding pattern than another.

This approach is particularly congenial to sociologists, who dominate academic criminology. It is why they focused so effectively on gangs – groups of individuals – when studying juvenile delinquency and much less satisfactorily on young arsonists and murderers. Crime can always be viewed as a reflection of the milieu in which it originates. After all, different countries often have very different kinds and rates of homicide, and it may well be more enlightening to look at a national ethos rather than at the traits of particular homicide offenders.

Chief among the proponents of an organizational focus are M. David Ermann and Richard Lundman. They enumerate characteristics of organizational deviance under five headings: (1) The act must be contrary to norms maintained by others outside the organization. (2) The act must be supported by the internal operating norms of the organization and conflict with the organization's formal goals. (3) New members of an organization must be socialized to accept rationalizations and justifications that support actions contrary to external norms. (4) To be organizational deviance, as opposed to individual deviance, the action of an individual must have support from fellow workers. This support may be passive or active. (5) Organizationally deviant acts must have support from the dominant administrative coalition of the organization. This support too may be passive or active.[55]

An organizational focus is made explicit in the definition by Laura Schrager and James F. Short, Jr. of the arena of white-collar crime that concerned them. They were interested in

> the illegal acts of omission or commission of an individual or a group of individuals in a formal organization in accordance with the operative goals of the organization, which have a serious physical or economic impact on employees, consumers, or the general public.[56]

A recent focus on organizational climate as an essential feature of corporate crime is found in Diane Vaughan's study of a 1977 Ohio case in which Revco Drug Stores was guilty of double-billing the state for more than a half-million dollars. Revco had become hopelessly befuddled in its attempts to file for legitimate reimbursements for drugs it had dispensed under the state Medicaid program.[57] More than fifty thousand of its claims had been rejected by state computers. It thereafter created fictitious claims, submitting again for the same drug that the state already had paid for, and merely reversing numbers on the reimbursement claim. The company was caught only because a podiatrist had been prescribing narcotics, and state agents, checking his drug record, stumbled upon the Revco fraud. Vaughan focused on characteristics of Revco and those of the state bureaucracy to explain the crime. She noted, for instance, that government rules for drug reimbursements had contributed to Revco's difficulties in compliance. Some of the government rules seemed at times to defy mastery, for instance. She notes that at no time did Revco officials define what they had done as a "crime." Statements made by corporate officials, she points out, suggested that they saw themselves as the victims and not as the offenders.

Organizational emphases offer a number of research advantages. For one thing, they hold out the prospect of pinpointing elements of a corporate environment that are criminogenic and may be susceptible to remedial action. Otherwise, the operative wisdom is that action against law-breaking company officials merely leads to their being replaced by other persons who quickly follow in their law-breaking footsteps. Ultimately, of course, the difficult linkage has to be made between what are presumed to be significant organizational traits and the perception of such matters by the persons engaging in the violative acts. It does not matter what an organization stands for either formally or informally if persons within the organization are not moved by these considerations. Another difficulty may exist in the moral realm. Blaming organizations for deficiencies that seemed to be linked to law-breaking takes some of the sting out of the condemnation, just as it does if you insist that murder is not the fault of a killer but fundamentally a reflection of the subculture in which that person was nurtured and of the larger social system which allowed that subculture condition to exist. Perhaps an organizational approach is healthy in this respect: It might depersonalize and moderate blameworthiness. But perhaps it might also serve to numb any sense of individual responsibility for personal actions. The matter obviously is complicated: Adjudication might best be left to later times and other writers.[58]

Concluding Comments

It is apparent that the criminological study of white-collar offenses is enjoying a vibrant, buoyant period. It seems likely that most of the perspectives noted above will expand and flourish. We will have further detailed empirical work, with its precision purchased at the necessary price of reducing complex matters to operational terms. We certainly will see a proliferation of studies carried out from an organizational perspective, and it can be hoped that independent scholars such as Clinard will pursue whatever matters intrigue them and will continue to add to our basic information. In short, things look promising, though perhaps less so for white-collar offenders than for white-collar scholars. Certainly, the efficacy of present legal arrangements for dealing with corporate crimes is apt to come under increasing critical scrutiny,[59] and there will surely be further work to determine how seriously public opinion regards white-collar crimes. At the moment, studies indicate that those which produce harm equivalent to that inflicted by street offenses are considered to be similarly serious.[60]

The tendency for legal and social science positions regarding white-collar crime to conflict at times may be a healthy sign of attempts to produce satisfactory delineations of the subject matter that satisfy criteria important to researchers and writers in both disciplines, or it may be a lamentable indication of territorial jealousies and games of intellectual one-upmanship. Assuredly, the field would be helped to prosper intellectually if economics and management scholars could be persuaded to pay more attention to it; their neglect reflects, I suspect, the presumed priorities of their disciplines as well as political predilections.

The study of corporate crime and of other forms of white-collar crime, as I see the matter, stands as an especially important venture for academics, persons uniquely positioned in contemporary society to examine those things which interest and concern them. Unexamined exercise of power has always been a major source of social difficulty. There may be a peril that honest persons are unreasonably stigmatized; but that has never been the fundamental issue, only an unacceptable side effect. The major problem has been that power is used and abused in ways that are hidden from sight or regarded as sacrosanct and beyond scrutiny. It is against this condition that work on white-collar crime is directed.

NOTES

1. Edwin H. Sutherland, "White-Collar Criminality," *American Sociological Review* 5 (1940): 1-12.
2. For material on Sutherland's background and work, see Gilbert Geis and Colin Goff, "Introduction," in Edwin H. Sutherland, *White Collar Crime: The Uncut Version* (New Haven: Yale University Press, 1983), ix-xxxiii.
3. Sutherland, "White-Collar Criminality," 2.
4. Howard Odum, "Edwin H. Sutherland, 1883-1950," *Social Forces* 29 (1951): 348.
5. Jerome Hall, "Edwin H. Sutherland, 1883-1950," *Journal of Criminal Law, Criminology and Police Science* 41 (1950): 394.
6. Edwin H. Sutherland, *White Collar Crime* (New York: Dryden, 1949), 210.
7. Micah 1:1-16 and 2:1-12. See also Hans Walter Wolff, *Micah the Prophet*, trans. Ralph D. Gehrke (Philadelphia: Fortress Press, 1981).
8. Robert Heilbroner, *In the Name of Profit* (New York: Warner, 1973), 200.
9. Robert G. Caldwell, "A Re-examination of the Concept of White-Collar Crime," *Federal Probation* 22 (March 1958): 30-36.
10. Ernest W. Burgess, "Comment," to Frank E. Hartung, "White-Collar Offenses in the Wholesale Meat Industry in Detroit," *American Journal of Sociology* 56 (1950): 34.
11. Paul W. Tappan, "Who is the Criminal?" *American Sociological Review*, 12 (1947): 96-102.
12. Edwin H. Sutherland, "Is 'White-Collar Crime' Crime?" *American Sociological Review* 10 (1945): 132-39.
13. Marshall B. Clinard, *The Black Market: A Study of White Collar Crime* (New York: Holt, 1952).
14. Richard Quinney, "Occupational Structure and Criminal Behavior: Prescription Violation by Retail Pharmacists," *Social Problems* 11 (1963): 179-85.
15. Donald J. Newman, "Public Attitudes Toward a Form of White-Collar Crime," *Social Problems* 4 (1957): 228-32.
16. Frank E. Hartung, "White-Collar Offenses in the Wholesale Meat Indus-

try," 25-34.

17. Robert E. Lane, "Why Businessmen Violate the Law," *Journal of Criminal Law, Criminology, and Police Science* 44 (1953): 151-65.

18. Roy Lewis and Rosemary Stewart, *The Managers* (New York: New American Library, 1961), 111-12.

19. Gilbert Geis, "White Collar Crime: The Heavy Electrical Equipment Antitrust Cases of 1961," in Marshall B. Clinard and Richard Quinney, eds., *Criminal Behavior Systems* (New York: Holt, Rinehart and Winston, 1967): 139-50.

20. U.S., Senate, Subcommittee on Antitrust and Monopoly, Committee on the Judiciary, 87th Cong., 2d Sess., 1961, "Administered Prices," *Hearings*, Parts 27 and 28; Joseph B. Gorman, *Kefauver: A Political Biography* (New York: Oxford University Press, 1971); Charles Fontenay, *Estes Kefauver: A Biography* (Knoxville: University of Tennessee Press, 1980).

21. See e.g., James S. Turner, *The Chemical Feast* (New York: Grossman, 1970); John C. Esposito, *The Vanishing Air* (New York: Grossman, 1970); Ralph Nader and Mark J. Green, eds., *Corporate Power in America* (New York: Grossman, 1973); Robert C. Fellmeth, *The Interstate Commerce Omission, the Public Interest and the ICC* (New York: Grossman, 1970).

22. U.S. Department of Justice, *National Priorities for the Investigation and Prosecution of White Collar Crime* (Washington, D.C.: Office of the Attorney General, 1980).

23. See e.g., Frank Pearce, "Crime, Corporations, and the American Social Order," in Ian Taylor and Laurie Taylor, eds., *Politics and Deviance* (Baltimore: Penguin, 1973): 13-41.

24. See e.g., National Institute of Justice, *Crime and the Abuse of Power: Offenses and Offenders Beyond the Reach of the Law?* (United States Discussion Paper for the Sixth United Nations Congress on the Prevention and Treatment of Offenders).

25. See e.g., Arnold J. Heidenheimer, ed., *Political Corruption: Readings in Comparative Analysis* (New York: Holt, Rinehart and Winston, 1970); Victor T. LeVine, *Political Corruption: The Ghana Case* (Stanford: Hoover Institution Press, 1975).

26. See e.g., J. R. Shackleton, "Corruption: An Essay in Economic Analysis," *Political Quarterly* 49 (1978): 25-37; Joseph S. Nye, "Corruption and Political Development: A Cost-Benefit Analysis," *American Political Science Review* 61 (1967): 417-27.

27. Stanislaw Pomorski, "La Corruption de Functionnaires devant les Tribanaux Sovietiques," *Revue d'Etudes Comparatives Est-Ouest* 14 (1983): 5-22.

28. Michael Levi, *The Phantom Capitalists: The Organisation and Control of Long-Firm Fraud* (London: Heinemann, 1981).

29. W. G. Carson, *The Other Price of Britain's Oil: Safety and Control in the North Sea* (Oxford: M. Robertson, 1982).

30. Council of Europe, European Committee on Crime Problems, *Economic Crime* (Strasbourg: Council of Europe, 1981).

31. Ibid., 11-12.

32. Ibid., 18-36.

33. John Braithwaite, *Corporate Crime in the Pharmaceutical Industry* (London: Routledge & Kegan Paul, 1984).

34. Ibid., 305-06.

35. Ibid., 334.

36. John C. Coffee, Jr., " 'No Soul to Damn: No Body to Kick': An Unscandalized Inquiry into the Problem of Corporate Punishment," *Michigan Law Review* 79 (1981): 386-459.

37. Marshall B. Clinard, *Corporate Ethics and Crime: The Role of Middle Management* (Beverly Hills: Sage, 1983).

38. Ibid., 120-21.

39. Ibid., 153.

40. Marshall B. Clinard, Peter C. Yeager, Jeanne Brissette, David Petrashek, and Elizabeth Harries, *Illegal Corporate Behavior* (Washington, D.C.: Government Printing Office, 1979).

41. Marshall B. Clinard and Peter C. Yeager, *Corporate Crime* (New York: Free Press, 1980).

42. Clinard, *Corporate Ethics and Crime*, 10.

43. Clinard and Yeager, *Corporate Crime*, 317-18.

44. Sanford H. Kadish, "Some Observations on the Use of Criminal Sanctions in Enforcing Economic Regulations," *University of Chicago Law Review* 30 (1963): 423-49.

45. Christopher D. Stone, *Where the Law Ends* (New York: Harper & Row, 1975).

46. Unsigned book review, *Michigan Law Review* 80 (1982): 978.

47. Leonard Orland, "Reflections on Corporate Crime: Law in Search of Theory and Scholarship," *American Criminal Law Review* 17 (1980): 501-20.

48. Herbert Edelhertz, "White-Collar and Professional Crime," *American Behavioral Scientist* 27 (1983): 109-28.

49. Ibid.

50. Brent Fisse and John Braithwaite, *The Impact of Publicity on Corporate Offenders* (Albany, N.Y.: State University of New York Press, 1983).

51. John Hagan, Ilene H. Nagel, and Celesta Albonetti, "The Differential Sentencing of White-Collar Offenders in Ten Federal District Courts," *American Sociological Review* 45 (1980): 802-20.

52. Stanton Wheeler, David Weisburd, and Nancy Bode, "Sentencing the White-Collar Offender: Rhetoric and Reality," *American Sociological Review*, 47 (1982): 641-59.

53. See generally Harriet Pollack and Alexander B. Smith, "White-Collar vs. Street Crime Sentencing Disparity: How Judges See the Problem," *Judicature* 67 (1983): 175-82.

54. Susan Shapiro, *Wayward Capitalists* (New Haven: Yale University Press, 1984). My review is based on the original manuscript.

55. M. David Ermann and Richard J. Lundman, "Deviant Acts by Complex Organizations: Deviance and Social Control at the Organizational Level of Analysis," *Sociological Quarterly* 19 (1978): 55-67.

56. Laura Shill Schrager and James F. Short, Jr., "Toward a Sociology of Organizational Crime," *Social Problems* 25 (1977): 407-19.

57. Diane Vaughan, *Controlling Unlawful Organizational Behavior: Social Structure and Corporate Misconduct* (Chicago: University of Chicago Press, 1983).

58. See generally Thomas J. Bernard, "The Historical Development of Corporate Criminal Liability," *Criminology* 22 (1984): 3-17; John T. Byam, "The Economic Inefficiency of Corporate Criminal Liability," *Journal of*

Criminal Law and Criminology 73 (1982): 582-603; Brent Fisse, "The Duality of Corporate and Individual Criminal Liability," in Ellen Hochstedler, ed., *Corporations as Criminals* (Beverly Hills: Sage, 1984): 69-84; Rob Kling, "Computer Crimes as Organizational Activities," *Computer/Law Journal* 2 (1980): 403-27; Stanton Wheeler and Mitchell Lewis Rothman, "The Organization as Weapon in White-Collar Crime," *Michigan Law Review* 80 (1982): 1403-26.

59. John Braithwaite and Gilbert Geis, "On Theory and Action for Corporate Crime Control," *Crime and Delinquency* 28 (1982): 292-314; Gilbert Geis, "A Research and Action Agenda with Respect to White-Collar Crime," in Herbert Edelhertz and Thomas D. Overcast, eds., *White-Collar Crime: An Agenda for Research* (Lexington, Mass.: Lexington Books, 1982): 175-202.

60. See e.g., Francis T. Cullen, Bruce G. Link, and Craig W. Polanzi, "The Seriousness of Crime Revisited: Have Attitudes Toward White-Collar Crime Changed?," *Criminology* 20 (1982): 83-102; Francis T. Cullen, Richard A. Mathers, Gregory A. Clark, and John B. Cullen, "Public Support for Punishing White-Collar Crime: Blaming the Victim Revisited?" *Journal of Criminal Justice* 11 (1983): 481-93; Leslie Sebba, "Attitudes of New Immigrants Toward White-Collar Crime: A Cross-Cultural Exploration," *Human Relations* 36 (1983): 1091-1110; Henry N. Pontell, Constance Keenan, Daniel Granite, and Gilbert Geis, "White-Collar Crime Seriousness: Assessments by Police Chiefs and Regulatory Agency Investigators," *American Journal of Police* 3 (1983): 1-16.

—————— CHAPTER 5 ——————
TOWARD MORE EFFECTIVE REGULATION
OF CORPORATE BEHAVIOR

Ton DeVos

The regulation of corporate behavior in America is an interesting phenomenon; interesting both because of its history (or maybe its relative un-history) and its nature. Even though most of us consider government intervention in managerial autonomy an established fact of American politics, serious questions can be raised about its authenticity and its effectiveness. In other words, much of what has been called regulation may not really have been regulation and most of what has been attempted may have been predestined to fail. This essay seeks to deal with that issue and does so based upon the premise that the drive to modify corporate behavior has been basically quixotic and will remain so unless the proponents of regulation and critics of the corporate world make some considerable adjustments in their strategy, including their research agenda.

Critics and champions of interventionist policies generally agree that the Progressive Era and the New Deal years were the timeframes in which the basic structure for government regulation of business was conceived and developed. Richard Hofstadter and others even called that period the Age of Reform.[1] Several social critics have argued, however, that the reforms instituted in that era were superficial and were carefully "managed" by the more powerful and perceptive leaders of the business community.[2] They point out that the anticorporate feelings of the farmers and other victims and adversaries of the business community were cleverly used in enacting the sort of legislation and defining that state role which would least hurt and hopefully even serve the basic interests of the nation's captains of industry and finance.

Whether one totally accepts their argument or not, these critics raise some valuable issues. First of all, they remind us that politics is not a zero-sum game. In the Age of Reform business did not lose all the power it had, and the farmers, organized labor, small businessmen, and consumers did not become omnipotent. American business retained a considerable amount of influence over the affairs of state even though appearances may have been different.[3] Secondly, they reaffirm that both the beliefs of the general public and the continuing power of the organized business community have enabled the latter to substantially shape and adapt to the political initiatives of the reformers. While it may be valid to allege that government has "gotten on the back" of American business, the question may well be raised whether that figure of speech should not be interpreted to mean that business was "undergirding" government rather than that the government was significantly impeding the attainment of the business community's ultimate objectives.[4] The point is that the American people have consistently bought the laissez-faire argument and have thereby allowed the regulation of corporate behavior to be of much less magnitude than is generally portrayed.

Part of the explanation why this political dynamic has continued to prevail lies in the nature and quality of the role played by the academic community. Gilbert Geis's essay in this volume details both the general history and a review of the more recent work done by criminologists. He raises two issues that deserve to be pursued in terms of the role played by both the criminologists and other academicians.

Geis, first of all, suggests that the work of American social scientists on corporate behavior has passed through several phases. My contention would be, however, that even though it may be possible to identify different periods of intensity and approach to the academic analysis and critiquing of corporate behavior, the academic community's overall stance has been supportive of corporate America. Academicians not only have tended to share in the general public's belief system, they also have shown that they know where their financial and political support is coming from and what sort of accommodation is required for that support to remain forthcoming.

Those social scientists who have taken critical views of corporate behavior have generally been latecomers and few in number.[5] Criminologists have not been the only critical ones; some have been political scientists and economists. Each of these groups, however – until recently – tended to take rather narrow views. David Truman and Grant McConnell, for example, as people in their discipline would be expected to do, limited their work to an examination of the role of organized business in electoral and legislative politics.[6] Very few political scientists have talked about the responsibility of corporations for the indirect and long-range political consequences of their productive, distributive, and financial activities. Economists, in turn, have tended to focus on such activities as trusts and combinations and the impact these have on the competition and pricing systems.[7]

A number of academics have been left on the outside of the political dialogue by wording their criticisms in rather ideological and polemical terms, reflecting the sort of distrust and disdain for business to which Geis refers.[8] Some have gone so far as outrightly rejecting the capitalist system.[9] It is understandable that the business community has responded to such rhetoric with equal passion, readily painting the academic critic to be naive if not nihilistic. The political fact is that the general public and their public officials have consistently given more credence to the rhetoric of the business community than to what rather early in the Age of Reform became labelled as muckraking.[10]

This type of confrontational posturing that has been the hallmark of the interaction between the critics of corporate America and the defenders of the business community seems to be a natural outgrowth of the American civic religion. The citizenry in general continues to see free enterprise as the engine of social and economic progress and as the cornerstone of democracy. The bulk of the nation's academics also find the benefits and promises of the market system to far outweigh its costs. The radical critiques strike most people to be irresponsible if not the sour grapes of envious underachievers.

The conduct of a productive political dialogue is impeded also by the public's tenacious belief in the right of privacy of person and property, a belief that has severely limited the execution of systematic third-party research on corporate America. Owners and managers have been consistently reluctant to grant access to their premises, records and employees to anyone whose investigation they cannot control or for studies that do not promise to significantly improve the productivity of their workers and efficiency of their organization.[11] Systematic research also has been impeded by the widespread conviction that employees owe their corporation absolute loyalty. Such organizations in this country have never been considered to be real or potential democratic institutions and as all hierarchical political systems demand strict obedience, owners and managers expect employees not to divulge company secrets or practices to "outsiders."

Thus, there exists a situation wherein a small percentage of social scientists have taken a critical look at corporate behavior, and a number of those who have attempted the research have been severely handicapped in their access to data. Those social scientists who have been critical generally have been unable to refrain from being polemical. What they have said and written, therefore, has had minimal effect on the operations of corporate America.

A second point is Geis's observation that the research interests of criminologists have shifted from a predominant emphasis on white-collar crime in the personal and occupational sense to white-collar crime in the organizational sense, i.e., in terms of the behavior of particular firms or categories of firms. The same sort of focusing has occurred in the studies of other social scientists, such as political scientists. While most of their earlier works concerned the activities of business pressure groups, recent and current studies have paid much more attention to the activities of firms, whether they be multinational corporations, defense contractors, environmental polluters, or sponsors of political action committees.[12]

This shift in focus to a certain extent can be related to some of the recent changes in the political interests and perspectives of the general public and thus American academe. The nation lost some of its innocence in the sixties and seventies, and academics then began assuming greater responsibilities as critics of the social and political status quo. It proved virtually impossible for them to ignore such things as the thalidomide babies, the political assassinations, the urban riots, the debacle in Vietnam, OPEC and the oil embargo, the overthrow of Allende, the infant formula problem in Third World countries, and the rapidly deteriorating quality of the nation's air and water, to mention only a few disturbing developments. Even though some of these had little apparent connection with the business world, more and more people wanted answers as to who and what were responsible, where and why the system failed, and what could be done to prevent further occurrences. The climate was in fact ripe for the projection of scapegoats. Big business could not escape being a natural target; some of its members were indeed deeply involved with some of the events and concerns.

It is ironical that the basic beliefs of the American people about the virtues of business have not really changed much in spite of the critical rhetoric of the sixties and seventies and the emergence of public interest and other reform lobbies. The election and reelection of President Reagan can only partially be explained in terms of his personal charm and charisma. Much of the credit should go to his team's (and his personal) ability to appeal to occasional dominant but always latent American conservatism.[13]

It is true that ITT, United Fruit, and the big oil firms, were the objects of public wrath for a while and that certain definitions of unacceptable corporate behavior were entered into the statute books. However, it seems that again few of the reforms and criminal sanctions systems have turned out to be of great consequence. Some may even be described as having backfired. The system of public financing of presidential election campaigns, for example, not only left the door open for candidates to stay out of the system if they can raise their own money, it also spawned a mushrooming of political action committees. Business and single-issue interest groups seem to have become distinctly more influential than they had been for decades. Single-issue and conservative coalition politics has been used very effectively to remove from office such key personages in the reform movement as Senators McGovern, Church, Bayh, Magnuson, and Nelson. The electorate readily turned its back on reform again and reendorsed the dogma that the government "should be taken off the back of the American people" (and particularly the business community). They seemed to not show much concern anymore about right or wrong corporate behavior.

Our conclusion has to be that both academic scrutiny and legal regulation of socially costly corporate behavior is probably going to remain sporadic and of rather limited effect for some time to come. The American political-economic belief system—and that of the developed world as a whole—has not changed much and will change only very slowly, if at all. Waves of commitment to regulation will come and go. If such should result in the adoption of public policy and vast regulatory authority in new or existing agencies, by the nature of the situation one might predict that both the policy and the regulatory authority in time will probably either atrophy or be virtually repealed. The business community is powerful, very imaginative, and well-organized, while the public interest will remain nondescript and underorganized. At the same time reformers will remain moody and shrill of tone, if not also unconsciously guilt-ridden about how they are interfering with that magical wealth-machine, the market economy.

Two things might overcome this inertia. We, who have an interest in defining certain behavior as unacceptable, must enlarge, if not amend, our research and action agenda. In addition we must do all we can to communicate our findings and policy suggestions in terms that do not automatically generate defensive responses and reactions. All constructive critiques should be clearly targeted to the enlightened self-interest motivations of the relevant audience and in particular to those of corporate management.

The first item to be added to the research agenda should be a careful assessment of the various techniques of behavior modification. For example, defining certain behavior through law enforcement or civil litigation is only one alternative, and frequently not the most effective. For lawmakers to accept and incorporate such a definition into the code can present a substantial problem in itself.[14] Then, if the potentially affected parties are politically powerful, the odds are that the definition desired by the reformers will turn out to be modified to make it more acceptable and passable and/or the enforcement clauses will be watered down.[15]

Having regulation on the book then is only half the victory. Many a regulation has been undermined by lethargic or totally counterproductive enforcement. Since most regulatory agencies and executive departments are on friendly terms with their constituent groups, enforcement of an unfriendly regulation naturally will not be very vigorous and effective. Inversely, in the cases in which the enforcement agency is adversarial to its constituency, the chances are that the regulated parties are either going to do all they can to change the personnel assigned to that agency, obtain the repeal of the regulation, or find ways to circumvent it. Pitting wits against wits in a game of legal reform with only incidental or lukewarm public support does not seem to be the most successful method to obtain long-lasting modification of corporate behavior.[16]

The only time that the strategy of legal regulation can be successful is when the general public can be activated and/or an effective coalition can be forged whose strength and solidarity outweighs that of the parties to be regulated. Both of these are extremely rare circumstances and depend on the unacceptable behavior producing such undeniably high costs and such calloused response from the perpetrators that a virtual stampede of emotion is unleashed. Even many of these moods of passion, however, wane in time and the new law and enforcement expectations, which may have resulted from the burst of initiative, will probably – as suggested above – remain effective for only a limited period of time. Under such circumstances, corporate behavior will be modified only if it is judged advisable by management and only if it does not unduly undermine the corporation's ability to attain its basic goals.

Legal regulation is certainly not the only coercive strategy employed to obtain corporate behavior modification. Results have been obtained also by such procedures as consumer boycotts, public information campaigns, and pressure by institutional investors.[17] Consumer boycotts themselves have limitations. The damage done by the objectionable corporate action, for example, has to be distinctly demonstrable and of such a nature to generate a passionate public response. Boycott actions, furthermore, are much more effective if the cause can be made salient to some existing, well-organized interest group. It is equally important that the target corporation(s) either have a conscionable management team or be economically vulnerable to a boycott.

One thing that is imperative for an effective consumer boycott is a viable public information program.[18] The same is true for most campaigns that seek legal reform. It is, therefore, highly advisable that researchers and reform advocates pay more attention to the question of what sort of informational activities work best with what audiences. The fact that many product lines have their own consumer publics, for example, suggests the use of different media and slants that fit the particular situations. While scholarly meetings and publications are integral parts of the research and reform process, effective political and economic action require communication between the research community, the public policymakers, and the general public.

Even though legal regulation, consumer boycotts and more effective communication technology can be helpful in modifying corporate behavior, the greatest promise for effective, long-lasting behavior modification lies in changes in intracorporate motivations. Voluntary action by an aroused and enlightened management team avoids all the potential resentments and maneuverings that can result from the application of coercive techniques. A pragmatic realization on their side that acceptable behavior pays is also more productive of change in corporate conduct than the dogmatic adversarialism toward "ivory tower academics," which results from polemical encounters.

Most corporations intend to be around for years to come. Their managers – like presidents and prime ministers – want to go down in the corporate history books as the one who guaranteed the long term viability of the firm rather than as the persons who endangered its survival or growth. They are – as such – open to reason and to credible and irrefutable evidence. While there exists a certain corporate myopia that focuses on short-term profit maximization and personal career improvement, it cannot honestly be said that such a perspective dominates all of the nation's corporate boardrooms. That some men and women are without scruples and others may be unaware of certain corporate activities, or their consequences, does not automatically mean that most corporate managers are not open to reason, will not learn, or cannot be morally persuaded. Corporations and management teams vary in their values, sensitivities, and degrees of openmindedness.

To enter into dialogue, however, both reformers and businesspersons must assume the responsibility for being rational and reasonable. Reform-minded researchers need to present the relevant facts clearly and in good faith. Businesspersons should shed any defensiveness and inclinations to dismiss reformers as idealists or uninformed observers and recognize value in the information supplied by those researchers who study facets of the enterprise that may have escaped corporate attention or been covered up by irresponsible subordinates.[19]

These observations lead to the second major area in which research activity has to be expanded, i.e., the construction of a body of salient data on the social costs of corporate activities. Social scientists – and others so inclined – need to examine critically the effects of the various productive, distributive, and financial activities of modern corporations. Some work has been done, mostly by investigative reporters. Chemical pollution, for instance, became prominent as a reform issue through the mass media's reporting of the personal tragedies at such dumpsites as Love Canal, although the media up to that point had paid little systematic attention to chemical dumping. Even if one admits that some practices just are not perceived to be unacceptable until the costs have become public, it is rather curious, if not naive, to suppose that one can, for instance, add a chemical to the environment without first seeking to determine what its consequences (and liabilities for the corporation) might be. That an organization does so without adequate research obliges the scientific and academic community to assume some responsibility on the issue. Within the social structure of every society there should be independent agents of curiosity, innovation, and caution for whom questions about the consequences of human action are crucial. If the academic community has fallen short in this respect and/or the general community has undermined the viability of academe's basic functions, both should redeem this situation.

A more systematic inventory needs to be made of the consequences and the categorization of the costs and benefits of human, including corporate, actions and structures. Enlightened self-interest will never substantially supplant the pursuit of narrow, short-term self-interest until more complete and accurate facts are available. The diminution of myths and adversarialism may well require the development of a better consensus about such basic things as the rules of evidence and the methods of computation and presentation of the data. This would require that the business community understand how the social sciences operate and that the social scientists demonstrate their scholarly responsibility.

One set of data that needs to be collected is specifics about the patterns of unacceptable corporate behavior and the apparent correlations between these and key characteristics of the firms. For example, while the popular notion is that multinationals have such tremendous power that they probably act howsoever and whenever they want, systematic research may well show that smaller firms are the prime perpetrators of unacceptable behavior. Finding the facts about the correlation between firm size and behavior patterns would not only help make law enforcement more efficient (in those behaviorial areas where legal regulation is being attempted), but would help better target persuasive communication that may result in voluntary behavior modification. Equally significant would be findings which indicate variances in behavior as they correlate with the industrial sector or product line in which the company is involved.

Another important issue is the relationship that exists between the company's behavior and its culture. The literature about multinational corporations, for instance, suggests that corporations which are ethnocentric have a tendency to be both rather unaware of and noncompliant with customs and regulations in their subsidiary locations.[20] Researchers should then take the next step and determine whether the firm's nationality is an important independent variable.

Another variable that should be measured is the age of the firm or the length of time it has been active in its industrial sector and product line. One would generally assume that experienced firms have learned what behavior is costly in terms of consumer and political reaction and which is not, but facts to bear this out are needed.

Not only do the characteristics of the firms need to be studied, the same may well be the case with regard to characteristics of the environment in which they operate. One of these would be the nature of the particular market or industrial sector. It was suggested earlier that one would expect somewhat different behavior from a monopolistic firm than from one which is part of a competitive market. It also is quite possible that different industries have varying traditions and forms of behavior.[21]

Another major area in which more systematic research should be done is the cost-benefit analysis of the type of economic system in which most of the world's business activity is carried out. While Marxist, Leninist, and other ideological analyses of Western political-economic systems abound, they do not have much of an audience among those whose behavior reformers seek to modify. The researcher's charge is to inventory the effects of system structures and processes and to clearly tag those that incur particularly high costs. Such systematic work would then facilitate the development of realistic plans for preventive or compensatory action.

Something that needs to be examined very honestly is the apparent tendency of corporate managers to make decisions in light of the bottom line of their balance sheets. When a manager's career success is primarily based on the production of profit and growth, and a firm's capitalization depends on the stocks and bonds market, the pressures for short-term profit maximization are intense. Individual entrepreneurs and partners in small firms generally base a number of their decisions on criteria other than how much money they could make how quickly. The emergence of the corporate form of business organization and the managerial class — as separate from the owning class —

appears to have produced some significant changes in business ethics.[22] Examination of this issue should also touch the investor as well as the manager. Studies that determine how people view their investments and the use made of their money, attitudes concerning priorities and values in terms of accumulation of assets as well as moral and ethical contingents on how the funds are being dealt with, and the manner in which the interest is earned would be enlightening as to investor behavior.[23]

A further area for investigation and open discussion is the phenomenon of rampant legalism and litigiousness. While rule-setting and conflict-settlement are unavoidable dimensions of human interaction – and significantly so in complex societies – the degree of adversarialism which has come to earmark this dimension of human interaction needs scrutiny. There undoubtedly is some relationship between the compulsive acquisitiveness referred to in earlier discussion and the "get-what-you-can" mentality which is involved therein. Similarly relatable is what some have identified as the paranoid style of American politics and society.[24] While product or service liability, to mention only one example of recent intensive litigation, is an understandable and necessary concept and practice, a thorough look has to be taken at the reasonableness of a number of awards juries have made customers and patients and the genre of attorneys this form of practice has generated.

An area in which a considerable amount of systematic work is being done but where much more is to be accomplished is the analysis of the implications of the global work and marketplace. No longer is the bulk of economic activities carried out within the confines of national jurisdictions by enterprises that rarely if ever operate in more than one nation state. More and more enterprises finance themselves and produce and market transnationally, and an ever-greater percentage of the global economic system's activities are generated by multinational corporations and their subsidiaries. Production networks are rapidly being rationalized globally. Multi-nationals shift production locations as labor and materials costs demand, market opportunities suggest, and changing political circumstances require. Some of these multinational enterprises are even described as geocentric in orientation, i.e., their company cultures do not primarily reflect the country of their origin or their headquarter's location. These types of companies are seen to have distinct interests and ways of doing things and rarely subordinate their interests to those of any nation state, including those of their home country.[25]

The globalization and denationalization of business activity presents two problems that need attention. The first one relates to enforceability of any rules or court decrees. In the absence of global enforcement structures, coercive transnational modification of corporate behavior through regulation would seem to remain elusive. The second problem is the prevailing disparity of power between multinational corporations and a number of national governments. Aspects for study would include the question of nationalism, transnational enforcement structures, and transnational solidarity.[26]

There are additional reasons why a more thorough analysis of the dynamics and consequences of the global work and marketplace is important in the quest to modify corporate behavior. The resulting systematic distribution of findings should help management to more fully understand the frustrations and activities of transnational labor, and vice versa. Such data could help both sides minimize the sort of dehumanized, impersonal perspective apt to prevail in a purely pragmatic, primarily confrontationist, mode of operation. Such a comprehensive analysis would surely show the degree of interdependence prevailing in the global community and the intermediate and long-term risks accruing from the narrow calculus that is involved in the short-term profit maximization mode of doing business. If it does, it can only promote the more effective utilization of the precarious inventory of mineral, energy, and human resources available on this planet and simultaneously makes it more possible to alleviate the sort of angry despondency politics that flows from persons and peoples who feel exploited and restrained in the attainment of their potential.[27]

Conclusion

However long-term or obtuse many of the above suggestions may be, it is my judgment that they have to be the basis or – at minimum – an integral part of the reformer's agenda. While some of the work suggested already has begun, more attention has to be given to its becoming more systematic and less ideological. The acquired findings finally should not only be measured in terms of their validity but also their communicability, particularly toward those constituencies whose interests are involved and/or who have the power to bring about change. Don Quixote was an admirable man, in some way, but he cannot be our model for the best use of our energy and spirit. As George Bernard Shaw observed:

> [Reformers] all agree that you cannot have a new sort of
> world without a new sort of Man. A change in heart they
> call it . . . It is not true that . . . Capitalism [is] the expres-

sion of human vice and evil will; on the contrary, [it is] largely the product of domestic virtue, of patriotism, of philanthropy, of enterprise, of progressiveness, of all sorts of socially valuable qualities . . . With such human material, we can produce a dozen new worlds when we learn both the facts and the lessons in political science the facts can teach.[28]

NOTES

1. Richard Hofstadter, *The Age of Reform* (New York: Alfred A. Knopf, 1952).
2. See, for example, Edward S. Greenberg, *Serving the Few: Corporate Capitalism and the Bias of Government Policy* (New York: John Wiley & Sons, Inc., 1974).
3. The socio-economic makeup of the Congress did not change substantially and neither did the sources of campaign funds. Campaign finances in the 1920s were dominated by the same firms that did so in the 1890s. This happened even though Congress had passed the Tillman and Federal Corrupt Practices Act of 1925. The Tillman Act prohibited direct contributions by corporations. Cf. Michael Malbin, "The Problem of PAC-Journalism," *Public Opinion* (December/January 1983): 15.
4. Ruling classes and interests do perpetuate the conditions of their own domination. The American system is no exception to that rule. See Michael Parenti's *Power and the Powerless* (New York: St. Martin's Press, 1978) and Thomas R. Dye's *Who's Running America?: The Reagan Years*, 3d ed. (Englewood Cliffs, N.J.: Prentice-Hall, Inc., 1983).
5. Note that Geis in his chapter suggests that sociologists did not deal with white-collar criminality until 1939.
6. David B. Truman, *The Governmental Process: Political Interests and Public Opinion* (New York: Alfred A. Knopf, 1951); Grant McConnell, *Private Power and American Democracy* (New York: Alfred A. Knopf, 1966).
7. See John Bates Clark, *The Control of Trusts* (New York: Macmillan, 1901); Elliott Jones, *The Trust Problem in the United States* (New York: Macmillan, 1921); Arthur Burns, *The Decline of Competition: A Study of the Evolution of American Industry* (New York: McGraw-Hill, 1936).
8. See Ch. 4.
9. See, for example, R. Edwards, M. Reich and T. Weiskopf, *The Capitalist System* (Englewood Cliffs, N.J.: Prentice-Hall, 1978); Immanuel Wallerstein, *The Origins of the Modern World System* (New York: Academic Press, 1974).
10. Mathew Josephson, Upton Sinclair, Ida Tarbell, and Lincoln Steffens earned that tag rather early for their work on the business elite, the meatpacking industry, Standard Oil, and corruption in the cities, respectively.
11. This researcher and many of his colleagues have found it much more dif-

ficult to obtain access to corporate personnel in American firms than to their counterparts in Europe (including American subsidiaries there).

12. Examples of this type of work are Richard Barnet & Ronald Müller's *Global Reach* (New York: Simon & Schuster, 1975); Abdul Said's *The New Sovereigns* (Englewood Cliffs, N.J.; Prentice-Hall, 1975); Raymond A. Bauer, Ithiel de Sola Pool & Anthony Dexter, *American Business and Public Policy* (New York: Atherton Press, 1963); Mancur Olson, *The Rise and Decline of Nations* (New Haven: Yale University Press, 1982); Charles E. Lindblom, *Politics and Markets* (New York: Basic Books, 1977).

13. The White House Office of Public Liaison, first operated in the Reagan administration, led by Elizabeth Dole and later by Wayne Valis, has as its prime responsibility to act as a brokerage house for an aggressive new business politics by organizing kitchen cabinets for particular policy areas. *New York Times* (10 March 1983): 13.

14. Just consider how long it took to get even the basic antitrust statutes. The Sherman Act of 1890 did not do the job; it required the passage of the Clayton and Federal Trade Commission Acts of 1914 to make for a workable package of regulations.

15. The Department of Justice in most administrations has not exactly stood out for arduous enforcement of anti-trust regulation!

16. Indicative of what will readily happen is the flurry of deregulation and dismantling of regulatory agencies occurring during the Reagan administrations.

17. One of the most publicized areas in which such strategies have been used successfully is in the campaign to modify the marketing practices of infant formula producers in the Third World. Even though the adjustment in marketing practices of such firms as Nestlé, Bristol-Myers, and American Home Products has to be partially credited to the actions of the World Health Organization, considerable impact was achieved by such groups as Infant Formula Action Coalition (INFACT), the International Nestlé Boycott Committee, the Interfaith Center for Corporate Responsibility, the Investor Responsibility Research Center, and the Sisters of the Precious Blood. Their seven-year boycott, sponsorship of proxy resolutions, visitations to management, etc. contributed significantly to the change in corporate behavior in the industry. See *The Dilemma of Third World Nutrition: Nestlé and the Role of Infant Formula*, a report prepared in 1983 for Nestlé, S.A. by Maggie McComas, Geoffrey Fookes, and George Taucher.

18. INFACT did organize the widespread distribution of the film *Bottle Babies*, which activated many (including Bill Moyers, who came out with his own CBS Report titled *Into the Mouths of Babes*), developed boycott literature, conducted a mock funeral for infant formula victims, and organized a national INFACT day in mid-April 1978.

19. There always have been and shall remain to be corporate leaders who carefully monitor their critics. Such reconnaissance can certainly help the business community guide the regulatory process rather than leave them to be victimized by strident opponents. See A. Lee Fritschler and Bernard H. Ross, *Business Regulation and Government Decision-Making* (Cambridge: Winthrop, 1980).

20. Amos Perlmutter, "The Tortuous Evolution of the Multinational Corporation," *Columbia Journal of World Business* 4 (January-February 1969): 9-18.
21. Although I would hesitate to list certain industries as particularly prone to commit unacceptable behavior, it is a fact that certain kinds of firms have been criticized much more than others as endangering the health and welfare of individuals. While some of the criticisms relate to the type of products and directness of its relationship to human health (e.g., chemicals), some of them result from management and marketing practices.
22. Single proprietor enterprises and firms tend to be smaller and thus less impersonal and remote from the clientele. Larger corporate enterprises have most of their decisions made directly or indirectly, i.e., under the guidance of the managerial professionals. The latter have different goals than client approval and friendship. See James Burnham, *The Managerial Revolution* (Bloomington: Indiana University Press, 1941).
23. All this does not suggest that profit is evil and that venture capital would remain as freely available as it is now if investors altered their behavior radically. However, the pursuit of profit in utter disregard for its consequences may legitimately be called socially irresponsible and counterproductive to the attainment of a way of life which rises above the dog-eat-dog ethic. Boyce Rensberger, "What Made Humans Human," *New York Times Magazine* (1 April 1984): 80-95, suggests that peaceableness and cooperation are the traits that began to distinguish the human species from its evolutionary ancestors.
24. Richard Hofstadter, *The Paranoid Style in American Politics and Other Essays* (New York: Alfred A. Knopf, 1965).
25. Perlmutter, "Evolution of the Multinational Corporation," 14.
26. Errant multinational corporations benefit from the fact that nationalism continues to prevail as the dominant ideology of these times. As long as that remains to be the case, transnational enforcement structures will continue to remain absent or falter and code-developing organizations like the Organization for Economic Cooperation and Development and the United Nations will have only very limited success in reaching agreement. Also, so long as the global recession is slow in turning around and unemployment and public revenue problems persist, national governments will never attain the solidarity among themselves which is required effectively to countervail the power of the major transnationals.
27. A greater comprehension of the global reality should help those in the general public sense the double standards which have been applied in the global work and marketplace. Such – in turn – should help to alleviate the kind of parody involved in the practice of considering only interests and retaliatory capabilities of the customers in one's own national jurisdiction while totally ignoring the best interests of those residing in jurisdictions that have very little or no coercive power over one's operation. While awareness certainly does not automatically produce behavior modification, the odds are that the chances of attaining modification tend to be much greater if and when the evidence is available. More systematic analysis and education about the dimensions of globality in socio-cultural and economic interaction appears to be a natural part of the reform strategy.

28. George B. Shaw, *Everybody's Political What's What*, 1944, as quoted in *G. B. Shaw: A Collection of Critical Essays*, ed. Ralph J. Kaufman (Englewood Cliffs, N.J.: Prentice-Hall, 1965).

CHAPTER 6
EFFICIENT CORPORATE HARM: A CHICAGO METAPHYSIC

John Byrne and Steven M. Hoffman

Introduction

With the emergence of the large business organization as a dominant institution in contemporary society, the traditional focus of economics and criminal law on the individual has been challenged. Efforts to adapt criminal law to reflect the realities of a pervasive corporate order have met with only mixed success. Indeed, one writer suggests that the application of criminal law to issues of corporate harm has resulted in such a "weak and undeveloped" idea of corporate criminal liability as to endanger the very notion.[1] Similarly, numerous problems have accompanied recent efforts in the field of economics to apply the conventional theory of the firm to complex organizations, especially the large corporation.

The mutual state of underdevelopment manifested in criminal law and economics' handling of corporations underscores the need for a coherent interdisciplinary theory of the area. An approach that is drawing increasing attention and interest is what is commonly referred to as the Chicago School approach to the economic analysis of law. Developed by lawyers and economists including Coase, Stigler, Becker, Posner and Elzinga and Breit, this framework seeks to direct the insights of economic theory to the task of revising corporate criminal law. This chapter focuses on the economic approach as a possible remedy to one problem in corporate criminal law, namely, the appropriate corporate sanction.

Elzinga and Breit[2] will be relied upon to illustrate both the specific policy attitude and the general normative orientation of the economic framework. This work provides in our view one of the most cogent expositions of the concepts, logic, and norms involved in the economic analysis of law and is additionally attractive for its practical tone, which keeps the volume largely free of the excess and zeal not infrequently exhibited by writings in this field. By focusing on their arguments, we hope that our own concerns with and objections to the economic approach are more clearly defined.

We begin with a review of basic concepts in the economic analysis of law and then summarize the major contributions made by Elzinga and Breit. A critical analysis ensues which concentrates on the building blocks of the economic framework: the rational actor model which these writers extend to explain corporate decisionmaking generally and criminal choice in particular; and the expectational calculus which they employ as a calibrator for corporate actions under conditions of uncertainty. We challenge the realism of these analytic constructs and argue that the defense mounted by Elzinga and Breit and others in favor of their use betrays an antagonism to the complexities involved in analyzing the corporate world. This antagonism results from a self-sealing quality in the economic analysis of law that disposes it to serve less as a theory of corporate criminal law than as some sort of guide to life. We conclude that the problem of devising criminal sanctions against corporations cannot be usefully addressed, much less resolved, within the economic framework as presently constituted. The need for an interdisciplinary theory remains.

The Coasian Framework: The Harm in Preventing Harm

To understand the debate over the problem of corporate criminal sanction, and in particular its recent focus on the economic dimensions of punishment, it is useful to begin with a review of the arguments credited by nearly all of the participants as having laid the foundations for the economic analysis of law. These arguments are contained in a paper by Ronald Coase which demarcated the concern of an economic analysis as the "actions of business firms which have harmful effects on others."[3]

In the article, Coase characterizes conventional legal analysis as follows: "The question is commonly thought of as one in which A inflicts harm on B and what has to be decided is: how should we restrain A?"[4] But, according to Coase, this approach fails to recognize the *reciprocal* nature of harm, a key concept in the economic analysis: "to avoid the harm to B would inflict harm on A." Recognition of this apparently obvious relation has a nonobvious consequence: "The real question that has to be decided is: should A be allowed to harm B or should B be allowed to harm A? The problem is to avoid the more serious harm."[5]

Armed with this insight, Coase challenges the traditional legal approach to the problem of business-induced harm on two grounds. First, he reasons that it is likely to ignore the consequences of legal arrangements of rights that may make efficient market transactions too costly. Second, even where the cost of scaling the legal wall is not prohibitive, a legal approach needlessly requires economic actors to divert resources away from productive activities and into the unproductive activity of making the law efficient in spite of itself.[6] The remedy lies in a new approach to law. Coase seeks to address the problem of harmful effects of business enterprise in a framework that renders rights as factors of production, understands the law as the codification of rights to employ factors of production to various ends, and evaluates law according to the opportunity costs created by the exercise of legal rights. By this measure, a legal system has as its aims the encouragement of maximum output and the reduction or elimination of the costs of engaging in economic exchange (i.e., what are termed transaction costs).[7] Interestingly, Coase shows that a legal system would not be necessary, or at least would be economically harmless, if there were no transaction costs. In such a case, economic actors would settle on the allocation of rights that in each instance maximizes output. While his argument invokes a fanciful history of law, it may also be understood as Coase's effort to assure the reader that the economic analysis will not forsake law entirely.

What distinguishes this approach, among other things, is that the meaning of rights and their relation to law is no longer to be found in what Coase regards as a one-sided consideration of harm (or benefit, as the case may be). Rather, law and rights are to emerge from the reciprocal give-and-take of rational agents seeking to maximize utility (wealth); a reflection of the logic of mutually beneficial exchange. In Coase's vision of society, the consequence of preventing harm is necessarily to cause harm. The aim of law must be to prevent harm only when it would not cause greater harm. The harm that results from the economic give-and-take is offensive and should be redressed *only* when total output might suffer and *then* only when preventing the harm would not reduce total output by a greater amount than allowing the harm to remain. The matter has been summarized nicely; "The real issue is: what party to the transaction is the most efficient in preventing the misallocation resulting from monopoly [that is, the harm]?"[8]

For economists, the Coasian framework brilliantly represents the communal belief: economic forces cannot be denied and legal arrangements will inherently be shaped by economic imperatives. For Coase, that the creation and enforcement of laws should be guided by this truth is obvious.

The Economics of Corporate Criminality

Elzinga and Breit[9] present a Coasian approach to the problem of antitrust violation. This work is widely referenced in the law and economics literature as an exemplar of both the economic approach to the design of sanctions against corporations and its value as a guide to policy in this area. From the vantage point of the economist, Elzinga and Breit's chosen focus on antitrust law is ideal since the explicit purpose of that body of law is to redress the ultimate economic crime of monopoly; what better place to argue the economist's case? A review of their analysis of the economics of antitrust sanctions is presented below. The review will proceed in two stages: the underlying decision-making model relied upon in the analysis is examined first; then their approach to punishment of antitrust violators is considered.

Corporate Criminal Decisionmaking

Elzinga and Breit predicate their analysis on the cardinal Coasian notion of the reciprocal nature of harm. In the antitrust context, this means recognizing that while the monopolist may harm the consumer (e.g., in the form of artificially high prices or unnecessary delays in bringing a product to market), efforts to restrict monopolistic behavior harms the monopolist (e.g., forcing the monopolist to surrender scale economies through reorganization).

> If liability is imposed on the consumer, a monopolist causes damage to the consumer of his product in the form of consumer's surplus lost. But if the liability is imposed on the monopolist through some form of antitrust law, the customer of the monopolist, in insisting through the law that the monopolistic behavior end, imposes a cost on the monopolist, the cost of lost monopoly returns. The question of "fault" is largely irrelevant in such a setting.[10]

Elzinga and Breit identify the central issue as the determination of the relative costs of the antitrust violation and the costs of enforcement of antitrust law, each weighed against the levels of corresponding benefits. It is this economic calculus rather than any pre-economic legal consideration of responsibility that is the focal point of the analysis.

The corporate sanction analysis developed by Elzinga and Breit depends upon a rational actor model to represent corporate decision-making as antitrust violations are contemplated.[11] The model relies on assumptions typically found in economic analyses of corporate behavior. First, the corporation is assumed to be a rational entity engaged in choosing among alternative actions in pursuit of maximum profit. Second, the corporation is regarded as unitary, speaking with one voice and acting linearly to fulfill basic goals. Third, while modes of organization may vary within the corporate world (differing degrees of centralization and hierarchy may be found, for instance), such variance is not expected to significantly alter corporate implementation of the maximizing algorithm. That is, the calculation of marginal costs and benefits is independent of the manner in which the corporation is organized. Finally, Elzinga and Breit employ a less common assumption that a particular risk distribution adheres in the corporate community, with risk aversive behavior being preferred. These views of the corporation are commonly associated with the work of Richard Posner and the Chicago School generally.

With these assumptions in hand, Elzinga and Breit are able to delineate the primary factors affecting corporate involvement in criminal activity. They include: the risk of detection and conviction, the predictability of punishment, the severity of the expected punishment, and the benefits of criminal violation. The risk of detection and conviction is conceived as a probability scale based on the corporate actor's perception of the effectiveness of corporate criminal law enforcement. The predictability of punishment affects the corporation's responsiveness to sanction systems. While all sanctions are convertible to monetary equivalents by rational actors,[12] it is essential that prospective corporate violators can ascertain the punishment, or range of punishments, they risk in criminal indulgence. Coffee has underscored the importance of predictable punishment to the logical operation of the rational actor model: if the punishment is not known, the decision calculus embodied in the model is prevented and the deterrent effect mooted.[13]

Whereas the first two factors involve the expectations of corporate actors about the future consequences of their acts, the remaining factors concern the economic quantities at stake in the criminal gambles, that is, the amounts to be won or lost. Severity of punishment represents the cost to the corporate violator if convicted (and if the expected sentence is imposed). This cost represents the potential loss to the corporation when deciding upon criminal activity and can be divided into two types: the direct costs of the imposed sanction (again, always expressible in money terms) and the indirect costs of litigation incurred in the corporation's unsuccessful defense of its behavior. Weighed against the cost of criminal activity are the potential gains, which include the direct profit from the illegal acts and the long-term benefit of reduced competition. The profit from illegal activity cannot alone justify its commission unless the rate of return associated with it is higher than that to be gained from the equivalent investment in legal activity. In other words, the opportunity cost of the illegal activity – the legal gains foregone – must be exceeded by the illegal profit plus the gains over time of being a monopolist.

Combining these four factors, Elzinga and Breit project the extent of corporate criminal behavior as a function of: (1) expected gain of antitrust violations, figured as the probability of successful violation[14] multiplied by the net benefits of criminal violation; and (2) the expected loss, figured as the money equivalent of the sanction (including litigation costs) multiplied by the probability of detection and conviction. Coffee's point discussed above may now be more readily seen: this corporate calculus requires certainty about the nature of the punishment to be formulated at all. The essential deduction of this model is given by Easterbrook, Landes, and Posner: "A firm will choose to comply with or violate the antitrust laws depending on whether its anticipated gain from the violation is greater or less than its expected liability."[15]

The Search for Efficient Corporate Punishment

Knowing how corporations will evaluate criminality,[16] the analysis then turns to the question of the most appropriate and effective legal sanction. Elzinga and Breit return to the Coasian framework to establish the proper criterion for assessing alternative penalties. They argue that because of the inherently reciprocal nature of harm, the key issue is whether the sanction as an allocation of harm produces, on net, more good than ill. Figured in this way, an optimal sanction is one which maximizes the value of total output.[17] Because output is at its maximum only when society has applied its resources towards their most valued ends, this criterion is another way of expressing the basic economic principle of efficiency; greatest output for a given input. The output is recognized as including both private and public goods; the optimal sanction is "determined by the intersection of the marginal social benefit and marginal social cost curves."[18] This intersection will correspond to "an antitrust approach that will maximize economic welfare and be consistent with the goal of approximating the benefits of perfect competition."[19] In other words, Elzinga and Breit are in search of an antitrust penalty that will deter inefficient monopoly – those instances where monopoly does not approximate the benefits of competition[20] – on the one hand and inefficient law enforcement on the other.

Their search begins with a survey of three traditional antitrust penalties: incarceration, structural relief (internal reorganization), and treble damages suits.

Incarceration

Employing the rational actor model, Elzinga and Breit find incarceration economically wasteful on at least two grounds. Because incarceration requires identification of individuals responsible for the antitrust violation, resources allocated to investigation necessarily must be substantial with often little likelihood of detecting the culprit. Elzinga and Breit suggest that, based on a review of antitrust cases, judges and juries are "understandably reluctant" to impose this form of punishment on a "well-dressed, wealthy, articulate pillar of the community" unless they can be certain that they are dealing with the business equivalent of the "common mugger or bank robber."[21] Thus, incarceration as a corporate criminal penalty suffers in the first instance from an excessive demand on legal resources relative to the level of punishment output obtained.

The second failing of incarceration is that it can only create costs for the legal system; it has conventionally no capacity to produce revenues for the system. This characteristic would not count against the sanction except that as Elzinga and Breit point out, there are sanction alternatives that encumber no resources while at the same time actually generating revenues, most notably, fines. Translated, this means that incarceration is inefficient in deterring corporate crime: "Whenever any penalty can give the same amount of deterrence at less cost, or additional deterrence for the same cost, that option is economically superior."[22] In other words, incarceration is bad business.

Structural Relief

A second form of sanction considered by Elzinga and Breit is structural relief, by which is meant some form of internal reorganization of the corporation, including dissolution, divorcement, and divestiture.[23] This sanction is predicated on the notion that anticompetive conditions stem from inordinate market power of individual firms. But this definition of monopoly is the cause of this sanction's major problems. If market power is the measure of monopoly, then presumably any one or more of the conventional criteria for defining market power would be adequate.[24] Elzinga and Breit, however, demonstrate the practical difficulty of applying these definitions. More importantly they argue that market power is only a symptom of monopoly; it is a necessary but not sufficient condition.

According to them, the proper measure of monopoly is the failure of a firm or industry to provide output at the least cost, or more precisely, to shift to the lowest available cost curve that competitive conditions would warrant.[25] Monopolists are able to resist pressures to minimize costs because of their "power over price" which they can manipulate through changes in quantity sold.[26] The difference between monopoly as a cost condition and as a circumstance of market power is basic. If a legal system uses the structuralist emphasis on market power, then large organizations become the target of antitrust prosecution. But

Elzinga and Breit argue that large organizations may in fact represent the most efficient means of production in certain markets. Citing Coase's theory of the nature of the firm,[27] they relate organizational scale to the cost of contracting, arguing that central planning brought about by increasing organization may more efficiently extend production than a series of smaller firms competing for market shares. Indeed, it is suggested that the existence of large organizations may be interpreted as evidence of the workings of competitive rather than monopoly markets: "Some entrepreneurs (or managers) will be less likely to make mistakes and can therefore efficiently organize a larger bundle of inputs (thus making for a larger firm) than other entrepreneurs."[28] Posner concurs in the view that fewer firms in some instances is preferable to numerous competitors.[29]

Thus, structural relief poses not only problems of wasteful use of law enforcement resources but may promulgate both directly through its application and indirectly through its deterrent effect an inefficient scale of business organization. The authors concede that the whole matter is somewhat iffy empirically, but urge that the legal system forego experimentation and instead observe the limits set by objective economic analysis for understanding monopoly.[30]

Private Action Penalty

There remains to be considered the most well-developed and extensive antitrust sanction in the American system, namely, the private action penalty of treble damages. Given the assumptions of the rational actor model and its tendency to revere the efficiency of the market, one would think that leaving the matter in the hands of private actors to deter monopoly would be the preferred action. Yet, Elzinga and Breit reject the private action penalty. They do so, however, not because of any detected inefficiency in this sanction's method of deterring antitrust behavior; rather the flaw is identified as its excessive efficiency in deterring crime. Briefly stated, the problem is that the private bar will tend to "overprosecute" and thereby deter monopoly beyond the point justified by economic efficiency.

It will do so according to Elzinga and Breit for three reasons. First, the private bar, in being a successful prosecutor, will discourage victims from taking corrective actions which are justified by their costs as weighed against the harm imposed upon them through monopoly. Or, what amounts to the same thing, victims will seek greater levels of victimization in order to increase the level of the treble damage award. Elzinga and Breit term this the "perverse incentives" effect. A second source of inefficiency is what they term the "misinformation effect." In this instance, the private bar increases the supply of damage allegations through nuisance suits beyond what is economically justified. They are able to do so because of the supposed risk aversiveness of corporations (an assumption strongly advocated but never empirically supported by Elzinga and Breit). This risk attitude makes them "tantalizingly vulnerable" to prosecution;[31] apparently, business does not learn from its collective experience. Faced with the highly complex and difficult calculation involving the certain costs of out-of-court settlement versus "the unpredictable payment of a relatively large (even if improbable) loss," many captains of industry submit to the private bar – this calculation is just too tough.[32] It should be noted that Elzinga and Breit must at least implicitly distinguish between the difficulty of this calculation and what the layman might mistakenly regard as the formally similar calculation of whether to engage in criminal acts. We leave it to the reader to discern the difference.

Finally, even when the perverse incentive and misinformation effects are small or absent, a private action approach exceeds the efficient level of sanction because it necessarily requires compensation of the private bar. As Elzinga and Breit observe, with this sanction "real resources are utilized not only in the conviction of violators but in the determination of damages . . . scarce resources that could be put to better uses."[33] This cost cannot be avoided because by the very nature of treble damage actions lawyers must be able to expect compensation for their efforts. Indeed, these legal entrepreneurs are entitled to profits in the same sense as any entrepreneur in a market. The court system being what it is, the result is that the private bar is able to produce more deterrence outputs per input of legal effort than other sanctions (such as incarceration and structural relief). Unfortunately, this level of individual production is beyond what market forces justify in terms of an overall level of economic efficiency. Thus Elzinga and Breit find the market an unreliable force for efficiency *within* the current legal architecture. But, they conclude that this problem can be easily overcome by altering the architecture.

The Optimal Solution – Fines

Based on the economic analysis of corporate legal sanctions, Elzinga and Breit reject conventional penalties because they either over- or underproduce deterrence relative to what would be called for in competitive markets *with* efficient legal arrangements. Their remedy is to devise a structure of fines administered through public enforcement which meets the Coasian requirement of efficiently allocating both corporate and judicial harms (i.e., the harms of monopoly vs. the harms of antitrust enforcement).

The economic advantages of fines are several. Because corporations are economic entities, economic punishments will be the most effective in influencing their behavior. Fines are also the least-cost economic punishment; according to Elzinga and Breit, "in terms of additional scarce resources, the cost of such a fine (once a violation has been detected and convicted) is in fact zero."[34] Second, a system of fines can costlessly bring the expected gain and loss functions into equality by simply varying the proportion of public antitrust enforcement resources devoted to detection and conviction. This is a significant advantage over private enforcement, which tends to drive the expected loss above the expected gain. Third, fines leave undisturbed the scale efficiencies achieved through time by increased organization, while simultaneously ensuring that corporate calculations of the net benefits of criminal activity take into consideration the relevant social costs (in the form of higher prices and misallocated resources of monopoly). This advantage of a fine system flows from the Elzinga-Breit rule that fines be set at a level equal to the marginal social cost of monopoly. Firms are then free to seek that level of organization which maximizes the "social benefits deriving from economies of scale."[35]

Thus, Elzinga and Breit are able to show that a fine system can be designed to precisely affect each factor in the corporate calculus — probability of detection and conviction, the cost of criminal activity, and its net benefits. Moreover, such a system is optimal because each factor in the model can be influenced according to the relative elasticity of the typical firm's calculus with respect to the factor. In this way, expected social gains are made to equal expected social losses, the equilibrium point of corporate crime. In the new legal architecture, corporations are free to invest in legal and criminal activity up to the point of this social equilibrium. Efficient monopolies are preserved and inefficient ones are penalized. At the same time, public enforcement of antitrust laws is constrained to a level which neither under- nor overproduces deterrence. The search for efficient corporate punishment is now concluded.

Failures of Realism

Elzinga and Breit represent their proposal for an optimal fine solution as grounded in realism, asserting that "it is the real world that concerns us."[36] This claim, as far as we can discern, means no more than they recognize that bargaining and negotiation are costly (transaction costs are positive). When one pushes past this concession to reality, however, there is little in the analysis that is grounded in the practicalities of either corporate decisionmaking or corporate criminality. The assumptions underlying the rational actor model and its application to the problem of corporate legal sanctions are far from realistic. Interestingly, a wealth of empirical evidence and conceptual challenges have already been formulated which cast doubt on both the assumptions and the general model itself. Yet this evidence is seldom considered in economic analyses of the law; indeed, Elzinga and Breit fail to reference this body of work.

In our view, the problem is not simply the lack of realism in such an approach, but an antagonism in the analysis generally toward the complexity and changeableness of reality. Elzinga and Breit's framework is indifferent and resistant to problems presented by contrary empirical findings and conceptual challenges that suggest that decisionmaking in large organizations is both a more complicated and less precise affair than they allow. As a result, their work offers little that would improve our understanding of corporate criminal decisionmaking. Indeed, it is easily shown that this analysis frequently leads us away from clear thinking about corporate criminal decisions. Yet, the framework contains nothing in its design which would force reconciliation of self-generated errors. In many instances, there can be no reconciliation because the arguments rest on data that cannot be collected or validated. As Coffee has argued, "it is a theory whose validity depends on data that cannot as a practical matter be gathered to verify or disconfirm it."[37]

Our discussion of the analytic properties of the economic analysis of law is divided into two parts. First, the representation of corporate decisionmaking by a rational actor model is examined. Discussion is then focused on the assumptions and implications of the expectational calculus used to describe corporate choice to violate antitrust statutes.

19th-Century Assumptions and 20th-Century Reality

The theory of the firm that underlies the rational actor model was written in all its essentials in the late nineteenth-century by William Stanley Jevons.[38] His theory bequeathed to contemporary economics the quintessential "economic man" who tirelessly calculates the effects of tiny increments of change in his commodity bundle to satisfy pleasure-pain preferences. Depending upon whether one is an objectivist or subjectivist, the refinement of von Neumann and Morgenstern's game theory[39] or Friedman and Savage's application of subjective probability to economic affairs,[40] to allow for the orderly assessment of uncertainty via an expectational calculus, completes the rational actor model used by Elzinga and Breit.

The most apparent difficulty in using this modified nineteenth-century model to describe contemporary corporate criminal decision-making is that it was constructed to stand for the thought patterns and behavior of an individual, not the twentieth-century corporation composed of many individuals, many products, many decisions, many values, and many goals. Economists for the most part, however, have been unconvinced that this obvious disjuncture between theory and reality requires significant repair of their ideas about firm decision-making. As Finkelstein and Thimm have observed, marginalist economics has always assumed the analysis of the firm could be extended "from a single-product to a multi-product firm as two- and three-dimensional Euclidian geometry would be extended to n dimensions. If the behavior of a single-product firm can be analyzed in two dimensions, and n product-firm could be considered to lie in n + 1 space and to have n independent variables in its profit function."[41] As with the existence of multiple products, the fact of many individuals, many goals, and so on has been regarded merely as a complication requiring extension but not reconstitution.

In the marginalist tradition, the firm is a "black box"; the process by which decisions are made may be eccentric, convoluted, and irrational without significantly affecting the character of the decision. The only relevant characteristic is that the decision process be directed finally toward the maximization of firm profit. Neither the number of individuals nor the layers of organization involved are expected to play a critical role in the decision process. But Berle and Means[42] demonstrated long ago (1932) that large organization influences both the nature of decisionmaking and its outcomes. With the rise of the stockholder corporation, the unitary decisionmaker gave way to a technocratic and managerial order which decided business strategy "on behalf of" the owners. This elite transformed the corporation into a multifaceted business and redirected the focus of business strategy away from profit maximization and toward expansion of sales, market influence through advertising, and the search for monopoly power within an otherwise competitive landscape.[43]

The rise of the managerial and technical elite had consequences far beyond the compromise of profit maximization. For example, it had the further effect of creating a tension between the economic objectives of the elite and the corporation's owners. Williamson's analysis of the modern corporation suggests that managers control profits and in fact lower them in order to improve their own economic circumstances; in other words, managers maximize their own interests and not the interests of the firm (although some limit must be observed, lest new owners and new managers result).[44] Leibenstein has extended the argument regarding the conflict between "firm owners" and "firm members."[45] While agreeing that profit maximization is inadequate as an objective function for large organization, he likewise questions the value of a managerial discretion model in which managers maximize a composite utility function of profits, sales, the firm's growth rate, and managerial perquisites. Efforts to achieve a maximum for this utility function are impeded by the size of the management group, the lack of individual manager control of the group decision environment, and the nonaggregative character of the individual objectives. As a result, "groups involve potential conflict, which puts into question certain basic concepts that are applicable to individuals" such as the existence of a single, unique utility function and the internal consistency of maximization strategies.[46]

The increased scale and complexity of organization has also been linked to the pursuit of nonpecuniary values in business. Fisse has noted that "[i]n bureaucratic practice, if not in economic theory, corporations are agencies having nonmonetary as well as monetary goals."[47] A host of nonmonetary goals have been found to influence decisions in large organizations, including power, security, community involvement, and X-efficiency.[48] These values are not easily accommodated in a model such as that used by Elzinga and Breit since they greatly cloud the issue of what counts as a gain or loss (and therefore what a fine on antitrust behavior would deter).

Even the idea that corporations are maximizers – without defining what they are maximizing or for whom – has been disputed in recent organizational studies. The work of what is now called the Carnegie School – Herbert Simon, Richard Cyert, and James March – portrays decisionmaking in organizational society as sub-optimizing.[49] Individuals face a reality in the age of organization where there are significant costs to learn, decide, and transact. These costs constrain the search to optimize and impel decisionmakers to seek satisfactory pleasure/ profits only. The answer to complexity in this world is "weakening the requirements for solution – by requiring solutions only to approximate the optimum, or by replacing an optimality criterion by a satisficing criterion."[50] For the firm, this means that:

> so long as profits are at a satisfactory level, management [may] devote the bulk of its energy and resources to the expansion of sales. Such a goal may, perhaps, be explained by the businessman's desire to maintain his competitive position, which is partly dependent on the sheer size of his

enterprise, or it may be a matter of the interests of management (as distinguished from shareholders), since management's salaries may be related more closely to the size of the firm's operations than to its profits, or it may simply be a matter of prestige.[51]

In sum, the empirical and conceptual analysis of organizations in this century suggests that growing organizational scale and complexity have affected the decision process of business in a way which precludes treatment of corporations as extensions of nineteenth-century "economic man." The importance of profit as a maximand has been diluted; the focus of internal organizational decisionmaking has shifted to discretionary actors and groups (in particular, managers); nonmonetary values have grown in importance in the development of business strategies; and the rationality of maximization has been undermined.

This would seem to leave the marginalist theory of the firm without much empirical or analytic value to the problem of explicating corporate criminal decisionmaking. Its decisionmaker, the isolated individual, is an inappropriate surrogate for the modern corporation. Further, its method of decisionmaking, maximization, is unavailable or irrelevant in many cases. And its decision goal, profit, faces stiff competition from other organizational goals. Why and how corporations commit crimes is suddenly no longer straightforward. These difficulties naturally pose serious problems as to the efficacy of Elzinga and Breit's proposed system of fines. Insofar as the deterrent impact of fines is predicated on their influence on a unitary corporate profit maximization function, the existence of multiple maximands within large organizations confounds and may actually block the deterrence message. In the absence of an unambiguous deterrence circuit, the capacity of fines to establish an equilibrium price for corporate crime which clears the market at a social optimum is suspect. As a result, antitrust violations can vary independently of the efficiency point envisaged by a fine system with no clear damper on their growth. Finally, if fines cannot be counted on to change firm behavior, victims remain victims. The only certain effect of fines would be their eventual absorption by the weakest link in the offending corporation's market sphere—the shareholders, workers (as a result of plant closings, for example), or consumers. In this respect, law will constitute a sort of Darwinian instrument for toughening the victim population.

The Wonderland of Economic Expectation

Efforts to operationalize the expectational calculus (expected gains reduced by expected losses) supposed in the rational actor model meet with similar problems of realism. That calculus employs probabilities to stand for the perceived risks of criminal activities by corporations. As a method of risk measurement, probability lends to the rational actor model the aura of precision required to make credible its promise of a decision pattern which will optimally allocate business and law enforcement resources. Indeed, the capacity for precision is vital to the proposed fine policy: if this sanction approach is to influence firm behavior *efficiently*, the future must be accurately anticipated in order that corporations can choose the socially optimal organizational scale and level of criminal participation. It should be noted, therefore, that in the rational actor model probability cannot stand for the layman's inexact sense of the "chance" that an event will occur. It must observe the mathematical properties of a probability distribution in order to yield a logically coherent and predictable image of expectation. Similarly, expected utility, as used by Elzinga and Breit, must correspond to the mean value of a frequency distribution; not just any approximate idea of future benefit or cost will do when it is their effect at the margin that is all-important. This does not rule out the possibility that probability might be subjectively based. But even subjective probabilities must conform with the basic mathematical axioms of probability generally.

The use of probability to transform uncertainty into a well-ordered function of economic risk has been debated in economic circles throughout this century. Specification of how uncertainty affects and is incorporated into market activity is obviously essential. But despite the elegance, rigor, and conciseness of the probability approach, questions regarding its adequacy remain. The challenges to this approach are wide-ranging and cannot be fully explored here. We have limited our discussion to two basic problems: the first concerns the technical requirements of probability specification; and the second revolves around the joint probability or collective expectation of several actors.

Formally, the model put forth by Elzinga and Breit requires corporate actors to estimate four probabilities: the probability of being detected and convicted for an antitrust violation, the probability of being assigned a particular fine,[52] the probability of success (increased wealth) and loss (decreased wealth) scenarios flowing from the criminal activity, and the probability distribution of different "foregone opportunities" scenarios (i.e., the probable outcomes of legal actions not undertaken as a result of the decision to engage in antitrust violations). The base of information which would support their estimation is certainly enormous. Minimally, corporations would need to anticipate the economic results of a long list of their own conceivable actions, the actions of other economic agents which might bear upon the outcome(s) of the corporation's criminal act(s), and the future market for their own goods and close substitutes. With this information base, firms could form the latter three probabilities. In addition, violators would have to engage in an expectational speculation of the activities of regulatory and judicial agencies which might lead to their detection and conviction.

The data collection requirements alone would seem to prevent precise probability estimations by corporations. It would appear more reasonable to assume that even large business organizations would respond to such complexity in the manner described by Simon and others,[53] namely, that they would "satisfice" by limiting their search for information in the hope of reducing the requirements for successful action. But satisficing in this case could threaten the efficiency of the Elzinga-Breit fine system. The behavioral influence attributed by them to fines is predicated on their incorporation in an expectational calculus of ill-gotten gains against the imposed costs of the court. If corporations fail to attempt such a calculus, then the efficiency effect of a fine system is short-circuited. The likely result in the event of detection is that corporations will seek to plea bargain, in which case fines lose their avowed superiority at least over the private action penalty. They will overproduce deterrence in the same way that treble damage nuisance suits do and for the same reason – by failing to perform the calculus (because it is too difficult) sub-optimal harm allocation results.[54] Thus, the fine system proposal, to be credible, *requires* that potentially offending corporations engage in probability estimation, even if done sloppily. And so we are forced to accept another level of unrealism to rescue the model.

Things become murkier as one inquires further into the matter. In addition to the data collection requirements, corporations are confronted with a second technical task – applying probability rules to the mass of information gathered. These include: (1) the "completed list" rule – that all alternatives are known and accounted for in the probability specification;[55] (2) the distributive rule – as the number of alternatives considered increases, the probability of at least some alternatives must decline and vice versa (in other words, the probabilities sum to one); and (3) the frequency rule – the probability of an event varies with the frequency of its occurrence. It should be noted that these rules apply regardless of the data that support the probability estimation; whether firms are supposed to calculate the probabilities from impressions, "insider" information, business statistics, or whatever, compliance with all of these rules is necessary.

The analytic value of these rules to theorizing about economic decisions under uncertainty, however, has been challenged. Perhaps the strongest critic is G. L. S. Shackle who has presented his arguments against the probability approach in comprehensive detail over the last three decades.[56] We do not presume to summarize this effort here, but only to indicate some relevant highlights.

Regarding the "completed list" rule, Shackle has pointed out that this is tantamount to assuming certainty as the essential background of economic decisionmaking: "probability, in all its treatments despite their diversity, engages itself to distribute *certainty*, that the truth will be found amongst the members of some given list of answers, or classes of answers."[57] If all alternatives are known, then an economic actor is not "surprised" by the future; the future cannot be "disbelieved."[58] While time may pose an obstacle to knowing the particulars of what will actually occur, the future is nonetheless fully anticipated. In this sense, probability as an epistemic system delivers time still-born. This would seem a particularly ill-suited notion for Elzinga and Breit's probability of detection *and* conviction, because it means that corporate actors are presumed to know all possible legal consequences of their illegal activities, including whether and how they might be prosecuted. Since prosecutors, by definition, would not even be in possession of evidence of a violation when this probability is calculated, the presence of this term in the expectational calculus gives a truly other-worldly quality to the analysis.

The distributive and frequency rules also imply odd things about the decision process. For example, in the case of the distributive rule, the arrival of a new possibility, however remote, must affect the distribution of probabilities. The effect, of course, may be small. The problem is not with the magnitude of the distributive effect, but instead with the logic imposed by this rule on the formation of expectations.

> [T]he numerical assessments of different answers to a given question [i.e., probabilities] are required, essentially, to be proper fractions summing to unity, that is, together representing the certainty that, between them, the answers include all possibilities. This logically necessary feature of a *distributive* expression . . . has one implication which seems to be generally overlooked and ignored. It implies that one of the chief disabilities of some proposed answer, regarding its power to influence action-decisions, lies simply in the *number of its rivals*. To increase the number of rival answers

is to reduce . . . the probability which can be assigned to particular answers.[59]

In other words, a business manager's expectation about a particular future event A—high payoff for an antitrust violation—must vary according to the number of other future events he can imagine, regardless of his judgment about the certainty of A's occurrence. Such a procedure concentrates attention on the fickle—the rise and demise of alternatives with the "news" of the moment—which may be nothing more than an expression of social fashion, idiosyncracy, neurosis, etc. This is hardly the sort of decision process that is conjured by claims of efficient deterrence.

Probability theory does include a corrective to overemphasis upon the fickle. The frequency rule causes events considered in a probability distribution to be weighed according to their numerousness. Application of this rule to expectations, however, simply substitutes one problem for another. Now the manager's expectations about event A and other conceivable outcomes are to be weighted by business trends. Probability is a frequency distribution and represents what is known about the historical occurrence of events under consideration; that is, probability is a summary of historical knowledge: "[Probability] is knowledge about a particular, identified set of circumstances in an identified, 'proper-named' historical context, a set of observations made on some occasion which can be located on the calendar and on the map and on a list of persons who made them."[60] While such weighting provides some antidote to the myopia of short-term thinking, it does so by grounding forecasts of the future on knowledge of the past. But as Shackle has observed, the future by its nature is beyond knowledge and therefore "expectation is origination, not reason . . . it cannot be understood by the principles of logic alone."[61] This has implications for the possibility of probable inference: "When the materials of certainty are incomplete, no manipulation of those that are present will change ignorance into knowledge."[62] A procedure which encases expectation in what is known, indeed varies expectations predictably according to what is known, strains its association with rationality.

Shackle argues that probability rules are entirely sensible treatments of outcomes which are repetitive and regular in nature, and which have their standing in a definable continuity of events. But their application to human decision under uncertainty distorts our understanding of the conditions involved. The essence of human decisions about the future is their nonrepetitive character involving choice among "rival hypotheses"—outcomes that cannot mutually occur—

which nonetheless coexist for the chooser; that is, "choice is amongst things which do not yet exist except in thought."[63]

To accurately portray economic decisionmaking under uncertainty, a nondistributional concept of expectation is needed. Shackle has developed a method called "focus-values" which proposes to accomplish this. Whether one is persuaded by Shackle's proposal is not the issue here. Rather, what is at stake in the acceptance of any nondistributional method is the recasting of expectation against a background of "irremediable uncertainty,"[64] with the consequence that the economic world can no longer be rendered self-contained or self-determined. But it is precisely these consequences of a nondistributional method which make it an unsuitable tool with which to rehabilitate the expectational calculus in Elzinga and Breit's model. The effect of fines, as conceived by Elzinga and Breit, is fully internalized by all corporate actors *because* of the probability rules. Although these rules distort our understanding of corporate expectation, they at least ensure that the net benefits of all alternatives are compared. It is the inherent property of a distributional scale that a complete comparison is made. In contrast, a nondistributional scale does not promise a full accounting of all possibilities. A fundamental disadvantage, therefore, accompanies a more realistic treatment of corporate expectation: it cannot promise that the actions of corporations will always be efficient. If a repair of Elzinga and Breit's model were to be guided by Shackle's criticisms, it would no longer be possible to presume a corporate mind and to fully determine the thoughts of corporate decisionmakers. As a result one could not claim to know the responses of corporations independent of the circumstances that shape these responses. Only a hermetic economic world can deliver with certainty the optimality ordained by Elzinga and Breit for fines.

If there are drawbacks to the use of probability in conceiving individual expectation, its applicability to collective expectation is more problematic. In the case of collective expectation, it is necessary that either a consensus exists among individuals about the future or that the risk attitudes of individuals conform. The condition of consensus almost certainly cannot be met. Consensus implies that individual probabilities can be aggregated somehow to yield a single number for the collective. Insofar as individual probabilities are derived from subjective judgments, such aggregation is precluded because there is no common scalar for performing the summary operation. This leaves the possibility that orientations toward risk agree.

Is there reason to believe that managers and other decisionmakers in corporations share a common attitude toward risk? And specifically, is there reason to believe that an aversive attitude as assumed by Elzinga and Breit prevails? One might argue that "the market" imposes a discipline on organizational actors forcing them to recognize a mutual reality of costs and competition, to seek an accommodation of their differences, and to internalize a common attitude toward risk. A variant of this argument has been offered by Posner[65] to discount the possibility that managers might reduce corporate profits in pursuit of personal gain. But in the case of attitudes toward risk, at least, the discipline exercised by the market may actually lead managers to adopt riskier dispositions than their superiors. As Coffee[66] has suggested, pressure on middle managers to show a profit for their sphere of organizational responsibility, coupled with the insecurity of their positions, may actually encourage them to take greater risks, including those involved in illegal acts, in order to protect or enhance their place in the corporate hierarchy. At any rate, because of their place in the hierarchy, they will experience different pressures from those of their superiors and as a result will recognize and act upon different risks. Furthermore, Coffee has noted that psychological and other studies of risk behavior suggest that individuals are likely to be risk preferrers rather than averters when in the shelter of a group; this is the so-called "risky shift phenomenon."[67] If anything, this work points to the possibility that market discipline and the nature of corporate decisionmaking attenuate conditions needed to establish a consistent attitude of risk, especially an attitude of risk aversion, among corporate members. Certainly, the *ipse dixits* (as Coffee characterizes them)[68] which are cataloged by Elzinga and Breit in support of their presumption of corporate risk aversiveness cannot resolve the question.

This is not to deny the possibility that policies and procedures can be formulated which purport to express a corporate sense of risk. But it is far from evident that corporate actors will carry forward this uniform expectation in their decisions. Indeed, the segmented nature of large organizations documented in the research on organizational behavior militates against the achievement of a collectively observed approach to expectaction. Therefore, without a rational basis for believing that either condition necessary to the formation of a collective expectation can be met, there is little to recommend it as an analytic construct. And, correspondingly, there is even less to recommend a single prevalent substantive disposition such as risk aversiveness.

Admitting as much, however, would be fatal to Elzinga and Breit's analysis. The abandonment of the assumption of risk aversion loosens, if not unravels, the relationship between fines and deterrence. Elzinga and Breit's own graphs concede that risk-neutral or risk-preferring actors will be affected more by the certainty of punishment than by its severity.[69] If the risky shift phenomenon is prevalent in large organizations, or if managers find that risking corporate assets as opposed to their own is less risky for them, the deterrence claim for fines dissolves.

Not only is risk aversion crucial to realizing the projected outcome for fines, it is also what prevents the specific fine system championed by Elzinga and Breit from inducing its own perverse incentives. Losses under Elzinga and Breit's proposed single fine of 25 percent of pre-tax profits are capped; but, obviously, potential benefits are not. Fines levied against violators, therefore, will never liquidate their holdings. In addition, fines are to be exacted from all profits during the "period of anticompetitive activity" (an interesting question of fact unto itself). Thus the 25 percent amount may or may not be equivalent to the harm value capitalized by the monopolist over the anticompetitive period. Elzinga and Breit are quite clear on the point: "The 25 percent figure is not to be taken as either an estimate of the firm's profits attributable to its antitrust violation or an estimate of the misallocative damage done to society by the firm's anticompetitive activity."[70] Modesty prevents them from designing a fine equal to the harm – "the present state of economic knowledge does not enable these estimations to be made with confidence." Anyway, "rather than being concerned with compensation, our proposal is directed toward deterrence."[71] However, once corporations are freed from the conservatism of risk aversion, a rational response to this sanction approach would seem to be: Gamble on monopoly when the stakes exceed 25 percent of "normal" profits. In other words, decisionmakers are encouraged to acquire a taste for risk, an orientation patently inconsistent with the goal of deterrence.

A second perverse incentive is set in motion when antitrust enforcement agencies vary the level of detection and conviction activity to optimize deterrence. While Elzinga and Breit recognize that either the level of enforcement activity or the level of the fine can be adjusted for this purpose, they seem to suggest that the former is the more practical and perhaps efficient approach.[72] In any event, altering the fine is limited by the possibility that a firm will be bankrupted, an eventuality clearly proscribed by Elzinga and Breit as jeopardizing the root goal of maximization of output.[73] If we now assume that a deterrence equilibrium exists and that prosecution efforts score a number of successes in a brief period of time, antitrust officers pledged to the efficient solution must worry that the deterrence signals sent out could discourage not only inefficient monopoly but efficient ones as well. In other words, an oversupply of deterrence is imminent. Given the expectational acumen of corporations assumed by the model, certainly they would have little problem discerning the implication and would launch monopoly efforts during the anticipated lull in prosecution. Even if they were caught (presumably because of some oversight in their calculations), firms could amortize their fines as downpayments on investments in future more lucrative violations resulting from an eventual decline in the supply of deterrence. This would appear to be what Lee has argued more abstractly to result from trading off fine and detection-conviction levels.[74]

The expectational calculus of the Elzinga-Breit framework, then, presents the reader with several hurdles to be overcome by the imagination. While the amount of information required to construe the future is sizable, the corporation is to be deemed equal to the task; indeed, it can be counted upon to pursue and organize the data efficiently. Creative faculties are then summoned to discipline the data via probability rules so that a well-ordered vision of the future is achieved. This vision transcends the chaos of the organization's parts — the disagreeing, conflicting individuals who would otherwise muddle the corporate sense of risk. Appropriately, the elementary materials for this imaginative exercise are the thoughts and images of the future possessed by corporate members. It is well that the corporate body can pull together these materials and realize the necessary imperative: Be Risk Averse. For without this realization, the efficient solution is denied.

Those not able to imagine the corporation in possession of these powers, it would seem, lack the special metaphysical sense necessary to enter the wonderland of economic expectation.

Self-Sealing Analysis

The rational actor model and the expectational calculus together portray an organizational decision process which bears little resemblance to what researchers of the subject have found. Ordinarily, distortions of the magnitude associated with the application of these analytic constructs to organizational contexts would be sufficient to force at least some reformulation. Nonetheless, we can expect the economic analysis of law generally and specifically to avoid addressing the problems that have been raised.

Why is this so? In part, change will be resisted out of self-interest. Repairs of Elzinga and Breit's analysis, for example, would almost certainly threaten the proposition that fines are the optimal solution. But there is a more fundamental reason.

The rational actor model and the expectational calculus on which the economic analysis of law entirely depends are built on conjectures about mental states and processes. As such, there can be little hope of measuring and evaluating data relative to these models. In other words, these models can neither be expected to repair nor recalibrate themselves with the arrival of new information. This in itself is not untoward; the study of society and social institutions such as law necessarily requires conjecture on matters for which there is no hope of measurement. But the economic approach to this problem is distinctive. It can be summarized in two steps. First, there is the postulate that human thought, decision, and action collectively emerge from a black box; that is, they cannot be analyzed by attention to (research on) the internal workings of actual human beings because they are essentially mysterious. Instead, we know about mental states and processes solely and conclusively by the *results*. Thus, although preferences rule, there is no way of studying them—there is no accounting for tastes.[75] All that we can do is allow the results of preferences to stand for the processes by which they are created and acted upon; in the economist's shorthand, this is the utility notion of value. A second postulate is that although the whys or hows of thought, decision, and action cannot be known, the method by which each is weighed (measured) and ordered (evaluated) can logically be represented as rational. That is, while the black box nature of mental states and processes precludes direct access to the data, how the data are organized, filtered, and manipulated can be expressed in terms of a pure logic of choice as an analog of human reason. Specifically, this analog is directed toward maximization of values assigned to the data (utilities).

These two postulates need to be juxtaposed to understand their implications. On the one hand, we are told that the workings of the social world are predicated on mysterious elements—the incomprehensible mental states and processes of human beings. On the other hand, we are assured as to precisely what is transpiring at any moment in this world—the mysterious elements are being evaluated and the maximal values being determined. Said another way, the first postulate announces that *direct* measurement of the objects of analysis—thoughts, decisions, and actions—is beyond analytic possibility; the second tells us that there exists a surrogate for the measurement of mental states and processes that precisely specifies what will be the results. Indeed, the surrogate—utility maximization—is logically unassailable. Thus, what the rational actor model and expectational calculus present is a closed system of thought that is fully determined and self-fulfilling. Analysis of the central objects of study is precluded, while the surrogate measurement of the unmeasurable informs us of what the answer would be were we able to study the objects.

Fundamentally, this confers upon economic arguments derived from the rational actor-expectational calculus construct the status of assured truth. Investigation within this framework becomes an exploration into the thoughts available within the closed system. Liebhafsky in his review of the law and economics literature characterizes the analysis as just that: "[it] consists of a discovery of the meaning of the assumption originally made."[76] The truths found by this mode of economic analysis cannot be disturbed by reality. From the first postulate, it is clear that no empirical evidence can be assembled to defeat these truths. The second postulate, moreover, indicates in any event that all the empirical evidence ever needed for this mode of analysis has already been collected, analyzed, and summarized in the truth of maximization. As Leff concludes:

> "[S]ince people are rationally self-interested, what they *do* shows what they value, and their willingness to pay for what they value is proof of their rational self-interest. Nothing merely empirical could get in the way of such a structure because it is definitional. That is why the assumptions can predict how people behave: in *these* terms there is no other way they can behave."[77]

Understood in this way, Elzinga and Breit's search for the optimal corporate punishment constitutes a coherent rendering of the deductions available on this matter from the standpoint of the rational actor-expectational calculus construct. The lack of realism found in their description of corporate decisionmaking, and the lack of any detailed attention to the realities of antitrust detection, apprehension, and conviction, are understandable since the enterprise was never intended to engage these areas. Their work faithfully sticks to its subject and even eschews potential demands that it infer beyond its "data" which, as they frequently remind us, is "the present state of economic knowledge."

For just this reason, Elzinga and Breit admonish against conceiving the efficient fine as equal to the extent of the harm.[78] While they are confident that individuals can accurately and comprehensively identify costs to them (and even to others if given the proper incentives), the authors recognize that the extent of economic knowledge to date is such as to foreclose the possibility of an objective account of costs, particularly those of monopoly.[79] The point should not be lost as technical detail of the argument. The economic analysis is not prepared to vouch for estimates of an essential economic quantity – cost – in any specific empirical context (at least this is true if one does not regard perfect competition as empirically possible). Yet, it is fully prepared to assure us that this economic quantity is accurately known and completely accounted for in the (inaccessible) mental states and processes of human beings. This is one example of Elzinga and Breit staying within the limits of their "data"; the economic analysis of law "presented in such a way that while it is in form empirical, it is almost wholly nonfalsifiable by anything so crude as fact."[80]

Elzinga and Breit outline a new antitrust sanction policy which directly follows from their investigation of a closed system of thought. They know what corporations will think and how they will act in response to a fine of 25 percent of pre-tax profits and, therefore, empirical or other inquiry into either the corporate world or law enforcement is not needed. This approach – moving directly from a deductive exercise to policy – is by no means unusual. Indeed, the Chicago version of economic analysis of law is replete with examples of such leaps of faith. Thus, Becker is prepared to reorganize criminal law in light of formal equations that can never be empirically tested yet which prove that crime is most efficiently deterred by punishments directed to lower criminal wealth;[81] Becker and Stigler propose to prevent malfeasance in law enforcement by the efficient use of (what else) income bribes;[82] Rubin stands ready to counsel us on how to restructure appeals so that the inherent efficiency of economic forces is allowed fully to work on judge-made law;[83] and Posner is eager to rewrite constitutions that would ensure efficiency in the allocation of rights.[84] An especially daring example of this kind is Ehrlich's analysis of the deterrent effects expectable from capital punishment in which he manufactures the necessary data ("synthetic data" as it is called) to describe mental states and processes of potential murderers in order to establish the efficacy of the death penalty.[85] Not surprisingly, the data confirm the model's inferences.

Self-sealing analysis of the kind found in law and economics can only confirm the validity and value of its assumptions. There can be *no* other conclusion.[86] In this sense, such analysis presents the reader with stories about what has always been, always is, and always will be – the inevitable, unassailable forces of economic order. The economic analysis of law resembles less a theory in an analytic sense than a guide to life.

Economic Analysis of Law as a Guide to Life

Some members of the law and economics community appear to recognize that indeed what they have to offer is akin to a guide to life. For them, the essential truth of economic order is everywhere evident.

Priest observes:

> [T]he tendency of the set of all legal rules to become domi-
> nated by rules achieving efficient as opposed to inefficient
> allocative effects is substantially more pervasive than
> might be thought. It will be shown that efficient rules will
> be more likely to endure as controlling precedents regard-
> less of the attitudes of individual judges toward efficiency,
> the ability of judges to distinguish efficient from inefficient
> outcomes, or the interest or uninterest of litigants in the
> allocative effects of the rules. Furthermore, it will be
> shown that this tendency toward efficiency is a characteris-
> tic of the common law process so that the content not only
> of the common law itself, but also of the legal interpretation
> of statutes or of the Constitution, is subject to forces press-
> ing toward efficiency.[87]

He needs only the disarmingly simple assumption "that transaction
costs in the real world are positive" to arrive at this observation; that
and the closed system of thought embodied in the rational actor-
expectational calculus construct.

Another practitioner of the art avers that efficiency is inescapable
because it is the motive of an evolutionary process which eternally
shapes law.

> We have thus shown that if rules are inefficient, parties will
> use the courts until the rules are changed; conversely, if
> rules are efficient, the courts will not be used and the effi-
> cient rule will remain in force. An outside observer coming
> upon this legal rule would observe that the rule is efficient;
> but this efficiency occurs because of an evolutionary proc-
> ess, not because of any particular wisdom on the part of
> judges. If judges decide independently of efficiency, we
> would still find efficient rules. Intelligent judges may speed
> up the process of attaining efficiency; they do not drive the
> process.[88]

To demonstrate this point, Rubin requires but three formal equations
into which facts can never intrude.

Understanding the basic forces at work throughout society and history, it is possible via the economic analysis of law to discover "an
alternative moral system" that is self-contained and complete. Posner
offers that "rights can be derived from [the economic theory of law]
itself; they do not have to be postulated."[89] This lends to the economic

analysis of law a special power: it is able to deduce moral guidance directly from the eternal truth of efficiency, without the discomfit of complex reality interfering. Coase has recently urged economists and social analysts in general to take heed of the "decisive advantage" associated with "the treatment of man as a rational, utility-maximizer" and extend the successes enjoyed in the field of law to other branches and disciplines of knowledge.[90] Presumably, this would include the handling of moral issues that surround and confuse those areas as well.

The depth of enthusiasm for spreading economic analysis to other fields is genuinely felt. These men honestly believe that efficiency is good, all other things being equal, and do not understand why the message would be resisted. What, then, are the norms which guide the efficient life found so irresistible by these writers? In particular, what are these norms with respect to law? While Elzinga and Breit seek to tackle only a part of the problem, many of the normative implications to be drawn from this mode of analysis are made clear in their discussion of antitrust penalties.

They perceive the guide to life offered by the economic approach in practical terms. The force of economic realities, including the inherent costs of law (i.e., the reciprocal harm theorem), compel the search for an efficient solution to the problem of devising sanctions against corporate offenders. In this sense, efficiency is a practical ideal and its moral direction also practical. From this humble ground, Elzinga and Breit describe practical norms for addressing the historic legal concerns with redress (compensation), the moral standing of the victim under law, the rehabilitation of offenders, and the need for law to express principles of fairness and equity.

They observe that the optimal fine will function as forecast only if corporations can be certain that this punishment, and not the treble damages of private suits, awaits them. Otherwise, corporations are forced to engage in a calculus characterized by a high degree of uncertainty and, being risk averse, will continue to undertake a strategy of minimizing maximum losses through out-of-court settlements. Therefore, Elzinga and Breit advocate a system of fines without victim compensation: "A severe monetary exaction paid to the state by violators should be the sole instrument of antitrust enforcement."[91] They do not seek to deny victims any form of redress, but instead limit redress to simple injunctive relief without damages.[92] This is consistent with the Coasian analysis which denies moral or other priority to victims. In the Coasian framework, harm is always reciprocal, with victim and criminal regarded simply as legal categories, continuously subject to redefinition to meet the objective of efficiently allocating harm; they are not moral types. If nothing else, the Elzinga-Breit position is symmetrical in this regard: as there is no perpetrator to kick or soul to damn where corporate violation is concerned,[93] so there is no corresponding victim to protect or compensate. Indeed, the very notion of victim is suggested to be irrelevant to social concerns about monopoly.[94]

Without a victim, and therefore the need for victim compensation, a potential problem arises for this approach, namely, the detection of an antitrust violation. As Elzinga and Breit point out, the traditional source of information regarding violation has been the victim(s). They claim, however, that eliminating victim compensation will not significantly diminish the historic role of the victim-informant. The reasons given are interesting, to say the least:

> [t]he costs of providing such information are so low and the gains (even without compensation) so adequate that such information will continue to flow into the enforcement agencies . . . At only minimal costs, without even the services of legal counsel, [the victim] can write an enforcement agency about its belief. The payoffs in doing so, even in the absence of treble damages, are still very real. If the antitrust agency successfully prosecutes . . . the informer may benefit through lower prices. In fact, the incentives for an informer . . . may actually be increased in the absence of treble damages because of the concomitant elimination of moral hazard counterincentives [i.e., malfeasance in private antitrust actions].[95]

At one level the argument appears bizarre. It is difficult to believe that lower prices will actually occur and accrue to the informant, or that such a circumstance will be seen as adequate incentive to report violations. Moreover, the faith expressed by these two economists in the relative virtue of government officers is not only incredulous but extravagant: even theories which entertain the possibility of rational governments do not advise confidence in official virtue. But we believe that this reading of the argument misses the most important point. What Elzinga and Breit are after, in our view, is the notion that antitrust enforcement should not be a function of the extent of victimization. An optimal fine system implies, instead, that enforcement ought to be varied according to the extent and size of the inequality between corporate expected gains and losses from antitrust activities. Thus, the efficient solution decouples enforcement from victimization. Neither the existence nor number of victims is to be of legal concern; only the efficiency of the violation. In this respect, law is accorded no role of rehabilitation of offenders. So long as the recipro-cal harms are the most efficient, victims and offenders may prosper.

Then there is the problem of fairness and equity in a system that denies the need for compensation and the relevancy of victimization. Elzinga and Breit suggest that there is a natural inclination in Ameri-can society to believe that "a standard of equity or justice demand[s] that parties aggrieved by illegal anticompetitive practices" ought to be recognized and compensated.[96] Unfortunately, the "present state of economic knowledge" precludes the ability to achieve perfect equity.[97] Once again, the Coasian framework resolves the moral dilemma: "The real question is how much is society willing to give up, in the form of real income, in order to achieve the normative end of perfect equity, that is, full restitution?"[98] As Elzinga and Breit astutely observe, "Equity, unlike butterflies, is not free."[99] What this implies, of course, is that equity, like any other public goal, must undergo the test of recip-rocal harm before it can be accepted as a design objective of the legal architecture.

The practical ideal, then, is associated with a distinctive normative view of antitrust justice. If implemented, the business of antitrust law will be to define and protect a world of corporate activity where there are no legal victims, there is no need for compensation of aggrieved parties, enforcement seeks not to reduce victimization but to make it efficient, rehabilitation is avoided on the moral ground of efficiency, and equity is resolved according to the principle of reciprocal harm. Justice in this world will be served when monopoly is required to be efficient and "victims" are forced to pay their fair share.

This normative view finds nothing of intrinsic value in the judicial process itself and, therefore, dwelling on issues associated with that process is not regarded as necessary. Elzinga and Breit are not callous about the plight of victims and their demand for redress. But treating these matters within the judicial process is, in their view, ultimately self-defeating. From their perspective, only if incentives are redirected in the first place toward efficient allocation of harm can victimization, equity, and so on be addressed in a lasting sense.

The assumption that results are what matter is logically correct if one assumes that human beings are (mostly) about the maximization of pleasures. Outside the paradigm, however, the logic fails. As Weinrib has pointed out, justice is not solely and, in some instances, not even primarily, concerned with results. Both judicial outcomes *and* the process that creates them involve significant rights and values. Ignoring this fact leaves the process of justice as pure instrumentality. We no longer care how justice occurs; any means will do. As Weinrib notes, this is equivalent to arguing that dropping a golf ball in a hole eighteen times amounts to having played a round of golf.[100]

Attacks on the economic guide to life for normative weaknesses such as these often are rebutted by practitioners who argue that the guide was never intended to deal with such matters and cannot be expected, therefore, to offer coherent advice on them. This is an interesting admission as to the limits of the economic analysis of law. Michelman has characterized the defense nicely: "noneconomic considerations," so the argument goes, are to be "left for others – philosophers, or maybe poets . . . hard-headed lawyers [and economists] cannot fathom that other spongy stuff." [101] But at bottom this dodges the issue. When efficiency is held up as the all-purpose norm against which all others are to be gauged, this is not a display of deference on moral concerns, but a poorly disguised assertion of normative priority. Its effect is to shield efficiency from precisely the analysis of its normative foundations that is required. Apparently, it is believed that assuming the role of moral eunuch absolves the analyst of normative responsibility, which is to confuse impotence with discretion.

In the final analysis, however, the economic guide to life is not a modest proposal and cannot be defended by an appeal to practical ideals. Tullock applies economic reason (and, as he repeatedly reminds, "high school algebra") to demonstrate why.

> A person who feels that the evidence is such that he has a certain probability of conviction will, if he is rational, confess if he is given a suitable reduction in sentence . . . There is . . . no obvious reason why we should find this undesirable. People would only confess to a crime of which they are innocent if the evidence against them is strong enough so that they feel there is a reasonable probability of conviction. The sentence to be given to them . . . would be appropriately discounted in terms of the evidence against them.[102]

There is nothing formally different in this argument from those typically offered in the economic analysis of law. What is desirable can be discerned without bringing in the spongy stuff once one realizes the truth of efficiency. The solution is obvious:

> we . . . work out the most efficient legal system and we, then, enforce it by use of the courts and police forces. But we should also indoctrinate a similar ethical code. Under this system . . . the ethical system becomes subordinated to the law rather than *vice versa*.[103]

Sooner or later, the economic analysis of law comes to moral abso-lutism. Tullock's "revision"[104] is but one version.

The Theodicy of Moral Paradox[105]

Some will conclude (and many already have) that The Economic Analysis of Law is ideology masquerading as analysis and will charge that the framework is either unwilling or unable to take responsibility for its normativity. We certainly would not quarrel with this conclu-sion. But there is an additional, by no means incompatible, interpreta-tion which we would like to offer.

Our interpretation harks back to the following observation of Liebhafsky:

> This literature has been produced largely by economists who know no law and a handful of lawyers who have learned their economics from these same economists, all of whom are bound together by their acceptance of eighteenth-century hedonism and a philosophy produced under the influence of two ripe apples—one observed fall-ing by Newton and the other eaten by Adam and Eve.[106]

Under the influence of these apples, The Economic Analysis of Law presents but another extension of economic liturgical practice—promise the faithful that through the empowerment of greed the unin-tended consequence (think of gravity) will be advancement of the public good. Moral intentions need not play a role in the proceedings; anyway, their conscious consideration can only confuse the issue, increase costs, and lead to harm (reciprocal, of course). Economics' defense of the free market in all things is an effort to elevate moral paradox to virtue.

NOTES

1. Brent Fisse, "Reconstructing Corporate Criminal Law: Deterrence, Retri-bution, Fault and Sanctions," *Southern California Law Review* 56 (1983): 1144.
2. Kenneth G. Elzinga and William Breit, *The Antitrust Penalties: A Study in Law and Economics* (New Haven: Yale Univerity Press, 1976).
3. Ronald H. Coase, "The Problem of Social Cost," *Journal of Law and Eco-nomics* 3 (1960): 1-44, as reprinted in William Breit and Harold M. Hoch-man, eds., *Readings in Microeconomics*, 2d ed. (New York: Holt, Rinehart and Winston, 1971): 423.
4. Ibid., 424.
5. Ibid.

6. One is reminded of the historic distinction in political economy between those who produced and those who appropriated output from the productive classes. Lawmakers, like Ricardo's landowners, would appear in the Coasian framework to make their way in society by acting under the illusion that "what they had transferred . . . they had created": W. Stark, ed., *Jeremy Bentham's Economic Writings*, vol. I (London: Allen and Unwin, 1952), 234.

7. Indeed, Posner suggests that the essential rationale for a legal system is to prevent the emergence of prohibitive transaction costs in the market system, "If the initial assignment of some right – say, to clean air – will not affect the wealth of any assignee appreciably, then regardless to whom the initial assignment is made, either a market system (if transaction costs are not prohibitive) or a legal system designed to simulate the outcomes of such a market (if transaction costs are prohibitive) will ensure the final assignment of the right to whoever derives greater value from having it." Richard A. Posner, "Utilitarianism, Economics, and Legal Theory," *Journal of Legal Studies* 8 (1979): 108.

8. Elzinga and Breit, *The Antitrust Penalties*, 83.

9. Elzinga and Breit, *The Antitrust Penalties*.

10. Ibid., 83.

11. See Simeon M. Kriesberg, "Decisionmaking Models and the Control of Corporate Crime," *Yale Law Journal* 85 (1976): 1091-1129.

12. E.g., Elzinga and Breit, *The Antitrust Penalties*, 123.

13. John Collins Coffee, Jr., "Corporate Crime and Punishment: A Non-Chicago View of the Economics of Criminal Sanctions," *American Criminal Law Review* 17 (1980): 427.

14. Actually, Elzinga and Breit's analysis of corporate criminal decisions is limited to those organizations successful in the economic game. Whether or not an individual corporation behaves in the manner described is irrelevant; those that do will survive and prosper, those that do not will, without government assistance, fail, according to this logic.

15. Frank H. Easterbrook, William M. Landes and Richard A. Posner, "Contribution Among Antitrust Defendants: A Legal and Economic Analysis," *Journal of Law and Economics* 23 (1980): 345.

16. This probability is not the same as the inverse of the probability of detection and conviction. Successful violation involves: (a) enjoying one of the gain scenarios that accompanies violation rather than one of the loss scenarios; and (b) foregoing less profitable legal alternatives that would have transpired had the corporation not chosen to violate the law. Both are probability scales in their own right.

17. See Elzinga and Breit, *The Antitrust Penalties*, 112.

18. Ibid., 13.

19. Ibid., 16.

20. As we shall shortly discuss, not all monopolies are inefficient, according to Elzinga and Breit. See their discussion of scale economies, ibid., 99-106.

21. Ibid., 97,43.

22. Ibid., 123.

23. See ibid., 43.

24. Elzinga and Breit consider five criteria for measuring monopoly market

power: a firm's market share, joint market shares of leading firms, a firm's profit, a firm's absolute size, and a firm's (or industry leaders') price behavior. Ibid., 106.

25. Elzinga and Breit, *The Antitrust Penalties*, 99-106.
26. See Richard A. Posner, *Antitrust Law: An Economic Perspective* (Chicago: University of Chicago Press, 1976), 8.
27. Ronald H. Coase, "The Nature of the Firm," *Economica* (November 1937): 386-405.
28. Elzinga and Breit, *The Antitrust Penalties*, 106.
29. Posner, *Antitrust Law*, 15-18.
30. See Elzinga and Breit, *The Antitrust Penalties*, 107.
31. See ibid., 91.
32. Ibid.
33. Ibid., 96.
34. Ibid., 150.
35. Ibid., 100.
36. Ibid., 82.
37. Coffee, "Corporate Crime and Punishment," 442.
38. See William Stanley Jevons, *The Theory of Political Economy* (New York: MacMillan and Company, Ltd., 1871).
39. John von Neumann and Oskar Morgenstern, *Theory of Games and Economic Behavior* (Princeton: Princeton University Press, 1944).
40. Milton Friedman and Leonard J. Savage, "The Utility Analysis of Choices Involving Risk," *Journal of Political Economy* 56 (1948): 279-304.
41. Joseph Finkelstein and Alfred L. Thimm, *Economists and Society: The Development of Economic Thought From Aquinas to Keynes* (Schenectady, N.Y.: Union College Press, 1981), 354.
42. A. Berle and G. Means, *The Modern Corporation and Private Property* (New York: MacMillan and Company, Ltd., 1948; 1st ed. 1932).
43. See generally Joan Robinson, *The Economics of Imperfect Competition* (London: MacMillan and Company, Ltd., 1933); Edward H. Chamberlin, *The Theory of Monopolistic Competition* (Cambridge: Harvard University Press, 1938); John Kenneth Galbraith, *The New Industrial State* (Boston: Houghton Mifflin, 1967).
44. See Oliver E. Williamson, *Markets and Hierarchies: Analysis and Antitrust Implications: A Study in the Economics of Internal Organization* (New York: Free Press, 1975).
45. See Harvey Leibenstein, "A Branch of Economics is Missing: Micro-Micro Theory," *Journal of Economic Literature* 17 (1979): 477-502.
46. See ibid., 481.
47. Fisse, "Reconstructing Corporate Criminal Law," 1154.
48. Ibid., notes at 1154-55.
49. See James G. March and Herbert Simon, *Organizations* (New York: Wiley and Sons, 1958); Herbert A. Simon, "Theories of Decision Making in Economics and Behavioral Science," *American Economic Review* 49 (1959): 253-83; Richard M. Cyert and James G. March, *A Behavioral Theory of the Firm* (Englewood Cliffs, N.J.: Prentice-Hall, Inc., 1963).
50. Herbert A. Simon, "Rationality as Process and as Product of Thought," *American Economic Review* 68 (May 1978): 12.
51. William J. Baumol, *Economic Theory and Operations Analysis*, 2d ed.

(Englewood Cliffs, N.J.: Prentice-Hall, Inc., 1965), 296.

52. Even with the 25 percent pre-tax profits rule (see Elzinga and Breit, *The Antitrust Penalties*, 134-36) the corporation must anticipate what revenues and costs will be counted by the court, something that cannot be known with certainty before the sanction is administered.

53. See text and references to Note 49 above.

54. See Elzinga and Breit, *The Antitrust Penalties*, 91.

55. G. L. S. Shackle, *Epistemics and Economics: A Critique of Economic Doctrines* (Cambridge: Cambridge University Press, 1972), 369-71.

56. See ibid.; and G. L. S. Shackle, *Expectations in Economics* (London: Cambridge University Press, 1949); *Decision, Order and Time in Human Affairs* (London: Cambridge University Press, 1961); *Imagination and the Nature of Choice* (Edinburgh: Edinburgh University Press, 1979).

57. Shackle, *Epistemics and Economics*, 400.

58. Ibid., 399-406.

59. Ibid., 399 (emphasis in original).

60. Ibid., 403.

61. Ibid., 444.

62. Ibid., 392.

63. Ibid., 365.

64. Ibid., 407.

65. Richard A. Posner, *Economic Analysis of Law*, 2d ed. (Boston: Little Brown and Company, 1977), 303-05.

66. John C. Coffee, Jr., " 'No Soul to Damn: No Body to Kick': An Unscandalized Inquiry into the Problem of Corporate Punishment," *Michigan Law Review* 79 (1981): 393-94.

67. Coffee, "Corporate Crime and Punishment," 465-68.

68. Ibid., 466.

69. Elzinga and Breit, *The Antitrust Penalties*, 122-26.

70. Ibid., 135.

71. Ibid.

72. Ibid., 115-16, 129-32.

73. Ibid., 135.

74. Dwight R. Lee, "On Substituting a Socially Costless Penalty for Costly Detection," *International Review of Law and Economics* 3 (1983): 179-85.

75. Except, interestingly enough, Stigler and Becker have proved (in the same manner that everything is proved in this mode of analysis – with formal equations manipulating the inaccessible) that "tastes . . . are the same to all men": George J. Stigler and Gary S. Becker, "De Gustibus Non Est Disputandum," *American Economic Review* 67 (1977): 76.

76. H. H. Liebhafsky, "Price Theory as Jurisprudence: Law and Economics, Chicago Style," *Journal of Economic Issues* 10 (1976): 27.

77. Arthur Allen Leff, "Economic Analysis of Law: Some Realism About Nominalism," *Virginia Law Review* 60 (1974): 457 (emphasis in original).

78. Elzinga and Breit, *The Antitrust Penalties*, 135.

79. See generally, ibid., 103-04; Milton Friedman, *Price Theory: A Provisional Text* (Chicago: Aldine Publishing Co., 1962); James Buchanan, *Cost and Choice: An Inquiry into Economic Theory* (Chicago: Markham Publishing Co., 1969); James E. Buchanan and G. F. Thirlby, eds., *L. S. E. Essays on Cost* (London: Weidenfeld and Nicolson for the London School of Eco-

nomics and Political Science, 1973).

80. Leff, "Economic Analysis of Law," 456.
81. Gary S. Becker, "Crime and Punishment: An Economic Approach," *Journal of Political Economy* 76 (1968): 169-217.
82. Gary S. Becker and George J. Stigler, "Law Enforcement, Malfeasance, and Compensation of Enforcers," *Journal of Legal Studies* 3 (1974): 1-8.
83. Paul H. Rubin, "Why is the Common Law Efficient?" *Journal of Legal Studies* 6 (1977): 51-63.
84. Posner, "Utilitarianism, Economics and Legal Theory."
85. I. Ehrlich, "The Deterrent Effect of Capital Punishment: A Question of Life and Death," *The American Economic Review* 65 (1975): 397-417.
86. This closed analytic system was elevated to epistemological status by Friedman in his grounding of "positive" economics on the prediction of reality "as if" it were what economists believe it to be: Milton Friedman, *Essays in Positive Economics* (Chicago: The University of Chicago Press, 1953), 3-43. An interesting defense of this epistemology has been offered by Boland who argues that critics have not let "as if" be "as if"; for, when examined on its own terms, surprisingly enough, it is internally consistent and logical. Thus, "Friedman's essay is an instrumentalist defense of instrumentalism. That may be interpreted to mean that Friedman's methodology is based on an infinite regress, but if it is then at least it is not internally inconsistent or otherwise illogical. The repeated attempts to refute Friedman's methodology have failed, I think, because instrumentation is its own defense and its *only* defense": Lawrence A. Boland, "A Critique of Friedman's Critics," *Journal of Economic Literature* 17 (1979): 522 (emphasis in original).
87. George L. Priest, "The Common Law Process and the Selection of Efficient Rules," *Journal of Legal Studies* 6 (1977): 65.
88. Rubin, "Why is the Common Law Efficient?," 55.
89. Posner, "Utilitarianism, Economics and Legal Theory," 109.
90. Ronald H. Coase, "Economics and Contiguous Disciplines," *Journal of Legal Studies* 7 (1978): 201-11.
91. Elzinga and Breit, *The Antitrust Penalties*, 150.
92. Ibid., 144.
93. See Coffee, " 'No Soul to Damn: No Body to Kick.' "
94. Elzinga and Breit, *The Antitrust Penalties*, 83.
95. Ibid., 144.
96. Ibid.
97. Ibid., 145.
98. Ibid.
99. Ibid., 146.
100. Ernest J. Weinrib, "Utilitarianism, Economics and Legal Theory," *University of Toronto Law Journal* 30 (1980): 321-22.
101. Frank I. Michelman, "Norms and Normativity: The Economic Theory of Law," *Minnesota Law Review* 62 (1978): 1029-30.
102. Gordon Tullock, *The Logic of the Law* (New York: Basic Books, Inc., 1971), 182-84.
103. Ibid., 256.
104. Ibid., 257.
105. This phrase is borrowed from a brilliant study on moral issues raised by

unfettered capital. We hope the authors appreciate our use of the phrase. See J. Raines, Lenora Berson, and David Gracie, eds., *Community and Capital in Conflict: Plant Closings and Job Loss* (Philadelphia: Temple University Press, 1982).

106. Liebhafsky, "Price Theory as Jurisprudence," 40.

CHAPTER 7

SANCTIONS AGAINST CORPORATIONS: THE LIMITATIONS OF FINES AND THE ENTERPRISE OF CREATING ALTERNATIVES

Brent Fisse

Corporate crime is now generally recognized as an important social problem[1] but the search for adequate solutions still continues. One conspicuous task which remains is that of devising effective sanctions against corporations.[2] The type of sanction now used most extensively – monetary exaction through cash fines or penalties – has been widely criticized, essentially on the ground that its deterrent capacity is usually weak.[3] Yet, what alternatives are there? Dissolution, disqualification from government contracts, production bans, and other forms of incapacitation have often been made available[4] but, whatever the possible attraction of any analogy to imprisonment, these forms of sanction are extreme and, if used, can easily cause worse side effects (e.g., layoffs of workers) than the harm prevented. There are more promising possible alternatives, however, namely stock dilution (equity fines), probation, publicity orders, and community service orders. The aim of this commentary is to outline the nature of these alternatives and to review their potential by exploring the main advantages they might have over fines or monetary penalties.

Three preliminary matters need to be settled. The first is that the scope of discussion does not extend to sanctions against individual persons convicted of offenses committed on corporate behalf, but is confined to sanctions against corporations in those cases where, for reasons of efficacy or justice, it is necessary for proceedings to be issued against a corporate employer in addition to, or instead of, an officer or employee.[5] Second, although our main focus is upon criminal sanctions against corporations, it should be realized that stock dilution, probation, publicity, and community service can also be used as civil penalties or remedies, depending on the circumstances of their application: Just as exaction of money can take the form of fines, monetary penalties, or damages, these alternative means of regulation can be deployed as criminal sanctions or civil penalties or remedies, depending on the manner and purposes of their use.[6] Third, it will be assumed that corporations can manifest fault in a genuinely corporate and blameworthy sense and that, consistent with fundamental principle, intentionality or negligence is a condition of criminal liability.[7]

Limited Deterrent Threat of Fines or Monetary Penalties

Legislation against corporate crime relies almost totally on fines or civil monetary penalties as the means of sanctioning corporate violators.[8] Civil remedies (e.g., injunctions, compensatory orders) are also available, but clearly they provide an inadequate substitute for punishment. Where it is necessary to punish corporations, should heavy reliance continue to be placed on fines or monetary penalties? The answer to this question is much in doubt because, although fines or monetary penalties are advantageous in some respects (notably ease of administration, noninterference in the internal affairs of corporations, and recoupment of the costs of enforcement), they are subject to a number of severe limitations.

To begin with, fines or monetary penalties against corporations are targeted at the corporate entity and not at any personnel who should be held individually accountable for the offense involved. This would matter little if any personnel at fault were proceeded against criminally or even civilly, but proceedings against corporate officers or employees are not always brought.[9] Given the limited resources of enforcement agencies it seems inevitable that the targets of prosecution will often be corporations and that individual accountability frequently will be attainable only by pressurizing corporate defendants to take internal disciplinary measures. Fines or monetary penalties poorly reflect this strategy of enforced self-regulation since they provide no guarantee that a corporate defendant will in fact take disciplinary action. Moreover, corporations have incentives which tend to inhibit disciplinary reaction: A disciplinary program may be too disruptive, too embarrassing for those exercising managerial control, or too fertile a source of evidence for subsequent civil litigation against the company or its officers. In short, the impact of enforcement can easily stop with a corporate pay-out, not because of any socially justified departure from the traditional value of individual accountability, but rather because that is the cheapest or most self-protective course for a corporate defendant to adopt.

A second limitation of fines or monetary penalties against corporations is that courts and legislatures have rarely been willing to set them high enough to provide a real deterrent.[10] Under the Australian Trade Practices Act, for instance, the maximum fine ($50,000 under s.79) or monetary penalty ($250,000 under s.76) is low compared with the profits which may flow from misleading advertising or restrictive trade practices. Even where the maxima are much higher, as in the case of antitrust offenses in the U.S.A., the EEC, and West Germany, the actual amounts imposed in practice usually have been low.[11] Moreover, account must be taken of the low risk of prosecution and conviction; as is a matter of public knowledge, proceedings tend to be launched only in a select range of cases.[12] Accordingly, as many commentators have suggested,[13] why not resort to much higher fines or monetary penalties? This solution has severe limits, however, because corporate defendants often do not have the resources to pay fines or monetary penalties in the amount required for effective deterrence.[14] As Coffee has explained, fines against corporations are confronted by a "deterrence trap":

> The maximum meaningful fine that can be levied against any corporate offender is necessarily bounded by its wealth. Logically, a small corporation is no more threatened by a $5 million fine than by a $500,000 fine if both are beyond its ability to pay. In the case of an individual offender, this wealth ceiling on the deterrent threat of fines causes no serious problem because we can still deter by threat of incarceration. But for the corporation, which has no body to incarcerate, this wealth boundary sets an absolute limit on the reach of deterrent threats directed at it. If the expected punishment cost' necessary to deter a crime crosses this threshold, adequate deterrence cannot be achieved. For example, if a corporation having $10 million of wealth were faced with an opportunity to gain $1 million through some criminal act or omission, such conduct could not logically be deterred by monetary penalties directed at the corporation *if the risk of apprehension were below 10%.* That is, if the likelihood of apprehension were 8%, the necessary penalty would have to be $12.5 million (*i.e.* $1 million times 12.5, the reciprocal of 8%). Yet such a fine exceeds the corporation's ability to pay. In short, our ability to deter the corporation may be confounded by our inability to set an adequate punishment cost which does not exceed the corporation's resources.[15]

Third, cash fines or penalties against corporations pose a monetary threat which is not well tuned to the nonfinancial values that partly govern organizational decisionmaking. Although it is often said that corporate activity is normally undertaken to reap some economic benefit and that corporate decisionmakers choose courses of action based on a calculation of financial costs and benefits,[16] nonfinancial values are also important. Managerial motivation, like human motivation in general, is not confined to satisfaction of monetary want but includes the urge for power, the desire for prestige, the creative urge, and the need for security. Since fines or monetary penalties against corporations touch upon these managerial motivations only obliquely, their sanctioning capacity is necessarily limited. Furthermore, although profit may be the predominant goal of business corporations from an external viewpoint, the profit goal is often overshadowed within a corporation by the more immediate goals of organizational sub-units. This phenomenon has been well described by Stone:

> As corporations become more complex, they tend to subdivide into various departments according to geographical divisions (manufacturing areas and distribution territories), functionally defined groups (finance, sales, advertising, legal) . . . The central organization cannot leave each of those groups at large to realize 'profit' as it sees best. Rather, the farther and farther down the operational ladder one moves, the more the 'profit goal' has to be translated into subgoals – targets and objectives for the shop, the department, the plant, the division, the subsidiary. It is these subgoals that define the task environment of the people actually engaged in production at such a plant, not some abstract 'corporate profit'.[17]

It should also be remembered that corporate personnel conceive their own ends in terms which may diverge substantially from the goals of their corporation or its organizational sub-units. For instance, lower management may falsify pollution compliance reports to avoid closure of an obsolete plant, not so much to maximize profits for the firm as to save their own jobs or reputation in the local community.

Finally, fines or monetary penalties against corporations are supposed in theory to catalyze reform of organizational compliance systems, but in practice change need not occur. Corporate managers may decide to treat fines as recurrent business losses for shareholders or workers to bear. Depending upon competitive pressures, those losses might even be passed directly on to consumers.[18] Preventive procedures or policies may be revised, but there is no obligation to react in this way, even when the offense subject to sentence resulted from palpably defective organizational controls. In this regard, it is instructive to consider the findings of Hopkins' empirical study of the impact of prosecutions and fines under the Australian Trade Practices Act.[19] In the seventeen case histories of misleading advertising studied, the offenses committed by fifteen of the companies were interpreted as largely attributable to defective standard operating procedures after prosecution. Nine of these fifteen companies changed their operating procedures accordingly. Two made minor changes, which were less than fully satisfactory. Two further companies made no changes and for the two remaining companies information was unavailable. The conclusion drawn by Hopkins was that:

> [w]here defective operating procedures were involved . . . the prosecution can be said to have led to significant organizational improvement in at least 60 percent of cases. On the face of it the prosecutions have had a substantial preventive effect on the companies concerned.[20]

However, in approximately 40 percent of the cases studied, the companies concerned failed to provide a responsive program of organizational reform. The further conclusion may thus be drawn that, although fines or monetary penalties maximize corporate freedom by trusting corporations to exercise adequate internal control, they are inept where, as unfortunately is far from uncommon, companies cannot be trusted to institute adequate crime-preventive controls.

Stock Dilution (Equity Fines)

One possible alternative to fines or monetary penalties is stock dilution, an imaginative approach recently proposed by Coffee.[21] The proposal, in essence, is this:

> [W]hen very severe fines need to be imposed on the corporation, they should be imposed not in cash, but in the equity securities of the corporation. The convicted corporation should be required to authorize and issue such number of shares to the state's crime victim compensation fund as would have an expected market value equal to the cash fine necessary to deter illegal activity. The fund should then be able to liquidate the securities in whatever manner maximizes its return.[22]

This proposal could be finetuned to advantage in various ways, as by providing for a statutory list of appropriate beneficiaries of the shares created (e.g., in the context of environmental offenses, conservation foundations; for consumer protection offenses, consumer organizations) but the basic idea – watering-down shares rather than exacting money – is a classically straightforward instance of lateral thinking.

The main advantage of stock dilution, as compared with cash fines or monetary penalties, is that they would sidestep the deterrence trap which arises when the liquid assets of a corporation place an upper limit on monetary punishment, and where this upper limit is less than the amount required to deter corporate crime.[23] To put the point simply, by appropriating fixed as well as liquid assets, the sanction of stock dilution raises the upper limit of the amount collectible. Moreover, the upper limit is raised further by the capacity of stock dilution to reach future assets in addition to current assets: The public seizes not just whatever cash the company can find to pay a fine or monetary penalty but a share in future earnings as well as ownership rights in its plant, equipment, and property investments. The basic explanation for this, as Coffee has indicated, is that the market valuation of most companies vastly exceeds their cash resources:

> the equity fine is a response to the basic precept of the economist that the value of the firm is the discounted present value of its expected future earnings. If one recognizes that this "going concern value" of the firm typically exceeds its "book" or liquidating value, then the real deficiency of cash fines is that they cannot be paid out of expected earnings, but it is precisely this source of value against which the equity fine is levied. To give an example, a young company with excellent prospects may have a very low book value, limited cash resources and little borrowing capacity with financial institutions. Yet, because of its expected future growth, its stock may trade at a high price-earnings multiple. It is essentially immune from high cash fines because it has only modest liquid assets, and thus it may be tempted to risk legal sanctions. But an equity fine permits society to reach its future earnings today by seizing a share of the firm's equity (which is, of course, equal in value to the market's perception of the discounted present value of those earnings).[24]

A related advantage of stock dilution over a fine or monetary penalty is that shareholders would bear the burden rather than persons beyond the circle of corporate profit-sharing. Fines or monetary penalties large enough to achieve deterrence are at risk of being passed on to consumers as higher prices, or to workers through layoffs or cutbacks in employment opportunities.[25] By contrast, stock dilution (equity fines) would not occasion the same unwanted spillovers: shareholders would bear the burden just as other losses are borne by them when the company in which they have invested is unsuccessful.[26]

Useful as punitive stock dilution orders would be as a means of outflanking the deterrence trap, standing alone they could not be expected to overcome the other major limitations of fines or monetary penalties against corporations (namely, circumvention of individual accountability, lack of congruence with nonfinancial values in organizational decisionmaking, and nonassurance of organizational reform).

Equity fines would affect shareholders more significantly than would cash fines or penalties and hence securities analysts and stockbrokers might begin to caution against buying into companies with inadequate compliance systems. Moreover, if severe equity fines were in fact imposed, shareholders might also insist upon internal disciplinary action by management. Thus, there could be more chance that punishing the corporate entity would result in the disciplining of individuals within the organization. The point to be stressed, however, is that there would be no guarantee of this: Shareholders might still decide to cut their losses and let managers pursue the business of making money or, as another option, exit towards other investment opportunities instead of remaining to express their voice.[27]

As regards congruence with nonfinancial values in organizational decisionmaking, the sanction of stock dilution would also fall short. Dilution of stock value could have some adverse effects upon corporate and managerial prestige and power, yet the deterrent impact would remain predominantly financial. Coffee has urged that equity fines would play on managerial fear of hostile takeover bids, on the basis that vesting a large marketable bloc of shares in a free agent such as a crime victim compensation fund would make a corporation a more inviting target for a takeover operation.[28] However, to the extent that takeovers are not obstructed by legal or political constraints upon anticompetitive behavior, the bloc of shares created by an equity fine would normally have to be very large indeed to create any serious risk of takeover for a large company.

Nor would stock dilution ensure that corporate defendants take adequate organizational precautions against re-offending. By reason of the greater possible severity of equity fines, corporations could be put under more pressure to take such precautions, but that increase in pressure would stop short of intervention by the state in the internal workings of the organization. Accordingly, like cash fines or penalties, punitive stock dilution orders would not guarantee the correction of violation-prone procedures or policies; the organization would remain a black box prodded by the law only from outside.

Probation

Although it is sometimes said that corporations are inappropriate subjects for rehabilitation,[29] this overlooks corporate probation, a sentence used increasingly in the United States.[30] Moreover, a variety of proposals have now been advanced for the more extensive utilization of this option, probation being a convenient platform upon which to base a number of more particularized sanctions.[31] Of these more particularized sanctions, the main possibilities are probationary orders mandating internal discipline or organizational reform.

Internal discipline orders have been advocated by the Mitchell Committee in South Australia, the suggestion being as follows:

> Essentially, internal discipline orders would require a corporation to investigate an offence committed on its behalf, undertake appropriate disciplinary proceedings, and return a detailed and satisfactory compliance report to the court issuing the particular order. In the event of unreasonable non-compliance corporate criminal responsibility would be necessary in some cases, but usually it would be sufficient to impose individual criminal responsibility on those personnel specified in the order as responsible for securing compliance. Unlike the system of Frankpledge, the object of internal discipline orders thus would not be to produce guilty individuals to the prosecuting authorities, but to cast part of the burden of enforcement squarely upon the enterprise on whose behalf an offence has been committed.[32]

At first glance, this proposal may seem unworkable in so far as it would require corporations to confess wrongdoing on the part of its officers or employees and then administer punishment itself.[33] However, this reaction is shortsighted because it overlooks the importance attached to internal discipline throughout the history of corporate regulation.[34] For instance, enforced internal discipline was expressly the policy adopted by the U.S. Securities and Exchange Commission in its successful campaign against foreign bribery during the mid-1970s. Faced with hundreds of likely corporate violators and thousands of individual suspects, the SEC implemented a "voluntary disclosure program" which pressurized the corporations into taking internal disciplinary action.[35] The basic strategy underlying such an approach, it should be emphasized, is to make a direct appeal to rational self-interest: If the corporation and its managerial personnel are threatened with severe sanctions in the event of noncompliance, compliance commends itself as the lesser of two evils.

It might also be wondered whether this approach would involve too great a sacrifice of due process for individuals subjected to corporate internal discipline because a defendant would not necessarily have any of the rights of an accused in criminal proceedings.[36] It would be misguided, however, to suppose that internal disciplinary systems should carry the same procedural protections as the criminal justice system: Subjection to internal corporate discipline, serious as it often can be, involves neither the expression of stigmatic condemnation by the state via a criminal conviction, nor the imposition of a sentence as harsh as that of jail.[37]

Organizational reform orders have been proposed, under various labels, by a number of reform agencies and commentators.[38] The common emphasis of these proposals is that corporate compliance policies and procedures should be revised under court scrutiny when organizational reform is necessary to guard against repetition of an offense.[39] This approach has recently been recommended under the American Bar Association's *Standards for Criminal Justice*[40] as Standard 18.2.8(a)(v):

> Continuing judicial oversight. Although courts lack the competence or capacity to manage organizations, the preventive goals of the criminal law can in special cases justify a limited period of judicial monitoring of the activities of a convicted organization. Such oversight is best implemented through the use of recognized reporting, record keeping, and auditing controls designed to increase internal accountability – for example, audit committees, improved staff systems for the board of directors, or the use of special counsel – but it should not extend to judicial review of the legitimate "business judgment" decisions of the organization's management or its stockholders or delay such decisions. Use of such a special remedy should also be limited by the following principles:
>
> (A) As a precondition, the court should find either (1) that the criminal behaviour was serious, repetitive, and facilitated by inadequate internal accounting or monitoring controls or (2) that a clear and present danger exists to the public health or safety;
>
> (B) The duration of such oversight should not exceed the five and two-year limits specified in standard 18.2.3 for probation conditions generally; and

(C) Judicial oversight should not be misused as a means for the disguised imposition of penalties or affirmative duties in excess of those authorized by the legislature.

It should be noted that the ABA proposal would not require the probation service to assume onerous new duties of corporate supervision: Where supervision is required, reliance would be placed on "an experienced corporate attorney, a firm of auditors, or a professional director."[41] Rather, the main question surrounding the ABA model is whether it goes far enough toward providing an effective sanction. The limitations imposed under Standard 18-2.8(a)(v)(A)(2), and (C) make the sentence of continuing judicial supervision remedial in nature whereas in cases of serious wrongdoing it is difficult to understand why corporations should not be punished in a way which requires them to take more extensive steps than those which can be imposed in the context of civil injunctive remedies. For instance, why should not a serious offense be punished by an organizational reform order requiring the corporate offender to develop and implement innovative compliance controls? One possible explanation for the conservatism displayed by the ABA proposal is the traditional conception of probation as a lenient sentencing option. If so, legislative provision should be made for explicitly punitive injunctions against corporations as well as for corporate probation.[42]

If internal discipline and organizational reform orders were available as probationary conditions or punitive injunctions, they would provide a means of overcoming the worst limitations of fines or monetary penalties against corporations. First of all, internal discipline orders would enable corporate offenders to be sanctioned in such a way as to promote individual accountability for corporate offenses: Unlike fines or monetary penalties, this type of sanction would be targeted directly towards those personnel who were implicated in the offense subject to sentence. Second, the deterrence trap which confronts attempts to impose heavy cash fines or penalties would largely be skirted by recourse to internal discipline or organizational reform orders: The deterrent impact of these sanctions would rest largely on financial or nonfinancial internal disciplinary sanctions and detraction from corporate or managerial power, and these are consequences which almost invariably can be borne by corporations without sending them into financial ruin. Third, internal discipline and organizational reform orders would be much more congruent with nonfinancial values in organizational decisionmaking: Corporate and managerial power would be affected directly, corporate and managerial prestige would be threatened at least to some extent, and the goals of organizational sub-units would be immediately relevant to probationary review of a company's compliance procedures. Fourth, as far as catalyzing organizational reform is concerned, organizational reform orders would provide the most obvious method of insisting that corporate defendants respond adequately to any structural or other institutional problems which have occasioned the commission of an offense.

Given these advantages over fines or monetary penalties, there is a strong case for introducing probation as a sanction against corporations. Numerous points of detail need to be settled and cast in suitable legislative form, but these should not distract attention from the need for a sanction capable of pressing upon the inner nerves of corporate governance and thereby achieving more effective deterrence and rehabilitation.

Publicity

A third possibility is to make adverse publicity available as a formal court-ordered punitive sanction (contrast merely remedial publicity under, e.g., corrective advertising orders).

This approach, which goes back to the English Bread Acts of the early nineteenth century, was suggested in 1970 by the U.S. National Commission on Reform of Federal Criminal Laws (the Brown Commission).[43] Section 405 of the Brown Commission's *Study Draft* provided in relevant part as follows:

> When an organization is convicted of an offence, the court may, in addition to or in lieu of imposing other authorized sanctions, . . . require the organization to give appropriate publicity to the conviction by notice to the class or classes of persons or sector of the public interested in or affected by the conviction, by advertising in designated areas or by designated media, or otherwise . . . [44]

This proposal was never implemented; however, the idea has enjoyed considerable support, partly because of a growing realization that most corporations are highly sensitive about their prestige as an interest over and above (although overlapping with) profits, and partly because of dissatisfaction with the deterrent capacity of fines or monetary penalties. Thus, in a recent case of toxic waste dumping in Los Angeles, the defendant corporation was ordered to advertise its crime in *The Wall Street Journal*; in the opinion of the judge imposing sentence, deterrence required a punishment that could not be regarded as "just another cost of doing business."[45] Beyond these concerns, adverse publicity is consistent with a shame-based system of morality, a philosophical underpinning laid by Peter A. French in the ensuing chapter.

In what respects might punitive publicity sanctions help to overcome the previously described limitations of fines or monetary penalties?

To begin with, adverse publicity orders against corporate defendants need not be exclusively corporate in orientation but, with the aid of probation, could also help to promote individual accountability. As Coffee[46] has argued, there is a valuable hint to be taken from the McCloy report[47] documenting Gulf Oil's bribery practices. The report, prepared by an outside counsel in response to SEC enforcement initiatives, not only triggered substantial procedural reforms but also hastened the resignation of officials named in it. Furthermore, the revelations in the report were such as to receive the attention of the press, and the report itself became a paperback bestseller. Taking this example as a starting-point, Coffee has proposed that corporate offenders be required to employ outside counsel to prepare a compliance report which names the key personnel involved and outlines in readable form what they did. Probationary pre-sentence reports would mandatorily be prepared "in considerable factual depth in the expectation that such studies will either find an audience in their own right or, more typically, provide the database for investigative journalism."[48]

Second, publicity orders would not fall into the deterrence trap created by limited corporate financial liquidity: Adverse publicity would be used to inflict loss of corporate prestige, without any need to inflict loss of money from cash resources. Ample evidence of the importance of prestige to modern corporations is provided by the amounts now spent on corporate image advertising campaigns.[49]

Third, publicity orders would be directed primarily toward the infliction of loss of corporate prestige, and hence would achieve congruence with this important nonfinancial value in organizational decisionmaking. To the contrary, it is sometimes suggested that the main aim of this type of sanction would be to inflict financial loss by discouraging consumers from buying the defendant's product.[50] This suggestion should be rejected: If infliction of monetary loss were the main aim, cash fines or penalties would be a more efficient way of achieving it.

Fourth, although adverse publicity orders would not guarantee any organizational reform of procedures or policies likely to result in a corporation re-offending, they could be used in such a way as to put public pressure on a defendant to move in that direction. Thus, it would be possible when framing a publicity order to pay explicit attention to the nature of the steps, if any, taken by a corporation to undertake institutional changes after the commission of an offense.[51]

Despite these potential advantages, skeptics have cast doubt on the extent to which corporate prestige is likely to matter to executives and have raised the specter of counterpublicity and other potential problems.[52] These and other questions have recently been the subject of an empirical study of the impacts of adverse publicity on 17 major U.S. and Australasian companies.[53] One of the main conclusions emerging from this range of corporate experience was that senior executives were deeply concerned over their perception that corporate prestige had been assaulted by adverse publicity even when the publicity had no adverse impacts on profits. It is also argued that the objections raised in the past to the idea of using shame and stigma as a means of controlling corporate behavior either are more fanciful than real or, if real, could be overcome by using formal publicity orders of appropriate design and application.[54]

Community Service

Community service has been required as a condition of probation or nonprosecution in several cases in the U.S.A. In the two best-known instances, *United States* v *Allied Chemical Corporation Company*[55] and *United States* v *Olin Mathieson*,[56] payment of money for charitable purposes was involved (in the former case, to establish the Virginia Environmental Endowment; in the latter, to set up the New Haven Betterment Fund). Likewise, in a more recent case where a highway construction company was convicted of fraudulent tendering for highway contracts, the defendant was required to donate $1.5 million to endow a professorship in ethics at the University of Nebraska.[57] This approach to sentencing, like that of imposing fines or monetary penalties, merely requires the defendant to write a check and, unlike the position in the case of fines or monetary penalties, gives the defendant a public relations bonus. By contrast, in *United States* v *Danilow Pastry Co., Inc.*,[58] six bakeries convicted of price-fixing were fined with substantial parts of the fines being suspended on the condition that the bakeries provide 12 months' free supplies of fresh baked goods to various needy organizations in the New York area. In imposing this sentence, the court emphasized two factors: First, fines commensurate with the gravity of the offenses would bankrupt the defendants and send them out of business; and second, substituted payment by means of free supply of products to welfare organizations would require the defendants to make "symbolic restitution" for their offenses by doing something more exacting and thought-provoking than merely handing over money to the state.

A detailed proposal for the legislative introduction of personally performed community service as a sanction against corporations has been advanced in another paper by the present author.[59] The basic statutory provisions envisaged are as follows:

(a) Where a corporation is convicted of an offense the court may make a punitive order (here referred to as a "community service order") sentencing the offender to undertake a project of community service in accordance with the subsequent provisions of this section.

(b) (i) The amount of community service required to be performed shall be quantified in terms of the actual net cost of materials, equipment, and labor to be used for the project.

 (ii) Unless provided otherwise the maximum cost of community service under a community service order shall be the same as the maximum amount of the fine or monetary penalty applicable to the offense for which the order is made.

 (iii) A project of community service shall be performed within two years of the date of sentence unless the court orders otherwise.

(c) (i) A project of community service may be either a project proposed by the offender and agreed to by the court or a project specified by the court.

 (ii) A project of community service shall be performed by personnel employed by the offender except where the court is satisfied that the assistance of an independent contractor is necessary to make the best use of the offender's own skills and resources.

 (iii) The personnel by whom a project of community service is to be performed shall include representatives from managerial, executive, and subordinate ranks of the offender's organization irrespective of nonimplication in the offense for which a community service order is imposed.

 (iv) An offender subject to a community service order shall specify which persons are to undertake the required project of community service and, in the case of employees, shall indicate their rank within the organization.

A community service sanction of the kind proposed above would require corporate defendants to undertake a socially useful program involving a commitment of time, effort, and available skills. Thus, in *Hartnell v Sharp Corporation of Australia Pty. Ltd.*,[60] an Australian case in which Sharp was fined $100,000 for misleading advertising in relation to a new range of microwave ovens, a court armed with the option of ordering a sentence of community service could have required Sharp to undertake various measures in aid of consumer protection. Apart from the possibility of deputizing the company to monitor the advertising of other firms in specified media over a given period, Sharp might have been called upon to assist the Standards Association of Australia in the research and development of safety standards for microwave ovens or in the testing of competitors' microwave products. Given the specialized talents and innovative capacity for which corporations are deservedly much-praised, little difficulty is likely to be experienced in finding suitable projects even if, as in the examples above, the projects chosen are tied closely to the particular context of the offense committed.[61]

Community service orders, like the other alternative sanctions canvassed, would be less vulnerable to the previously stressed limitations of fines or monetary penalties.[62] First, as far as promoting individual accountability is concerned, community service orders might help to stimulate internal discipline because, in being forced to allocate personnel to a project of community service, corporate defendants would be encouraged to ask those persons responsible for getting the company into trouble to perform the necessary acts of rescue. Second, a sentence of personally performed community service need not slip into the deterrence trap of limited corporate financial liquidity: A project of personally performed community service could take up slack organizational work capacity rather than absorb cash reserves. Third, community service orders would offer a means of impinging upon nonfinancial as well as financial motivations: Whereas cash fines or penalties require only the payment of money, personally performed community service would require the expenditure of time and effort. Last, however, most kinds of community service orders would lack the ability to provide any guarantee of adequate organizational reform after the commission of an offense. The exception to this would be a combined sentence of community service and probation requiring a defendant to develop innovative compliance controls and to prepare instructions and follow-up reports with a view to their use by other corporations as a freely available guide or model.[63]

The greatest potential difficulty is that the sanction of community service might give corporations too much opportunity for subterfuge and pre-varication.[64] This obstacle should not be exaggerated, however, for two main reasons. First, as in the case of corporate probation, independent special counsel or masters could be used to supervise compliance. Second, it seems implausible to regard corporations convicted of crime as dens of iniquity, and most convicted corporations are likely to have enough good faith to want to redeem themselves as soon as possible.

Conclusion

Fines or monetary penalties are now used extensively as a sanction against corporations, but stock dilution (equity fines), probation, publicity orders, and community service also merit consideration as additional sentencing options. These alternatives seem promising because, in increasing the variety of deterrent impacts achievable against corporations, they offer ways of angling around the major limitations of monetary sanctions. This is not to suggest that fines or monetary penalties have no useful role to play; in many instances, especially less serious offenses, fines are often an expedient and adequate solution. Nor is it suggested that any one alternative represents some ideal type of sanction against corporations; the anatomy of corporate crime is so diverse that effective sentencing requires courts and tribunals to be equipped with a range of available sanctions, not merely one.[65]

Accepting all of this, it will nonetheless be objected that the alternatives outlined – stock dilution (equity fines), probation, publicity, and community service – are too indeterminate in impact, too inefficient, or too restrictive of freedom to justify introduction.[66] Are these objections well-founded?

The initial objection is that the impact of probation, adverse publicity, or community service would be uncertain in impact whereas the quantum of cash or equity fines is fixed at a finite amount.[67] Superficially plausible as this objection may be, it seems unpersuasive. To begin with, the comparison in issue should concern the *actual* impact of sanctions, not their formally quantified level: Sentences of probation, adverse publicity, and community service can also be imposed in terms of some formally quantified level of expenditure. This being so, it must be wondered whether the actual impact of fines or monetary penalties on corporations[68] is any more predictable than the actual impact of probation, adverse publicity, or community service. For example, when executives at Ford in Detroit were interviewed about the impact of a $7 million environmental fine imposed on their corporation in 1973, the answer was that in a period when the demand for their cars was strong, the impact was minimal. But fortunes change quickly in the auto industry, and the impact of such a fine in the late 1970s or early 1980s would have been utterly different.[69] Beyond examples such as this, the point has already been made that, although fines or monetary penalties are supposed in theory to catalyze internal discipline or organizational reform, the actual impact may often be confined to payment of the monetary demand imposed.

Consider next the objection that the costs of administering sanctions other than fines or monetary penalties would make them inefficient. Is this objection tenable? In answering this question it is instructive to compare the position in the case of imprisonment. We do tolerate the extremely high inefficiency of imprisonment because fines of sufficient deterrent gravity usually cannot be paid by individual offenders.[70] If so, it may be argued that the relative inefficiency of alternatives to fines or monetary penalties against corporations should also be tolerated: The deterrence trap created by the limited financial liquidity of corporations forces us either to use fines or monetary penalties of insufficient deterrent gravity, or to resort to alternative sanctions which, although regrettably less efficient, offer more chance of effectively preventing corporate crime.

Finally, would equity fines, probation, publicity, and community service subject corporations to some overbearing regime of state control of corporate enterprise? There seems little risk of this happening. For one thing, the customary sentencing practice of imposing severe sanctions only for serious offenses is unlikely to be abandoned. For another, sentencing criteria could and should be devised so as to maximize freedom of enterprise in compliance systems;[71] one possibility would be to stipulate in the empowering legislation that, wherever practicable, corporate defendants be given the opportunity to indicate before sentence what disciplinary or other steps they propose to take in response to their conviction for an offense.

NOTES

1. See generally Edwin H. Sutherland, *White Collar Crime: The Uncut Version* (New Haven: Yale University Press, 1983); Marshall B. Clinard and Peter C. Yeager, *Corporate Crime* (New York: MacMillan, 1980); K. Tiedemann, "Antitrust Law and Criminal Law Policy in Western Europe," in L. H. Leigh, ed., *Economic Crime in Europe* (London: MacMillan, 1980): 39-56.
2. See generally Stephen A. Yoder, "Criminal Sanctions for Corporate Illegality," *Journal of Criminal Law and Criminology* 69 (1978): 40-58; Raymond Screvens, "Les Sanctions Applicables aux Personnes Morales dans

les États des Communautes Européenes," *Revue de Droit Penale et de Criminologie* 60 (1980): 163-90; Brent Fisse, "Reconstructing Corporate Criminal Law: Deterrence, Retribution, Fault, and Sanctions," *Southern California Law Review* 56 (1983): 1141-1246.

3. See e.g., United States v Danilow Pastry Co., Inc., 563 F. Supp. 1159 (1983); Christopher D. Stone, *Where the Law Ends: The Social Control of Corporate Behavior* (New York: Harper & Row, 1975), Ch. 6; John Braithwaite, *Corporate Crime in the Pharmaceutical Industry* (London: Routledge & Kegan Paul, 1984), Ch. 9.

4. See e.g., Henry D. Bosley, "Responsabilité et Sanctions en Matiere de Criminalité des Affairs," *Revue Internationale de Droit Penal* 53 (1982): 131-132; Screvens, "Les Sanctions Applicables aux Personnes Morales dans les États des Communautes Européenes"; Pierre Delatte, "La Question de la Responsibilité Penale des Personnes Morales en Droit Belge," *Revue de Droit Penal et de Criminologie* 60 (1980): 210; John Braithwaite and Gilbert Geis, "On Theory and Action for Corporate Crime Control," *Crime & Delinquency* 28 (1982): 308-09; Brent Fisse, "Responsibility, Prevention, and Corporate Crime," *New Zealand Universities Law Review* 5 (1973): 252-53; Yoder, "Criminal Sanctions for Corporate Illegality," 54-55.

5. See Brent Fisse, "The Social Policy of Corporate Criminal Responsibility," *Adelaide Law Review* 6 (1978): 371-82.

6. John Griffiths, "The Limits of Criminal Law Scholarship," *Yale Law Journal* 79 (1970): 1410-11.

7. See further Fisse, "Reconstructing Corporate Criminal Law," 1183-1213.

8. See e.g., Trade Practices Act, 1974-1984 (Aust'l.), ss.76, 79.

9. See e.g., Australia, Trade Practices Commission, *Fourth Annual Report, Year Ended 30 June 1978* (Canberra: Australian Government Publishing Service, 1978), 77; Brent Fisse, "Criminal Law and Consumer Protection," in A. J. Duggan and L. W. Darvall, eds., *Consumer Protection Law and Theory* (Sydney: Law Book Company, 1980): 183.

10. See Yoder, "Criminal Sanctions for Corporate Illegality," 47-48.

11. See C. S. Kerse, *EEC Antitrust Procedure* (London: European Law Centre Ltd., 1981), 178-181; but note the EEC Case of *Pioneer Hi-Fi* [1980] 1 C.M.L.R. 457 where a penalty of 4,350,000 units of account was imposed on Pioneer Electronic Europe. See further Virginia Morris, "The Fines Imposed in EEC Competition Cases in Light of the *Pioneer Hi-Fi* Decision," *California Western International Law Journal* 14 (1984): 425-62.

12. See e.g., Australia, Trade Practices Commission, *Annual Report 1981-82* (Canberra: Australian Government Publishing Service, 1982), 15-18, 78-80.

13. E.g., Kenneth G. Elzinga and William Breit, *The Antitrust Penalties: A Study in Law and Economics* (New Haven: Yale University Press, 1976), Ch. 7.

14. See e.g., United States v Danilow Pastry Co., Inc., 563 F. Supp. 1159 (1983).

15. John C. Coffee, Jr., " 'No Soul to Damn: No Body to Kick': An Unscandalized Inquiry into the Problem of Corporate Punishment," *Michigan Law Review* 79 (1981): 390.

16. See e.g., "Developments in the Law – Corporate Crime: Regulating Corporate Behavior Through Criminal Sanctions," *Harvard Law Review* 92 (1979): 1235.
17. Stone, *Where the Law Ends*, 43.
18. See Alan M. Dershowitz, "Increasing Community Control over Corporate Crime: A Problem in the Law of Sanctions," *Yale Law Journal* 71 (1961): 285-86.
19. Andrew Hopkins, *The Impact of Prosecutions under the Trade Practices Act* (Canberra: Australian Institute of Criminology, 1978).
20. Ibid., 21-22.
21. Coffee, " 'No Soul to Damn: No Body to Kick' ": 413-24.
22. Ibid., 413.
23. See e.g., United States v Danilow Pastry Co., Inc. 563 F. Supp. 1159 (1983); Kerse, *EEC Antitrust Procedure*, 184.
24. Coffee, " 'No Soul to Damn: No Body to Kick' ": 419-20.
25. See generally Dershowitz, "Increasing Community Control over Corporate Crime," 285-86.
26. See further Coffee, " 'No Soul to Damn: No Body to Kick' ": 414-17.
27. See further Fisse, "Reconstructing Corporate Criminal Law," 1235-37.
28. Coffee, " 'No Soul to Damn: No Body to Kick' ": 418.
29. See e.g., Bruce Otley, "Criminal Liability for Defective Products: New Problems in Corporate Responsibility and Sanctioning," *Revue Internationale de Droit Penal* 53 (1982): 158; John B. McAdams, "The Appropriate Sanctions for Corporate Criminal Liability: An Eclectic Alternative," *Cincinatti Law Review* 46 (1977): 992.
30. E.g., United States v Atlantic Richfield Co., 465 F.2d 58 (1972) and see generally James A. Geraghty, "Structural Crime and Institutional Rehabilitation: A New Approach to Corporate Sentencing," *Yale Law Journal* 89 (1979): 353-75.
31. See e.g., Coffee, " 'No Soul to Damn: No Body to Kick' ": 448-59; Geraghty, "Structural Crime and Institutional Rehabilitation."
32. South Australia, Criminal Law and Penal Methods Reform Committee, *Fourth Report, The Substantive Criminal Law* (Adelaide: South Australian Government Printer, 1977), 361-62.
33. See Richard Fox, "Corporate Sanctions: Scope for a New Eclecticism," *Malaya Law Review* 24 (1982): 46.
34. See Fisse, "The Social Policy of Corporate Criminal Responsibility," 382-84.
35. See Edward D. Herlihy and Theodore A. Levine, "Corporate Crisis: The Overseas Payment Problem," *Law and Policy in International Business* 8 (1976): 547-629; Jacqueline Wolff, "Voluntary Disclosure Programs," *Fordham Law Review* 47 (1979): 1057-82.
36. See Mark Crane, "Commentary: The Due Process Considerations in the Imposition of Corporate Liability," *Northern Illinois Law Review* 1 (1980): 42; Fox, "Corporate Sanctions," 46.
37. Brent Fisse and John Braithwaite, *The Impact of Publicity on Corporate Offenders* (Albany: State University of New York Press, 1983), 304-05.
38. See American Bar Association, *Standards for Criminal Justice*, vol. 3 (Boston: Little, Brown, 1980): 18.162-163, 18.179-184; Fisse, "Responsibility, Prevention, and Corporate Crime"; Christopher D. Stone, "A Slap on the

Wrist for the Kepone Mob," *Business and Society Review* 22 (1977): 4-11; Geraghty, "Structural Crime and Institutional Rehabilitation"; Lewis D. Solomon and Nancy Stein Nowak, "Managerial Restructuring: Prospects for a New Regulatory Tool," *Notre Dame Lawyer* 56 (1980): 120-40.

39. See generally Robert A. Katzmann, "Judicial Intervention and Organization Theory: Changing Bureaucratic Behavior and Policy," *Yale Law Journal* 89 (1980): 513-37.

40. Vol. 3, 18.162-163, 18.179-184.

41. Ibid., 18.182-183.

42. See further Fisse, "Reconstructing Corporate Criminal Law," 1156-57, 1164-65, 1223-24.

43. See generally Brent Fisse, "The Use of Publicity as a Criminal Sanction Against Business Corporations," *Melbourne University Law Review* 8 (1971): 107-50; American Bar Association, *Standards for Criminal Justice*, 18.177-79.

44. United States National Commission on Reform of Federal Criminal Laws, *Study Draft* (Washington, D.C.: United States Government Printing Office, 1970): §405.

45. *Los Angeles Times* (31 January 1984): 1.

46. Coffee, " 'No Soul to Damn: No Body to Kick' ": 429-34.

47. John J. McCloy, *The Great Oil Spill: The Inside Report* (New York: Chelsea House Publishers, 1976).

48. Coffee, " 'No Soul to Damn: No Body to Kick' ": 431.

49. See e.g., Nancy Yashihara, "$1 Billion Spent on Identity: Companies Push Image of Selves, Not Products," *Los Angeles Times* (10 May 1981): pt. 6, 1; Roy Birch, "Corporate Advertising: Why, How and When," *Advertising Quarterly* 57 (5) (1978): 5-9; Wally Olins, *The Corporate Personality: An Inquiry into the Nature of Corporate Identity* (New York: Mayflower Books, 1978).

50. E.g., Leonard H. Leigh, *The Criminal Liability of Corporations in English Law* (London: Weidenfeld and Nicholson, 1969), 159-60.

51. See Fisse and Braithwaite, *The Impact of Publicity on Corporate Offenders*, 298, 302.

52. See e.g., Herbert L. Packer, *The Limits of the Criminal Sanction* (Stanford: Stanford University Press, 1968), 361; Coffee, " 'No Soul to Damn: No Body to Kick' ": 424-29.

53. See Fisse and Braithwaite, *The Impact of Publicity on Corporate Offenders*.

54. Ibid., Ch. 21.

55. 420 F. Supp. 122 (1976).

56. *New York Times* (2 June 1978): D1.

57. *New York Times* (29 July 1983): 1.

58. 563 F. Supp. 1159 (1983).

59. See Brent Fisse, "Community Service as a Sanction Against Corporations," *Wisconsin Law Review* [1981]: 970-1017.

60. 5 A.L.R. 493 (1975).

61. See further Fisse, "Community Service as a Sanction Against Corporations," 984-85, 1001-03.

62. See generally, ibid., 1003-08.

63. Cf. Thomas C. Hayes, "Complying with EPA Rules," *New York Times* (16 January 1980): D 1.

64. See generally Fisse, "Community Service as a Sanction Against Corporations," 1011.
65. See generally Simeon M. Kriesberg, "Decisionmaking Models and the Control of Corporate Crime," *Yale Law Journal* 85 (1976): 1091-1129.
66. See generally Fisse, "Reconstructing Corporate Criminal Law," 1215-31.
67. See e.g., Coffee, " 'No Soul to Damn: No Body to Kick' ": 427, on adverse publicity.
68. See Fox, "Corporate Sanctions," 39.
69. See Fisse and Braithwaite, *The Impact of Publicity on Corporate Offenders*, 57.
70. Richard Posner, *Economic Analysis of Law*, 2d ed. (Boston: Little, Brown, 1977), 168-69.
71. Fisse, "Criminal Law and Consumer Protection," 194-99.

CHAPTER 8
PUBLICITY AND THE CONTROL OF CORPORATE CONDUCT: HESTER PRYNNE'S NEW IMAGE

Peter A. French

Perhaps the most quoted line in the long history of the discussion of corporate criminal liability is attributed to Edward, First Baron Thurlow, Lord Chancellor of England. The line is:

> "Did you ever expect a corporation to have a conscience, when it has no soul to be damned, and no body to be kicked?"[1]

Baron Thurlow was concerned with how to effectively punish a corporation that had committed a serious crime even though corporations cannot be thrown into jail and the cost of large fines can often be passed on to consumers. This is an important issue because the idea of corporate criminality will be an empty one if the law has no effective means of punishing a corporation that has been found guilty of a criminal violation, and the courts have been busy lately in hearing corporate criminal cases.[2] ("Corporate crimes" are not to be confused with crimes perpetrated by managers, accountants, etc., against their own corporations but, as I use the term, are those offenses that involve general corporate policy or decisionmaking, e.g., the manufacture of defective, life-threatening products, pollution of the environment, wrongful death in certain airline disasters, antitrust violations, and price-fixing.)[3]

Baron Thurlow's dictum is cemented in the foundation of the retributive views that, by and large, sustain our penal system. The firm hand of retribution, with its biblical "eye for an eye" authority, still commands the high ground of our thinking about the punishment of criminals,[4] and I think that it should. If a corporation has no body to kick (leaving to God the business of souls and eternal damnation), how can it retribute its felonious behavior? It has no eye to be exchanged for an eye it has blinded by unsafe working conditions. It has no neck to stretch for the wrongful deaths it has caused in product explosions. Or so the story is meant to go.

Retributivism, however, does not have to be understood in biblical bloodlust terms. Repayment need not always be made in kind. Capital punishment in the case of human murderers, for example, has in many jurisdictions been replaced by life sentences that carry possible parole stipulations, and the old Anglo-Saxon notion of *wergeld* is frequently utilized in settling wrongful death suits. The price of a human life may not always come cheap, but it is being set by the courts and paid by corporate offenders or their insurance carriers.

The idea that a corporation can pay a fine or a set sum to the relatives of its victim in a homicide case and thereby expiate its guilt is, however, regarded by many people as an affront to justice.[5] After all, the price of such punishment can be written off as another cost of business and, in the normal course of events, be passed on to the consumers of the corporation's products or services. Certainly, a whole corporation cannot, as Baron Thurlow knew, be tossed in jail. But, if the crime is a truly corporate one, it will also be an affront to justice to punish any individual employee or manager or director when such persons usually can demonstrate that they did not have the relevant intention nor the required capacities to constitute the *mens rea* required by the law for successful prosecution.[6] Vicarious liability or guilt by association in these instances is hardly likely to satisfy the demands of justice. Frankly, very few of these cases are really reducible to individual negligence, let alone intention or recklessness.[7] Most of the existing penal options such as license or charter revocation are usually ineffective. Fines and forced closings frequently hurt those who are the least closely associated with corporate decisionmaking, namely, low-level employees and stockholders.

Stockholders, of course, are protected by SEC regulations, and if they suffer from corporate punishment, that is a risk they undertook when entering the market. Often stockholders benefit from the undetected crime and may do so for a period of time. I see no reason why they ought not bear some of the burden of punishment. The stockholder, after all, is free to trade his or her holdings in the market and is never assured of a clear profit. Also, the stockholder might consider pressing a civil suit against the corporation that cost him or her a significant value in stock due to its criminal behavior. A class action suit by stockholders who claim damage under such conditions could have a second level retributive result. And if the corporation was forced to pay stockholders for losses due to corporate crime, additional deterrent aims of punishment might be accomplished.

Heavy fines, as we know, are likely to be recovered from the consumer in the form of higher prices. The limit to that practice, however, is set by the marketplace. The exceptions would be in public utilities or in other monopoly or semimonopolistic enterprises where consumers must deal with the criminal corporation or forego the service. Such corporations are generally regulated by government agencies, and pricing increases to offset penalties could be prevented if those agencies act in the best interests of the community at large.

It should also be mentioned with respect to the harming of innocent employees that when a human being is convicted of a felony and punished, his or her family and dependents are frequently cast into dire financial straits. The harm done to them, though they may be totally innocent of any complicity in the crime, may in fact far outweigh that done to the incarcerated felon. After all, the convicted criminal receives three meals a day and lodging. The family may be reduced to penury and find that meals are only a sometime thing, and then hardly nutritious. In many jurisdictions, little or no official interest is paid to these innocent sufferers. Why should it be paid to employees who work for offending corporations?[8]

Returning to the efficacy of punishment, the fining of corporations is just not perceived by the corporate world as punishment comparable to incarceration of the human felon. Therefore, many believe that at least as a practical matter and regardless of whether punishment is morally justified, corporations should not even be subject to the criminal law.[9] Such a view, however, is remarkably shortsighted and, worse yet, can lead to a number of socially unacceptable outcomes. If, as earlier noted, we can only punish individuals, and if we must do so in a defensibly just fashion, then many offenses must go unpunished because the offense will be peculiarly corporate. We will then lose an important avenue of social control over the most powerful institutions in our social system.

We are, however, not as restricted or unimaginative as may have been assumed. I propose to commend an alternative corporate punishment – adverse publicity – though I must stress that in isolation from other available sanctions (e.g., fines, probation orders), the punishment I have in mind will not likely have the full reformative or deterrent effects a concerned citizenry would desire. In some cases it will best be used only to augment other sentences, but in many cases it may have all of the desired punitive effects, retributive and deterrent.

The moral psychology of our criminal legal system surely is guilt-based.[10] Guilt historically is viewed as a form of debt either to the specific victim harmed or to the society as a whole. To expiate guilt, the guilty party must repay. Hence, the fine system. Punishment is an institutional vehicle of repayment and restoration. When the debt is retired the original *status quo* is restored. The Latin *debitum* in the Lord's Prayer and in Matthew 18:27 is translated in Old English as *gylt*. The substantive sense of *gylt* as debt is usually treated as the primary sense of the term. Hence, the popular expression "paying one's debt to society." There are, of course, a number of things one can do with debts that one cannot do with guilt. For example, debts can be transferred, guilt cannot. The family of the deceased may be bound to pay his outstanding debts, but they do not assume his criminal guilt.

Our notion of guilt, because it so directly associates with law violation, is a threshold notion. Either the defendant in a criminal case is guilty as charged or not guilty. Guilt is a minimum maintenance notion. Guilt avoidance involves meeting very basic standards of behavior. As should be expected, guilt-based moralities are statute-dominated and the primary concern is to be in a state of nonviolation. The spotlight is on the drawing of the boundaries of acceptable behavior, at the minimal level.

In contrast to a guilt-based morality, certain societies, and in part our own, emphasize development and maintenance of personal worth and image in comparison to exemplary models of behavior. In such moralities the central notion is shame rather than guilt.[11]

In a shame-based morality, evaluation of behavior is not made against rules or laws that set minimal constraints. Moral worth is measured against role or type models. Do you remember how your mother or your grandmother ingrained this type of morality in you? "Act like a human being, only a pig would do that," or "your brother or sister would never behave like that." To feel shame or to be shameful a person must come to regard one's behavior as having fallen below or short of what is expected of or associated with the role, station, or type to which one belongs. The feeling of shame is the feeling of inadequacy or inferiority.

A crucial element in a shame-based morality is stress on the individual's self-conception as measured against ideal models that are accepted by the person as appropriate to that individual's way of life. (Shame, by the way, is much more of a biblical notion than guilt, both in the Old and New Testament.) Shame is a visual concept. Its root meaning is to cover one's face or hide. It relates to the way one is seen, the way one's actions look to oneself and to others. Interestingly, the language indicates that being without any shame is not a respectable thing, while being guiltless is. That is because shame depends on a sensibility to oneself. The most dangerous persons are the brazen incorrigibles who, in Zephaniah's words, "knoweth no shame."[12] To be unaffected by shame is to be antisocial and, worse than that, to have no concern for self-image. Shame operates in the field of honor and self-respect rather than being associated with meeting legal and social obligations.

An adept penal system, I should think, would be one that could induce shame when there has been a notable incongruity with the accepted models and could utilize the visual and media capabilities of the society to heighten the awareness in the offending individual or corporation, as well as the community at large, of a serious discrepancy between actual behavior and the identity or image thought to be possessed or projected.[13] Importantly, shame cannot be purged by repayment. Shame is not translatable to debt. It is not a matter of paying a fine and restoring the *status quo*. To regain one's sense of worth, to reclaim one's desired identity, the shameful person must act in positive, creative, and even heroic ways so that he or she may again feel and be seen as worthy. Often the shameful persons must go well beyond what is ordinarily required to again value themselves. The greater the shame the more extraordinary and prolonged must be the behavior that reestablishes worth. Our current penal system only incidentally, accidentally, produces such a response in an offender. But there is a form of punishment that specifically derives from the concept of shame and that may again be utilized in this country: the Hester Prynne Sanction. Recall *The Scarlet Letter?*[14]

> The penalty thereof is death. But in their great mercy and tenderness of heart, they have doomed Mistress Prynne to stand only a space of three hours on the platform of the pillory, and then and thereafter, for the remainder of her natural life, to wear a mark of shame upon her bosom. "A wise sentence!" remarked the stranger gravely bowing his head. "Thus she will be a living sermon against sin."[15]

The Hester Prynne Sanction surely is not directly a monetary penalty. Adverse publicity, however, could contribute to the achievement of monetary deterrent and retributive effects by costing the corporation business when customers refuse to purchase products or services, but that cost may be negligible and so not constitute a real repayment for the crime. When applied to a corporate offender it threatens the company's prestige, its image.[16] The Hester Prynne Sanction, in fact, will be effective only if the criminal either or both regards social stigmatization as a matter of grave concern, or is concerned with personal moral worth, i.e., is not shameless. For the Hester Prynne Sanction to really work, the offenders must regard themselves as having acted disgracefully, as having significantly reduced their status in the community by their behavior. The criminals must think of themselves as unworthy of the kind of respect and consideration they previously enjoyed, as having fallen short of what can be legitimately expected of them. They must come to view the sanction as a legitimate damaging blot on their reputations; as a mark of their failure; as an exposure of their moral shortcomings; as an indicator of the disgust of others; as a signal that they must rebuild their identity.

The Hester Prynne Sanction is particularly suited to corporate offenders, because image and reputation are at the very heart of modern corporate life.[17] Little sustained success has ever been enjoyed by a company with a bad reputation. Official censure is not an inconsequential matter when corporate achievement depends on communal standing. In fact, the Hester Prynne Sanction might be far more effective in dealing with corporate offenders than with human criminals.

It is worth noting that in a recent study of seventeen major corporations that have suffered adverse publicity over an offense or serious incident (though such publicity was not court-ordered), executives at the middle and higher levels of management reported that loss of corporate prestige was regarded as a very major corporate concern.[18] Indeed, the loss of prestige was regarded as far more serious than the payment of a fine.

For a corporation to survive it simply must garner and nurture a good image among the constituents of its marketplace. Furthermore, framing corporate punishments in terms of adverse publicity orders is more likely to minimize the kinds of unwanted externalities that plague the kinds of sanctions now used by the courts against corporate offenders.[19] It is noteworthy that the U.S. National Commission on Reform of Federal Criminal Laws in their 1970 *Study Draft* supported use of something that sounds remarkably like Hester Prynne. The proposal was this:

> When an organization is convicted of an offense, the court may in addition or in lieu of imposing other authorised sanctions, . . . require the organization to give appropriate publicity to the conviction . . . by advertising in designated areas or in designated media . . .[20]

Sadly, the Commission's *Final Report*[21] lacked this recommendation due to strong corporate lobbying. My argument is directed toward a revival of the basic idea.

The almost universal corporate aversion to a tarnished image is, however, insufficient by itself to ground the Hester Prynne Sanction as a penal device. "Bad press" may be repugnant, but it is hardly penal and can be countered by corporate media campaigns intended "to put a different face on the matter." Quite simply, if this sanction is to be retributively penal, the convicted corporation must regard the adverse publicity to be not only noxious, but a justified communal revelation of the corporation's disgrace, its failure to "measure up."

Measure up to what? Against what standard, what model identity, is a corporation to judge itself and be judged by the institutions of social order and justice? *The Scarlet Letter* provides only the structural or formal aspects of the matter. Hester is judged unworthy against a model of human fidelity that was deeply embedded in the puritanical society of early Boston. That model was understood and internalized throughout her community. It was not a product of law, though surely many of the Bostonian laws were derived from the same set of conceptions that engendered the model. In the eyes of Boston, Hester was not just guilty of lawbreaking, she should be ashamed. The willful breaking of law in itself does not generate shame. Very few people, for example, who are caught driving at 60 miles per hour in a 55 mile zone, under ordinary conditions, report feeling ashamed of what they have done.

We have throughout the centuries articulated human ideal models.[22] They are a part of our history, legend, education, religion, and literature. But there surely are corporate ideal models as well. The content of those models need not here be specified, though we should expect to find such features as being profitable, socially responsive, and humane in them. Each corporation, just as each human being, formulates its own conception of worth and associates itself with an ideal of behavior. Just as human beings are disposed to be the kind of persons they value, corporations are guided, at least in part, by an attempt to successfully realize the corporate images they have adopted and to be viewed by the community as having the characteristics of ideal corporate models. Public relations and advertising departments, of course, play focal roles in every corporation's attempt to establish and nurture its social standing and its exemplary image in the community.

The courts have both the authority and the social credibility to force persons and corporations to confront their failures, to live up to the ideals of their types. Court-ordered adverse publicity should provide an institutionalized revelatory apparatus, the modern substitute for the pillory, where the offender stands contemptible before the community, forced to confront the fact of his or her, or its, inadequacy. Shame is, after all, an identity crisis.

The exciting aspect of the Hester Prynne Sanction, however, is that the suffering of adverse publicity alone does not restore the offender to communal grace and relieve the shame. Only positive corrective acts can do that, as Hester proved by her exceeding good deeds. But look where this gets us: the imposition of the Hester Prynne Sanction on a corporation can institutionalize and broadcast a corporate offender's behavior, thus arousing the appropriate social contempt, an internal approbation, and it can be the spark to ignite the kind of adjustments of its operating procedures, policies, and practices that are required for that corporation to again appropriate the model identity and regain moral worth in both its own eyes and those of the community.[23]

The Hester Prynne Sanction might have significant retributive and deterrent effects on corporations, but as a primary penal device some have thought it prone to fail for a number of practical reasons. In the first place, as we all know, government is a rather poor propagandist.[24] It is not very persuasive, and very rarely is it pithy. (Have you ever seen a catchy piece of government-written prose that could rival the output of Madison Avenue?) For the adverse publicity sanction to have the desired *in terrorem* effects, and when used, for it to have a genuine impact on an offending corporation's established image, the court will have to employ clever writers and publicists, not the run-of-the-mill bureaucratic scribblers who crank out the government's literature. Courts also risk soiling their own images by descending to the Madison Avenue level in order to produce effective penal outcomes.

Such concerns can be easily addressed. Courts have the power to write their orders in such a way that the cost of the adverse publicity is paid by the criminal corporation from its own advertising budget to a competitive agency (other than ones that carry its accounts) which will then manage a campaign as approved by an officer of the court (perhaps a college professor trained in advertising and marketing). The corporation will have to submit its previous year's advertising budget to be used as a starting line, a percentage of the advertising budget will be set aside for the adverse publicity campaign, and that percentage will be carried through all annual budgets until the expiration of the order. In this way, even if the corporation increases its advertising budget to attempt to entice sales, it will have to pay a higher adverse publicity cost. The court-appointed overseer will instruct the agency to expend all funds in the adverse publicity budget annually and to do so in outlets roughly equivalent to those used by the usual corporate advertising agencies, e.g., the agency will not be allowed to place adverse publicity in obscure small-town newspapers if the corporation does not generally advertise in such ways. The private sector would then be actively engaged in the penal process, and a whole new respectable area of advertising will provide jobs and new paths of expression for the creative imagination to wander.

A frequently voiced second concern is that the level of anticorporate "noise" in our society is so great as to devalue the effect of specific adverse publicity orders.[25] The newspaper editorialists, the campaigning politicians, the special interest groups, the conservationists, the

Naderites, the assorted movie and TV actors and actresses with various causes all contribute to a confusing cacophony of charges that are usually indirect, often unsubstantiated, and certainly not properly adjudicated. Can this noise be controlled? Probably not, and it is not a good idea to pursue such a line in a free country. The corporations attacked in such ways have the option of legal action to counter unfair criticism. Against this noise, however, a well-developed adverse publicity campaign against a particular corporate offender, identified clearly as court-ordered, is still likely to draw attention. The public may never be very discriminating, but generally the fact that a court has ordered a certain publicity campaign as punishment for a particular criminal offense should pierce the shield of apathy behind which the public hides from the onslaught of ordinary corporate criticism.

It will be suggested that corporations can dilute the Hester Prynne Sanction through counterpublicity.[26] There is no denying the power of Madison Avenue agencies to create clever and effective image-building, even in the face of severe public or government criticism. But the sanction can be written in such a way, as suggested above, to offset any corporate counterattack. Furthermore, the court has the power to order the corporation not to engage in any advertising directed specifically towards rebutting or diluting the sentence. If the corporation were to promote its own case after having lost in court and having received an adverse publicity sentence, it would be in contempt of the court and sterner measures would be justified. Oil companies such as Mobil mounted effective replies to the charges leveled against them during the energy crisis. Also corporations after *Central Hudson Gas & Electric Corp. v Public Service Commission*[27] clearly have first amendment rights to express opinions on matters of public concern.[28] Corporate rebuttals to adverse publicity orders, however, are not necessarily protected by *Central Hudson*, and the Mobil commercials were certainly not attempts to minimize the effectiveness of any adverse publicity court orders. The oil companies were only charged in the court of public opinion, and the response was a totally appropriate defense in that venue.

The Hester Prynne Sanction may prove efficacious in fraud, public safety, and felony cases, but some doubt it can be equally effective in regulatory cases. Gulf Oil, it will be remembered, made illegal campaign contributions in connection with the Watergate scandals.[29] The publicity was profuse, but there is little evidence that it hurt Gulf Oil sales. There are two things that seem appropriate in response. The first is to point out that in the regulatory cases questioned adverse publicity occurred in the ordinary media coverage of the events. It was not court-ordered in lieu of or in addition to some other penal sanction, e.g., a stiff fine. In effect, it was incidental, and as the story faded from the front page or the first fifteen minutes of the telecast, its intensity diminished. But it just may be the case that the Hester Prynne Sanction does not produce significant desired effects in the case of certain crimes. I make no claim that adverse publicity orders will always suffice to achieve the retributive or deterrent ends of the legal system. A mix of sanctions will undoubtedly be required. I would argue that adverse publicity orders are more likely than most other sanctions to produce what might be called rehabilitative outcomes, reformed corporations. Fines certainly are too easily assimilated to business costs.

The Hester Prynne Sanction, however, may produce much the same externalities as fines.[30] After all, if it is really effective, some say that it should lead to decreased sales, and the corporation's employees at the lowest levels could be made to suffer layoffs and other unwanted effects.[31] This should not overly concern us. Such externalities plague penal sanctions of all kinds. More to the point, however, the true question is whether the Hester Prynne Sanction is justifiable over the simple assessment of a fine when both produce basically equivalent externalities. I think that I have offered some firm reasons for the court to prefer, at least with regard to certain crimes, the Hester Prynne Sanction rather than or in addition to fines. The payment of a fine and the suffering of court-ordered and supervised adverse publicity are simply not equivalent punishments.

The celebrated case of *United States v Allied Chemical Company*,[32] in which Allied Chemical was fined $13.24 million after a no-contest plea to 940 counts of pollution of the James River and other Virginia waterways, is often cited as an example of creative sentencing leading to the development of an alternative to the traditional sanctions.[33] The Allied Chemical fine was reduced to $5 million when the company agreed to give more than $8 million to the Virginia Environmental Endowment. Strictly speaking, the court did not order community service, but it did accept the company's establishment of the endowment as mitigatory. In another case, *United States v Olin Mathieson*,[34] the company pleaded no contest to the charge of conspiracy involving the shipment of rifles to South Africa. The judge imposed a $45,000 fine after Olin Mathieson agreed to set up a $500,000 New Haven Community Betterment Fund. (The maximum penalty could have been $510,000.)

Although neither of these cases really involved the imposition of a community service sanction (the defendants essentially wrote a check), some legal theorists have recently argued that the lessons learned in them indicate the desirability of providing the court with such a sentencing option.[35] There are certain practical problems with this approach that warrant only brief mention. Perhaps the most serious is that the corporation's costs in buying or performing community service are tax deductible charity contributions, and standard court-imposed fines are, of course, nondeductible. Legislation, however, could correct this deficiency.

It must also be realized that the performance of community service is a positive, image-enhancing action. It can be expected to elevate the public opinion of the criminal corporation. In fact, the results of corporate community service projects and charitable contributions are likely to make a rather favorable impression on members of society, while the reasons why the donor-corporation embarked on its apparently altruistic ventures are likely to be forgotten or lost in the outpouring of grateful sentiment. An obvious corrective for this difficulty, is to invoke Hester Prynne in conjunction with community service sentencing. Simply, the court can require that the service project be clearly identified as court-ordered as a penalty for a specific criminal offense. Every association drawn by the corporation to its beneficence would have to include an adverse publicity reference to its criminal conviction as the reason for the service.

Although community service does not seem to stand on a par with Hester Prynne and the traditional sentencing options, should it be encouraged? I think there are reasons why its use should be very restricted and that it should never be used in isolation from other penal sanctions.

The socially conciliatory aspect of community service, the fact that such endeavors can restore lost prestige and polish tarnished images, makes such civic contributions a major avenue for corporations to regain status and acceptance lost through conviction and broadcast in accord with the imposition of a Hester Prynne sentence. A shamed company, as earlier noted, cannot simply buy its way back to social grace. It needs to perform especially worthy deeds to achieve restoration. Community service is certainly a type of action it needs to perform to achieve such ends. But for there to be worth in the doing of such deeds, they must be voluntary. If they are performed under a form of duress, they are not actions of the person compelled to perform them. Insofar as none of our principles of responsibility capture them for that person, they do not accrue to the moral credit of that person. They would seem to be extended acts of the judge who decided to whom and how much. The convicted corporation is little more than an instrument of the court's conception of social need. A recent Nebraska sentence is a case in point. A corporation convicted of bid-rigging in highway construction contracts was ordered to donate $1.4 million to establish a permanent professional chair in business ethics at the state university.[36]

The community service sanction, when conjoined to Hester Prynne (ideally) or to a fine, can, however, have a certain morally desirable outcome, beside the fact that some good was done (the service was performed or the donation to a worthy cause was made), regardless of the reasons for its performance. Forced charitable deeds might serve to inculcate a habit of social concern in the corporation. At the very least, the sentenced corporation might come to view a continuation of community involvement as a way to curry future judicial favor. Aristotle maintained that a person is good by doing good deeds, by getting into the habit of doing such things.[37] A community service sentence could start a corporation on the path to virtue. Hence, there may be a rehabilitative value in the sanction despite the involuntary nature of the service performed by the convicted company.

There is, however, a notable amount of uncertainty that such an outcome will ensue from this type of sentencing. It does not seem likely enough to be a justifying reason to use the sanction. In fact, the best reason for a judge to order community service would be to achieve the charitable ends themselves. The rehabilitation of the offending corporation would seem to be an incidental upshot. Judges, however, are not necessarily in the best position to decide on our social or charitable needs. Furthermore, other than monetary or time loss, the penalty relationship of the sentence to the crime may be remote.[38]

All of these factors militate against the use of community service orders in corporate criminal cases, unless they are augmented by stiff fines and/or Hester Prynne. In comparison with the other discussed sanctions, adverse publicity, with its primary shaming function, would seem to be preferable on both practical and moral grounds. In any event, it is clear that there are effective and morally justifiable sentencing options (though community service is the least preferable) that support the inclusion of corporate entities among those persons who are subject to the criminal law. Baron Thurlow's demurral on the notion of corporate criminal liability may be set aside. Corporations are not only intentional agents, moral persons, they are proper subjects of the criminal law and all of its fury. They can be stigmatized and they can be "kicked" in ways comparable to those imposed on human offenders.

NOTES

1. *The Oxford Dictionary of Quotations,* 2d ed. (Oxford: Oxford University Press, 1966), 547.
2. See generally Marshall B. Clinard and Peter C. Yeager, *Corporate Crime* (New York: Free Press, 1980).
3. See e.g., Brent Fisse and John Braithwaite, *The Impact of Publicity on Corporate Offenders* (Albany: State University of New York Press, 1983), Chs. 2-18, 317.
4. See e.g., J. Murphy, *Retribution, Justice, and Therapy* (Boston: D. Reidel Pub. Co., 1979); R. Singer, *Just Deserts: Sentencing Based on Equality and Desert* (Cambridge, Mass.: Ballinger Pub. Co., 1979); A. Von Hirsch, *Doing Justice: The Choice of Punishments* (New York: Hill and Wang, 1976). But see John Braithwaite, "Challenging Just Deserts: Punishing White-Collar Criminals," *Journal of Criminal Law and Criminology* 73 (1982): 723-63.
5. See generally Victoria Lynn Swigert and Ronald A. Farrell, "Corporate Homicide: Definitional Processes in the Creation of Deviance," *Law & Society Review* 15 (1980): 161-82; Brent Fisse, "Reconstructing Corporate Criminal Law: Deterrence, Retribution, Fault, and Sanctions," *Southern California Law Review* 56 (1983): 1141-1246.
6. See further Peter A. French, *Collective and Corporate Responsibility* (New York: Columbia University Press, 1984), Ch. 11.
7. See e.g., Fisse and Braithwaite, *The Impact of Publicity on Corporate Offenders,* 303.
8. See generally John C. Coffee, Jr., " 'No Soul to Damn: No Body to Kick': An Unscandalized Inquiry into the Problem of Corporate Punishment," *Michigan Law Review* 79 (1981): 401-02.
9. See e.g., Gerhard Mueller, "*Mens Rea* and the Corporation," *University of Pittsburgh Law Review* 19 (1957): 21-50.
10. See generally Walter Kaufmann, *Without Guilt and Justice* (New York: Delta, 1973).
11. See further Peter A. French, "It's a Damn Shame" (unpublished manuscript 1984). For a psychodynamic analysis of shame, see Helen M. Lynd, *On Shame and the Search for Identity* (London: Routledge & Kegan Paul, 1958).
12. Zephaniah 3:5.
13. See e.g., Fisse and Braithwaite, *The Impact of Publicity on Corporate Offenders,* 75-76, 214-215, 227, 298, 302.
14. Nathaniel Hawthorne, *The Scarlet Letter* (New York: Pocket Books, 1954; originally published in 1850).
15. Ibid., 63.
16. See generally Fisse and Braithwaite, *The Impact of Publicity on Corporate Offenders.*
17. See e.g., Wally Olins, *The Corporate Personality: An Inquiry into the Nature of Corporate Identity* (New York: Mayflower Books, 1981); Charles Channon, "Corporations and the Politics of Perception," *Advertising Quarterly* 60(2) (1981): 12-15; Nancy Yashihara, "$1 Billion Spent on Identity: Companies Push Image of Selves, Not Products," *Los Angeles Times* (10 May 1981): pt. 6, pp. 1, 17.
18. See Fisse and Braithwaite, *The Impact of Publicity on Corporate Offenders,*

Ch. 19.

19. Ibid., 308-09.
20. U.S., National Commission on Reform of Federal Criminal Laws, *Study Draft* (Washington, D.C.: U.S. Government Printing Office, 1970), 405.
21. U.S., National Commission on Reform of Federal Criminal Laws, *Final Report* (Washington D.C.: U.S. Government Printing Office, 1971), 3007.
22. See generally Kaufmann, *Without Guilt and Justice*; Fred L. Polak, *The Image of the Future: Enlightening the Past, Orienting the Present, Forecasting the Future*, vols. 1 and 2 (New York: Oceana Publications, 1961).
23. See references at Note 13 above.
24. See further, Coffee, " 'No Soul to Damn: No Body to Kick' ": 425-26; Fisse and Braithwaite, *The Impact of Publicity on Corporate Offenders*, 291-92.
25. Ibid., 426. See further Fisse and Braithwaite, *The Impact of Publicity on Corporate Offenders*, 294-95.
26. See further Coffee, " 'No Soul to Damn: No Body to Kick' ": 426; Fisse and Braithwaite, *The Impact of Publicity on Corporate Offenders*, 295-98.
27. 447 U.S. 557 (1980).
28. See generally Herbert Schmertz, *Corporations and the First Amendment* (New York: Amacom, 1978); William Patton and Randall Bartlett, "Corporate 'Persons' and Freedom of Speech: The Political Impact of Legal Mythology," *Wisconsin Law Review* (1981): 494-512.
29. See John J. McCloy, *The Great Oil Spill* (New York: Chelsea House, 1976).
30. Coffee, " 'No Soul to Damn: No Body to Kick' ": 427-28.
31. But see Fisse and Braithwaite, *The Impact of Publicity on Corporate Offenders*, 306-09.
32. 420 F. Supp. 122 (1976).
33. See further Brent Fisse, "Community Service as a Sanction against Corporations," *Wisconsin Law Review* (1981): 970-1017.
34. Criminal No. 78-30, slip. op. (D. Conn., June 1, 1978).
35. Fisse, "Community Service as a Sanction against Corporations." See also Ch. 7.
36. *New York Times* (29 July 1983): 1.
37. Aristotle, *Nicomachean Ethics*, tran. M. Ostwald (Indianapolis: Bobbs-Merrill, 1962), 33.
38. But see Fisse, "Community Service as a Sanction against Corporations," 1008-16.

CHAPTER 9
THE EXERCISE OF PROSECUTORIAL DISCRETION IN FEDERAL BUSINESS FRAUD PROSECUTIONS

Jed S. Rakoff

Valor is the better part of discretion. Only in an atmosphere free of constant second-guessing can a public official find the security necessary to make "hard," unpopular, sometimes heroic decisions. Of course, discretion, i.e., the power to make lawfully binding decisions on the basis of one's own considered judgment and conscience, invites not only valor but also arbitrariness, and arbitrariness invites — perhaps too reflexively — the imposition of procedures for review.

Comparatively few public officials enjoy the breadth of discretion accorded a prosecutor in deciding whether or not to commence a prosecution. The prosecutor may have to prove his case in court, but his decision to bring a case is subject to only limited review; and his decision *not* to bring a case is virtually unreviewable. Thus it is not surprising that academic commentators from K. C. Davis[1] to James Vorenberg[2] have called for placing greater restraints on the exercise of this considerable prosecutorial discretion through the imposition of administrative regulations and judicial review. But before accepting their recommendations, we should examine the effectiveness of existing restraints on the exercise of prosecutorial discretion. This chapter offers such an examination and attempts to convey some practical feel for how prosecutorial discretion is exercised, by describing its exercise in the decision whether or not to seek a federal indictment in a typical business fraud case.

This context was chosen not only because it is the area of the author's own experience, first as a prosecutor and now as a defense counsel, but also because business fraud cases — by virtue of their complexity, difficulty, likeness to civil cases and (sometimes) moral ambiguity — often require a very sensitive exercise of prosecutorial discretion. In this particular area, prosecutions most commonly proceed against individuals; the question of whether to prosecute a corporation in addition to, or in lieu of, its officers and employees has not arisen to the same extent as it has in other areas such as pollution offenses.[3] Moreover, the examples which arise are by no means confined to corporate crime in the sense of offenses committed on behalf of an organization.[4] My central concern, however, is not with the balance between individual and corporate criminal liability nor with the difference between corporate crime and white collar crime in some broader sense. The more fundamental question is whether the exercise of prosecutorial discretion should be governed by an additional regime of legal constraints.

Constitution-Based Limitations

Although there are few statutory restraints on prosecutorial discretion, the Constitution itself contains several such restraints, both express and implied, on the exercise of prosecutorial discretion. One express constraint is the Double Jeopardy Clause of the Fifth Amendment: "nor shall any person be subject for the same offense to be twice put in jeopardy of life or limb." This Clause has been rather narrowly interpreted by the courts. Even together with the related legal doctrines of res judicata and collateral estoppel, it bars only those prosecutions that are dependent for conviction on an issue of ultimate fact which has been clearly determined in the defendant's favor in a prior criminal proceeding involving the same parties. Since a single underlying criminal transaction can frequently give rise to a multitude of criminal charges involving different elements, and since it is frequently impossible to determine from a general verdict of acquittal what particular elements were necessarily determined in the defendant's favor, it is a rare situation where the Double Jeopardy Clause will provide a defense to a subsequent prosecution on a different charge.

Nevertheless, federal prosecutors regularly apply the policy of the Double Jeopardy Clause to decline prosecutions that would not be prohibited by the Clause itself. This, for example, is part of the basis of the Justice Department's so-called *"Petite* policy" (discussed below), which bars most federal prosecutions for transactions already prosecuted by state or local prosecutors or by other federal prosecutors. More generally, it is the common practice of federal prosecutors not to bring prosecutions that effectively enable them to get "more than one bite at the apple" unless such prosecutions fall into one of several reasonably well-defined exceptions.

Reference to the area of federal business fraud prosecutions will help illustrate this practice and also some of the exceptions to it. Defendants in federal business fraud prosecutions usually take the stand in their own defense and try to provide plausible exculpatory explanations for their involvement in the seemingly fraudulent activities of which they are accused. If, following the giving of such testimony, the defendant is acquitted, is it appropriate thereafter to prosecute him or her for perjury arising from this testimony? While the Double Jeopardy Clause would rarely bar such a perjury prosecution, and while no written directive of the Justice Department prohibits such a prosecution, it is the routine practice of federal prosecutors to decline such prosecutions. This is true even where, following the acquittal, new evidence is uncovered clearly demonstrating the perjurious nature of the defendant's testimony; for such an exception would frequently be little different from re-prosecuting the original charge itself on the basis of newly discovered evidence, an outright violation of the Double Jeopardy Clause.

Because, however, this practice is "discretionary," it offers the flexibility necessary to permit the occasional deviation mandated by exceptional circumstances. An example: In the late 1960s, a major attempt was made by so-called "organized crime" to infiltrate the over-the-counter markets in securities as a first step toward infiltrating the securities brokerage business generally. As part of an effort (ultimately successful) to stem this, an indictment was brought in 1970 in the Southern District of New York alleging criminal securities fraud on the part of sixteen organized crime defendants, including some of the major alleged "mob" figures in the country. But at the trial, although some of the lower echelon defendants were convicted, the upper echelon figures, after taking the stand and testifying in their own defense, were acquitted. In 1972, however, the decision was made to deviate from the general practice described above by seeking indictment of each of these previously acquitted figures, on charges of having given perjurious testimony at the prior trial. This decision was felt to be justified by three exceptional factors. First, following the original trial, evidence was uncovered strongly suggesting that the defendants had tampered with a juror. This was different from the ordinary kind of newly discovered evidence discussed above, in that it cast doubt on the legitimacy of the entire process by which the defendants had previously been acquitted. Second, a major grand jury witness who had become unavailable to testify at the trial because of secret complicity with the defendants was now willing to testify at the perjury trials. Again, this was not newly discovered evidence that the government had dredged up after the acquittals; rather, this was previously known evidence which the defendants had wrongly prevented from being placed before the trial jury. Third, all available information indicated that the defendants stood at the very pinnacle of some of the most heinous criminal enterprises in the country and yet would be difficult to bring before the bar of justice in the best of circumstances. These factors (similar to those which led to the jury-tampering prosecution of Jimmy Hoffa following his earlier acquittals on various substantive charges) led in this case to the perjury indictment of each of these major "Mafia" figures, and each was duly convicted.

The Equal Protection and Due Process Clauses of the Constitution also provide certain limitations on the exercise of prosecutorial discretion, notably a bar to "selective prosecution" and "vindictive prosecution." But as in the case of the Double Jeopardy Clause, the courts have interpreted these limitations quite narrowly. To establish a defense of "selective prosecution," a defendant must establish (often without benefit of discovery) both that s/he has been singled out for prosecution while others similarly situated have not generally been proceeded against and that the government's discriminatory selection of him or her for prosecution is based upon such constitutionally impermissible considerations as race, religion, or the desire to prevent one's exercise of First Amendment rights. Similarly, the doctrine prohibiting vindictive or retaliatory prosecutions appears to be applied only where prosecutors have retaliated against a defendant's exercise of such specially protected rights as First Amendment rights or the right to appeal.

Nonetheless, as in the case of the Double Jeopardy Clause, federal prosecutors have as a matter of discretion implemented the Constitution-based doctrines of "selective prosecution" and "vindictive prosecution" in ways that go well beyond their judicially enforceable application. For example, in recognition of the Supreme Court's dictum in *Blackledge* v *Perry*[5] that there is an appearance of prosecutorial vindictiveness in the discouragement of a defendant's right to appeal, federal prosecutors have routinely refused to enter into any post-conviction bargain with a defendant by which the defendant waives or compromises that right. This is so even though it is not uncommon for a just-convicted defendant to offer to waive his right of appeal if the prosecutor agrees not to "push" for a heavy sentence. Although this would be a tempting bargain if the prosecutor were to adopt a strictly adversarial viewpoint, the spirit (though not the letter) of *Blackledge* has led prosecutors to reject it. Conversely, since the Supreme Court has held bargaining for a guilty plea to be not only constitutionally sound but "a process mutually beneficial to both the defendant and the state" (*Corbitt* v *New Jersey*),[6] federal prosecutors have with equal uniformity entered into ordinary plea bargaining, notwithstanding academic criticism that such a bargain unfairly "coerces" a defendant into waiving his right to trial.

Ethical Imperatives

Numerous ethical standards for prosecutors are set forth in *Standards Relating to the Prosecution Function and the Defense Function*,[7] a set of ethical rules and guidelines drafted between 1964 and 1970 by a distinguished Advisory Committee and approved by the American Bar Association House of Delegates in February, 1971. Although these Standards have not been adopted by the Justice Department as "official policy," most federal prosecutors appear familiar with them and sensitive to their import. Particularly relevant to the exercise of prosecutorial discretion is Prosecution Standard 3.9b, which reads:

> The prosecutor is not obliged to present all charges which the evidence might support. The prosecutor may in some circumstances and for good cause consistent with the public interest decline to prosecute, notwithstanding that evidence exists which would support a conviction. Illustrative of the factors which the prosecutor may properly consider in exercising his discretion are:
>
> (i) the prosecutor's reasonable doubt that the accused is in fact guilty;
> (ii) the extent of the harm caused by the offense;
> (iii) the disproportion of the authorized punishment in relation to the particular offense or the offender;
> (iv) possible improper motives of a complainant;
> (v) prolonged nonenforcement of a statute, with community acquiescence;
> (vi) reluctance of the victim to testify;
> (vii) cooperation of the accused in the apprehension or conviction of others;
> (viii) availability and likelihood of prosecution by another jurisdiction.

In this author's experience, these are in fact the primary factors weighed by federal prosecutors in deciding whether or not to prosecute a given case or defendant. And while this Standard (like the others) has been criticized as being too loose and general to provide meaningful guidance, many of its directives have been elaborated into more specific rules governing the exercise of discretion.

For example, with respect to those business fraud cases that derive from civilian complaints, one of the "possible improper motives of a complainant" (Standard 3.9(b)(iv)) that receives very close scrutiny is whether the complainant is attempting to misuse the criminal process to collect a civil debt from his adversary. Indeed, the Manhattan District Attorney's Office will as a rule simply not prosecute a business fraud case where the complainant has already commenced a civil action against the alleged wrongdoer, both because of the risk that the criminal case will be misused as a weapon in the civil litigation and because of the need to preserve the relatively scarce resources of that office for cases where the victim is unable to obtain civil redress. Although the relatively greater resources of federal offices permit a less rigid approach, virtually all federal offices begin with a presumption against prosecuting cases where the civil complainant has already instituted a civil action. This presumption maybe is unfortunate, since it is perfectly natural for the victim of a business fraud to seek what redress he can in the civil courts, even while dutifully reporting the fraud to the police authorities. Moreover, if a main purpose of prosecuting the defrauder is general deterrence, it seems largely irrelevant whether or not the victim is seeking, or can obtain, civil redress. But, wise or foolish, the point is that Standard 3.9 has had some genuine impact on the exercise of prosecutorial discretion.

Unfortunately this is less obviously true of Standard 3.9(c), which provides that "In making the decision to prosecute, the prosecutor should give no weight to the personal or political advantages or disadvantages which might be involved . . . " Where the prosecutor is a politically nominated, publicly elected official, adherence to this Standard is sometimes little more than a pious hope. Even in consciously nonpolitical prosecutors' offices, however, the serpent still enters the garden in the guise of the media, for it is an unusual prosecutor who is not secretly pleased by positive media coverage and not-so-secretly sensitive to media criticism. Moreover, in those situations where to the lure of publicity itself is added its possible future transmutation into political power, the tendency to let media impact affect prosecutorial judgment may become very strong.

However, it is not so easy to prescribe the proper relationship between the media and a prosecutor's office, not only because of the obvious role of the media in exposing incompetence and corruption and in providing a basis for democratic debate and public choice, but also because of the need for media coverage to achieve the prosecutor's legitimate aim of achieving general deterrence through well-publicized prosecutions. In the case of business frauds (not an area of high media interest on the whole), the number of cases that can be prosecuted is necessarily a very small percentage of all such crimes committed, and hence considerations of general deterrence, and of media coverage, loom large in the selection of what cases to prosecute. Moreover, since business frauds are typically perpetrated by reasonably well-informed, educated persons acting not on impulse but on the basis of preconceived schemes, such crimes would seem to be particularly subject to deterrence by highly visible, publicized prosecutions.

Thus, something of a ready-made rationale exists for targeting high-visibility figures and for seeking maximum media coverage of these prosecutions.

While the author regards this rationale as suspect, the point is that the impact of the media on the exercise of prosecutorial discretion is complex and arguably both salutary and dangerous. It is unlikely, however, that more rigid regulation or judicial review of the exercise of prosecutorial discretion could meaningfully resolve these difficult issues; more likely, it would only render them still more complicated.

Internal Guidelines

The 95 United States Attorney's Offices are not governed by formal regulations but, so far as written directives are concerned, chiefly by the provisions of an unwieldly, multi-volume melange of policies, guidelines, legal analyses and helpful hints known as the *United States Attorneys' Manual.*[8] The *Manual* is expressly for internal use only, and its provisions are not judicially enforceable. Internal enforcement of the provisions is sometimes lax and sometimes idiosyncratic; yet, most of the provisions are followed most of the time, perhaps because they generally correspond to older, oral traditions of federal prosecution.

Most of the provisions applicable to the exercise of prosecutorial discretion are set forth in Chapter 2 of Title 9 of the *Manual*. In addition, the most important of such provisions, along with commentaries, are gathered together in a pamphlet entitled *Principles of Federal Prosecution*, issued by the Department in 1980 and now publicly available. Typical of these provisions are those comprising the so-called "*Petite* policy," mentioned above. (The name refers to *Petite* v *United States*[9], in which the Supreme Court expressly deferred to the Department's policy in this area.) As set forth in the *Manual* at §9-2.142, the policy has two prongs. First, there is the "dual prosecution policy":

> The Department of Justice's dual prosecution policy precludes the initiation or continuation of a federal prosecution following a state prosecution based on substantially the same act or acts unless there is compelling federal interest supporting the dual prosecution.

The *Manual* then defines and illustrates what constitutes a "compelling federal interest" in this context. Second, there is the "successive federal prosecution policy:"

> The Department of Justice's successive federal prosecution policy precludes the initiation or continuation of a federal

> prosecution following a prior federal prosecution based on the same transaction unless there is a compelling interest supporting the subsequent prosecution.

Again, the *Manual* then undertakes to define and illustrate what constitutes the "compelling interest" exception in this context.

As noted earlier, the *Petite* policy is partly an example of the Department's application of Constitutional-based directives (in this case, the Double Jeopardy Clause) to situations beyond those reached by the letter of such directives. In addition, the *Petite* policy permits the efficient allocation of federal prosecutorial resources. The first prong of the *Petite* policy, dealing with dual state and federal prosecutions, also illustrates one of the most pervasive considerations affecting the exercise of federal prosecutorial discretion, *viz.*, a qualified deference to state authorities in the prosecution of crime generally.

Historically, primary authority over the prosecution of criminal activity was vested with the states, and this has largely remained true even in periods of expanding federal power. For example, one of the most common reasons given by federal prosecutors for declining to prosecute cases brought to them by civilian complainants is that the cases more appropriately fall within the jurisdiction of local prosecutors, even if some technical basis for federal jurisdiction might be found. While this is sometimes simply an easy way of disposing of unattractive cases, more often it represents a genuine deference to local authority.

There are, of course, certain kinds of crimes, such as narcotics offenses, which invite combined action by both state and federal authorities in joint "task forces." In addition, there are certain prosecutions which federal prosecutors tend not to defer, typically involving crimes that local prosecutors are either *unable* or *unwilling* to prosecute. Major business frauds exemplify the "unable" category, for they frequently require lengthy and complex investigations for which local prosecutorial offices often lack the necessary resources and expertise. Major political corruption cases exemplify the "unwilling" category, for where the target is a local political power, the local prosecutor, himself often an elected official of the same party, may be unwilling to undertake the necessary investigation and prosecution. There is, moreover, a symbiotic relationship between these two categories. Federal prosecutors in pursuing local official corruption have made extensive use of a statute originally aimed at business frauds, the federal mail fraud statute,[10] by analogizing such corruption to a fraud on the public. The resultant stretching of the mail fraud statute in official corruption cases has in turn extended its applicability to virtually every conceivable kind of business fraud, making it in effect an instrument for mapping the frontiers of business ethics.

Whether this is an appropriate use of criminal law, state or federal, is subject to debate; what seems less debatable, however, is that it represents, not an infringement upon state law enforcement, but rather the application of federal criminal laws to areas where state criminal law does not, as a practical matter, function. Thus, the claim that federal prosecutions in such areas represent an unwarranted invasion of state prerogatives is misplaced, for there is no indication that the states will exercise their prerogatives in such areas to any meaningful extent. So, the operative question in such cases is whether there should be any criminal prosecution at all or whether such matters should be left to civil remedies.

Internal Priorities

The policies and guidelines affecting prosecutorial discretion which are set forth in the *United States Attorneys' Manual* tend to remain relatively constant from year to year and from administration to administration. But each administration has its own prosecutorial points-of-emphasis, or "priorities," as to a lesser extent does each individual United States Attorney. Three kinds of priorities which affect prosecutorial discretion bear mention here.

First, each recent federal administration has, with much fanfare, "declared war" on one or another kind of crime. Under the Kennedy and, to a lesser extent, Johnson administrations, the target was organized crime and labor racketeering; under the Nixon and, to a lesser extent, Ford administrations, it was narcotics; under the Carter administration, it was "white-collar" crime and official corruption; and under the Reagan administration, it is once again narcotics and official corruption. But these rapid changes in priorities have not had a fundamental impact on the exercise of federal prosecutorial discretion, because each such prioritization has been accomplished, not so much by shifting federal prosecutorial resources from one area of prosecution to another, as by increasing the total amount of federal prosecutorial resources and directing the added increment to the prioritized area. Thus, for example, the Carter administration prioritized the prosecution of "white-collar" crime, not by decreasing the number of federal prosecutions in other areas, but by hiring additional Assistants to serve as "economic crime specialists" in the various federal districts. Similarly, the Reagan administration's attack on narcotics trafficking is being implemented, not so much by diverting resources away from the prosecution of other kinds of crime (although there has been some reduction in business crime prosecutions), as by securing special appropriations for the hiring of still more Assistants, who devote themselves to the prosecution of narcotics offenses.

A second kind of prioritization – one with more impact on the exercise of the prosecutorial discretion – has been the attempt of both the Justice Department and individual United States Attorneys' Offices to develop somewhat specific guidelines within each category of crime as to which cases to decline *ab initio*. For example, in the area of business fraud prosecutions, the Justice Department issued a report in 1980 entitled *National Priorities for the Investigation and Prosecution of White Collar Crime*,[11] which recommended that particular kinds of business frauds not be given "priority" (i.e., not be prosecuted) unless their impacts upon victims met certain threshold limits. For example, the threshold limit in the case of insurance frauds was a minimum of $250,000 in aggregate losses or two or more incidents perpetrated by the same person or persons; in the case of advance fee schemes, it was a minimum of $100,000 in aggregate losses or ten or more victims; in the case of criminal copyright violations, it was a minimum of $500,000 in aggregate losses and distribution in three or more states or countries; and in the case of securities frauds, it was simply a minimum of $100,000 in aggregate losses. For a while these "priorities" served as more or less binding guidelines in many United States Attorneys' Offices.

The promulgation of such specific guidelines may have pleased those commentators who believe that the limits on federal prosecutorial discretion are too indefinite and impressionistic. Conversely, however, one might fairly argue that such specific guidelines are wholly artificial, make the prosecutorial decision depend on one limited aspect of the criminal transaction, and create more evils than they eliminate. For example, thanks to effective surveillance by the SEC, some of the most massive and sophisticated business fraud schemes have been exposed before they could be fully consummated, with the result that the actual losses inflicted upon victims were slight, even though the intended losses were huge. Yet, consistent application of the aforementioned guidelines would preclude prosecution of such frauds. Perhaps for such reasons, these guidelines are no longer as rigidly followed as they were when first promulgated.

A third kind of priority is that formulated by a local United States Attorney or even one of his subordinates. Although such priorities create the possibility of "unequal" enforcement of the law in different parts of the United States, they are often reasonably responsive to particular local conditions. The relative concentration of criminal prosecutions for securities frauds in the Southern District of New York (itself the result of New York's position as the nation's financial capital) has been accompanied by the formulation of certain local priorities (some more enduring than others) as to which such cases should be prosecuted. One such priority, for a time, was an emphasis on prosecuting outside professionals involved in such frauds.

Obviously, securities frauds can rarely succeed without the help, or at least the acquiescence, of both an attorney and an accountant, and thus, as Judge Friendly stated in *United States* v *Benjamin*,[12] "the accountant's certificate and the lawyer's opinion can be instruments for inflicting pecuniary loss more potent than the chisel or the crowbar." In cases dating back at least to the 1930s, the United States Attorney's Office for the Southern District of New York prosecuted numerous accountants who helped these frauds to succeed, but comparable prosecutions against attorneys were rather less frequent. After a while the accusation was heard that the prosecutors, being attorneys themselves, were overly sympathetic to fellow attorneys caught up in dubious circumstances. Although many such cases were referred to the bar association for professional disciplinary measures, criticism was also voiced that the New York bar was reluctant to impose meaningful sanctions on its errant members. In 1973, the Southern District responded to these criticisms by announcing that hereinafter the conduct of attorneys in business fraud cases would be given particularly searching scrutiny. Internal steps taken to implement this policy ranged from keeping internal statistics on the number of attorneys indicted to personal monitoring by the Chief of the Criminal Division of all investigations involving lawyers. As result, there was, during the mid-1970s, a significant increase in the number of lawyers prosecuted for business frauds in the Southern District of New York.

The appropriateness of this "priority" was rendered more problematic, however, by the unexpected decision of the New York Court of Appeals in *Matter of Chu*.[13] *Chu* held that any attorney thereafter convicted of a federal felony would be automatically disbarred (whereas previously s/he was entitled to a hearing on whether the federal felony corresponded to a New York State felony). Because there are few federal misdemeanors but many minor federal felonies, particularly in the area of securities fraud, the *Chu* decision raised the question whether in many cases federal prosecution of an attorney for a relatively minor securities violation might lead to collateral punishment substantially disproportionate to the crime. Thereafter the priority given in the Southern District to the targeting of attorneys subsided and was not resurrected even when, some years later, the New York State legislature repealed *Chu.*

Practices, Customs and Traditions

Beyond policies, guidelines, and priorities, federal prosecutorial discretion is substantially shaped, and substantially limited, by practices, customs, and traditions that are orally conveyed from Assistant to Assistant. These unwritten "rules" are remarkably uniform even from office to office. For example, in every United States Attorney's Office with which this author is familiar, it is the general practice not to commence a prosecution if the Assistant investigating the case has a reasonable doubt about the putative defendant's guilt, even if the Assistant's superiors think the evidence of guilt is sufficient. The Assistant's superiors see their role as including the power to disapprove (typically on legal or policy grounds) a prosecution proposed by the Assistant, but not as including the power to resurrect a prosecution the Assistant has disapproved on the facts, except in extraordinary cases. This practice – which is akin to the division of power between trial and appellate courts – finds its justification in the better "feel" that the Assistant investigating the facts has for the facts themselves, even if s/he does not have the same policy perspective as his or her chiefs. Incidentally, however, this practice provides an important protection for an accused, in that it tends to focus the decision to prosecute on the particular facts of the individual case as opposed to the broader "deterrence" perspectives on which the chiefs tend to concentrate.

With respect to the particular area of business fraud prosecutions, a rather more controversial practice which has become common in many offices is the tendency, mentioned above, to use the criminal law to map (or, some would say, extend) the frontiers of business ethics. From one point of view, "test" cases should have no place in criminal prosecutions; society's most stringent sanctions should not be imposed on a defendant, regardless of how "immoral" his or her conduct may have been, unless he or she violated a known and certain legal duty to society. From another viewpoint, however, criminal sanctions may be viewed as the most effective deterrent against new and creative forms of fraud most likely to victimize the public, and a failure to invoke such sanctions may be seen as equivalent to giving free reign to the most artful swindlers.

A current example illustrative of these conflicting viewpoints involves the prosecution of "inside information" cases. Beginning in 1968, if not earlier, civil lawsuits under SEC Rule 10b-5 were held to lie against those investors privy to confidential business information who had some specific fiduciary duty that required them to either disclose the inside information or to refrain from investing on the basis of it. By 1980, the Supreme Court could speak of this application of Rule 10b-5 as "established" and trace its roots back to common law origins.[14] Nonetheless, civil lawsuits had no apparent effect in deterring unlawful trading on inside information, which trading became, if anything, more common.

Accordingly, in 1978 a federal criminal prosecution was commenced in the Southern District of New York against one Vincent Chiarella, who had taken advantage of the confidential information contained in the not-yet-public announcement of corporate takeover bids printed by the company for which he worked to make a "killing" on the stock market. At Chiarella's trial, the government persuaded the District Court to charge the jury that Chiarella could be convicted not only for defrauding his employer and the companies with which his employer did business, but alternatively, for defrauding the anonymous investors on the other side of his stock transactions, who were effectively cheated because they did not have the advantage of the confidential information he had stolen. This latter theory, though supported by many commentators, was not unequivocally embraced by prior SEC civil case law. But in affirming Chiarella's conviction, the Second Circuit adopted and even extended this approach by holding that "anyone – corporate insider or not – who regularly receives material nonpublic information may not use that information to trade in securities without incurring an affirmative duty to disclose."[15] This extension led the Supreme Court to reverse (although not without forceful dissents from Chief Justice Burger and Justices Blackmun and Marshall).[16]

Chiarella nicely illustrates the fine line between the properly aggressive prosecution of new kinds of fraud and the over-extension of the criminal law beyond the frontiers of established civil law (and, arguably, even of business ethics). But it is also important to note that the reversal in *Chiarella* did not lead the government to abandon its attempt to deter improper trading on inside information. Thus, in the three years since *Chiarella*, a dozen felony prosecutions for improper trading on inside information have been brought in the Southern District of New York, all resulting in convictions.

In conclusion, it may fairly be stated that while a prosecutor's decision whether or not to seek an indictment is not readily reduced to a formula, this does not mean that it is made without consideration of numerous familiar and acceptable points-of-reference. One may infer that it is precisely because there are so many perfectly legitimate considerations that may and should be taken into account in deciding whether or not to prosecute a defendant in any reasonably complex case that rigid rules would be counterproductive and that considerable discretion is necessary if the system is to operate with genuine fairness, let alone with wisdom and with courage.

NOTES

1. K.C. Davis, *Discretionary Justice: A Preliminary Inquiry* (Baton Rouge: Louisiana State University Press, 1969).
2. James Vorenberg, "Decent Restraint of Prosecutorial Power," *Harvard Law Review* 94 (1981): 1521-73.
3. See further Ch. 10.
4. On these matters of definition and scope, see Ch. 1, Note 1.
5. 417 U.S. 21, 27-28 (1974).
6. 439 U.S. 212, 222 (1978).
7. American Bar Association, Office of Criminal Justice Project, *Standards Relating to the Prosecution and the Defense Function* (New York: Institute of Judicial Administration, 1971).
8. U.S., Justice Department, *United States Attorneys' Manual* (Washington, D.C.: Justice Department, 1980).
9. 361 U.S. 529 (1960) (per curiam).
10. 18 U.S.C. 1341.
11. U.S., Justice Department, *National Priorities for the Investigation and Prosecution of White Collar Crime* (Washington, D.C.: U.S. Government Printing Office, 1980).
12. 328 F.2d 854, 862 (2d Cir. 1964).
13. 42 N.Y. 2d 490 (1977).
14. Chiarella v United States, 445 U.S. 222, 230 (1980).
15. 588 F.2d 1358, 1365 (2d Cir., 1978).
16. Chiarella v United States, 445 U.S. 222 (1980).

CHAPTER 10
CORPORATE RESPONSES TO ERRANT BEHAVIOR: TIME'S ARROW, LAW'S TARGET

Brent Fisse and Peter A. French

Corporate liability for wrongdoing traditionally has depended on proof of responsibility for causally relevant acts or omissions at or before the time the wrongdoing is manifested.[1] The present authors have recently challenged this orthodoxy by suggesting that corporate responsibility should also be assessed on the basis of a defendant's responses to prohibited harmcausing or risktaking.[2] The essay to follow pursues the implications which a reactive timeframe has for several major problems of corporate regulation. It will be argued that the law has more chance of success if the timeframe for enforcement is altered so as to place more emphasis on corporate responses to errant behavior.

Our starting point is the concept of reactive corporate fault.[3] Reactive corporate fault may broadly be defined as unreasonable corporate failure to devise and undertake satisfactory preventive or corrective measures in response to the commission of the *actus reus* of an offense by personnel acting on behalf of the organization.[4] This concept, which is latent in a number of decided cases,[5] reflects two practical realities:

(1) Communal attitudes of resentment toward corporations that stonewall or otherwise fail to react diligently when their attention is drawn to the harmful or excessively risky nature of their operations;[6] and

(2) Managerial practice in accordance with the principle of management by exception, whereby compliance is treated as a routine matter to be delegated to inferiors and handled by them unless a significant problem arises.[7]

Underlying these practical pillars of reactive corporate fault is the principle of responsive adjustment.[8] This is a principle of moral responsibility derived from the relativity between time and blameworthiness. The central notion is that:

[C]ertain moral considerations, primarily those that stress the integrity of a lifetime, require adjustments in behavior to

rectify flaws of character or habits that have actually caused
past evils or, on the positive side, to routinize actions that
have led to worthy results . . . [The principle of responsive
adjustment] entails that the intention that motivates a lack of
responsive corrective action (or the continuance of offending
behavior) affirms, in the sense that it loops back to retrieve,
the actions that caused the evil. By the same token, failure to
routinize behavior that has been productive of good results
divorces the previously unintentional action that had good
consequences from one's moral life.[9]

The concept of reactive fault and the principle of responsive adjustment offer a promising way of avoiding the contentious attribution of
criminal intentionality to a corporation.[10] Corporations can and do act
intentionally in carrying out corporate policies.[11] Almost invariably,
however, a boilerplate compliance policy will be in place,[12] and consequently it is indeed rare that a company displays any criminal intention at or before the time of commission of the *actus reus* of an offense.
The typical legal solution at present is either to impose strict liability
or to impose liability vicariously on the basis of the intent of a representative. The former approach avoids the issue by making intention
irrelevant at the level of attribution of liability (intentionality is relevant in relation to sentence). The latter approach (which is essentially
a form of strict liability) is based on representational rather than genuinely corporate intentionality.[13] If the fundamental criminal element of
mens rea is applied in the corporate sphere, thereby displacing strict or
vicarious liability, the focus must necessarily be on a corporate
defendant's policy. To achieve that focus in a workable way, it is possible to extend the timeframe of inquiry so as to encompass what a
defendant has done in response to the commission of the *actus reus* of
an offense. What matters then is not so much a corporation's general
policies of compliance, but what it specifically proposes to do to implement a program of internal discipline, structural reform, and compensatory or restitutionary relief.[14] The effect of this reorientation would
be to flush out blameworthy corporate intentionality more easily than
is possible when the inquiry is confined to corporate policy at or
before the time of the *actus reus*. For instance, consider the Firestone
500 tire scandal: It was impossible to show any palpable flaw in Firestone's general compliance policies, but relatively easy to regard the
company as blameworthy for adopting a reactive policy of not
promptly implementing a recall program in response to the over-
whelming evidence that the tire was unsafe.[15]

This advantage aside, a reactive timeframe generates useful ideas on several other important issues of corporate regulation. In particular, time's arrow reorients the following issues:

(1) State intervention in corporate internal affairs;
(2) Expected standards of corporate behavior;
(3) Individual accountability for corporate wrongdoing; and
(4) Design and application of sanctions against corporations.

State Intervention in Corporate Internal Affairs

The last decade has seen a stream of proposals for strengthening the control of corporate behavior by means of state intervention in the decisionmaking structure and procedure of private enterprise.[16] At the same time, many have opposed state intervention of this kind, partly on the ground of undue interference with managerial freedom, and primarily on the basis of economic inefficiency.[17] Various attempts have been made to find some satisfactory middle ground, most notably in the recent work of Christopher Stone and John Braithwaite.[18] The interesting thing about a reactive timeframe in the context of the debate about the limits of state intervention is that it suggests an additional compromise, namely, Enforced Self-Reaction.[19]

The leading work advocating increased state intervention in the internal affairs of corporations is Stone's *Where the Law Ends: The Social Control of Corporate Behavior*; the thesis advanced is that the law should focus directly on the processes of corporate decisionmaking:

> Instead of treating the corporation's inner processes as a "black box," to be influenced only indirectly through threats laid about its environment like traps, we need more straightforward "intrusions" into the corporation's decision structure and processes than society has yet undertaken.[20]

This thesis may have much to commend it, but how far should it be taken? Under what circumstances should there be resort to mandated decisionmaking structures, watchdog directors, or other intrusions into the black box of the corporation? The answer given by Stone is essentially that:

> the more intrusive the intervention, the more it should be reserved for a relatively narrow class of situations in which the warrant for doing so appears sufficiently strong, at least until we have had more experiences with them to evaluate.[21]

Accordingly, the mandatory appointment of special compliance directors is considered appropriate over a limited range of regulation, as in the case of recidivism ("demonstrated delinquency") or in the setting of a generically hazardous industry (e.g., asbestos manufacture, toxic waste disposal).[22]

The criterion recommended by Stone offers a moderate compromise, but how should it be applied in less extreme situations? Plainly, there are many first offenders and numerous generically nonhazardous industries. In this more typical context, should the state continue to treat the corporation's decisionmaking processes as an inviolate black box, or should some more interventionist strategy be adopted?

One leading model for the resolution of this issue is the American Bar Association proposal for continuing judicial oversight as a sentence against corporate offenders.[23] Under the ABA proposal, a sentence of continuing judicial supervision cannot be imposed unless there is a finding that:

> the criminal behavior was serious, repetitive, and facilitated by inadequate internal accounting or monitoring controls or . . . that a clear and present danger exists to the public health or safety.[24]

A weakness of this proposal is that the adequacy of a defendant's compliance and disciplinary measures will go unchecked by the sentencing court unless the case is severe enough to fall within one or another of the limited categories specified. Consider the application of the ABA proposal to antitrust offenses or offenses of misleading advertising or corruption. Offenses of these kinds may easily arise from defective standard operating procedures which, if uncorrected, create a real risk of repetition.[25] Unless the offense is "serious" and "repetitive" or there is a clear and present danger to public health or safety (as can sometimes happen with misleading advertising or corruption), a corporate offender is required only to write a check for the fine.

The practical significance of this weakness is confirmed by Andrew Hopkins' empirical study of the impact of prosecutions for misleading advertising under the Australian Trade Practices Act.[26] In 40 percent of the cases where the offense had resulted from deficient operating procedures, there was reason to suspect that no adequate changes had been made: the corporations were convicted and fined and accepted that fate without making any apparent effort to rectify the main cause of violation.

Is it possible to provide a better guarantee of responsive corporate action than that afforded under the ABA proposal and yet also avoid subjecting corporations to any excessive yoke of state control? There seems room for some optimism here. To begin with, it should be recognized that the ABA proposal appears to proceed on a false assumption, namely, that it is impossible for the courts to look into organizational responses to the commission of an offense unless they severely intrude into corporate internal affairs.[27] That assumption is false because it overlooks the possibility of requiring corporate defendants to file a compliance report detailing their responses to an offense and making judicial intervention contingent on the emergence of an unsatisfactory corporate reaction. This approach — Enforced Self-Reaction — revolves around the concept of reactive corporate fault and the underlying principle of responsive adjustment.

A legal framework for the adoption of the concept of reactive corporate fault and the principle of responsive adjustment would require a two-stage hearing.[28] In the first stage the main question in issue would be whether the *actus reus* of an offense or civil violation had been committed on behalf of (or by) the corporate defendant. If this element were established the defendant would then be required to prepare a compliance report indicating what steps it has taken or proposes to take by way of internal discipline, modification of compliance policies or procedures, and facilitation of redress to victims.[29] At the second stage the central issue would be whether the defendant has reacted satisfactorily to the harmdoing or risktaking proven against it at the first hearing. If the reaction were adequate the result would be an acquittal. If the reaction were unsatisfactory the result would be conviction on the basis of reactive corporate fault, and the defendant would be punishable in a variety of ways, including subjection to judicial supervision, punitive mandatory injunctions, and other interventionist sanctions. By structuring proceedings against corporations along these lines, resort to interventionist sanctions would thus be contingent on the failure of a defendant to comply with a court order requiring it to make a responsive adjustment to its earlier wayward behavior.

The point to be stressed is that Enforced Self-Reaction would preserve managerial freedom provided that a corporate defendant satisfies the court that it is committed to a program of effective responsive action; freedom of enterprise would be maintained, but the price of that freedom would be the exercise of reactive initiative and diligence. This represents an extension of Braithwaite's model of Enforced Self-Regulation.[30] Under that model, corporations are required to formulate their own regulatory standards, with state intervention being confined to the specification and enforcement of broad overarching goals and principles. By contrast, under the model of Enforced Self-Reaction, corporations are required to formulate their own reactive programs in response to violations of regulatory standards and on a case-by-case basis.

Enforced Self-Reaction would help to avoid the lax nonintervention which so often now arises when corporations are convicted and fined. Put simply, defendants could not merely write a check and thereby treat an offense as a business expense.[31] At the same time, the degree of intervention in the internal affairs of corporations would be minimized because emphasis would be placed on the ability of managers to devise their own reactive programs; only in the case of untrustworthy or careless corporations would direct intervention be necessary. This last-mentioned feature is particularly important in that, although there are some essential minimum requirements for effective corporate compliance systems, there are many variables (e.g., size of compliance staff) which can differ widely from company to company without necessarily affecting the efficacy of internal compliance; illuminating in this regard are Braithwaite's empirical findings, as discussed in his chapter, "Taking Responsibility Seriously."[32]

Given these potential advantages, Enforced Self-Reaction commends itself as a promising strategy for a wider range of offenses, including not only offenses dealing with matters of public health or safety but also those relating to antitrust, misleading advertising, or corruption.[33] Nor should Enforced Self-Reaction be restricted to cases of "serious" and "repetitive" criminal behavior.[34] For one thing, a relatively minor offense of say misleading advertising committed by a first offender may be the result of bad checking procedures which, if left unrectified, may create a substantial risk of serious offenses in the future.[35] For another, the degree of intervention in the managerial affairs of the company would be confined to requiring the preparation and submission of a satisfactory compliance report. It may also be added that Enforced Self-Reaction would be relevant in the context of violations that are continuous or discrete: The more continuous the pattern of violation the stronger the evidence of reactive fault and the greater the justification for escalating the standards of reaction demanded.

In summary, Enforced Self-Reaction has been suggested as an additional compromise solution to the risk of excessive state intervention in the internal affairs of corporations. Embryonic as this solution is, it seems to have more promise than an approach which, like that of the ABA proposal for judicial oversight, does not steadfastly seek to ensure adequate corporate reactions to violations.

Expected Standards of Corporate Behavior

The specification of legal standards of corporate behavior is a problematic enterprise for several reasons:

(1) rules of general application are universalistic, whereas effective regulation may require particularistic rule-making tailored to each corporation;

(2) rules of criminal prohibition need to be clear and precise in order to give fair notice, yet precise rules soon cause a proliferation of loopholes;

(3) rules of law cannot reach the high standards possible on a moral plane, but nonetheless project authoritative models of minimum compliance which tend to depress the standards expected morally; and

(4) rules of law promote conformity and stability, whereas social and corporate conditions are increasingly dynamic.

As we shall see, a reactive timeframe might well help to reduce the above tensions and thereby improve standard-setting in corporate regulation.

Reconsider the well-known case, *United States* v *Allied Chemical Corporation*.[36] Allied was convicted on 940 counts of water pollution resulting from the escape of the pesticide Kepone into the waterways of Virginia. The offense imposed strict responsibility, but suppose a statutory defense of due diligence had been available or that the offense had been defined in terms of causing pollution without taking due care and attention not to do so.[37] What standard of "due diligence" or "due care" would have been relevant within a *proactive* timeframe? How satisfactory would that standard have been?

To begin with, "due diligence" or "due care" imports an objective standard of care which, although not dictated by prevailing industry standards, takes those standards as a benchmark.[38] The objective standard derived from a consideration of prevailing industry practice may then be adjusted to take account of the individual circumstances of the defendant, but the extent of this adjustment is constrained by the universalistic ideal of imposing a standard consistently on all members of an industry. One difficulty with this approach is that there may in fact be no generally accepted standard for a compliance system within the industry concerned; as suggested by Braithwaite's study of safety compliance in the coalmining industry, the attitude within the industry may be that "you can't cookbook compliance."[39] Assuming however that some consensus does exist, what happens when a defendant has adopted a customary compliance system that, contrary to reasonable expectations before the event, proves inadequate? Assume, for instance, that Allied had installed a waste treatment plant of the kind then common in the chemical industry but that the Kepone experience brought to light an unexpected limitation of the plant. Assume further that this limitation could be overcome by adding a backup treatment facility using a special chemical degradation process which, given Allied's superior know-how and patents in this area, would cost Allied much less than any other company to install. Allied would have exercised due diligence prior to the outflow of Kepone residues and, unless we insert additional facts (e.g., careless maintenance of the waste treatment plant), would be entitled to an acquittal regardless of whether it attempted to install the backup treatment facility. Moreover, even if another outflow of Kepone residues were to occur under similar circumstances a year later, Allied might again be acquitted. Provided the waste treatment plant was still that typically used in the chemical industry, and provided the plant had been carefully operated, then presumably Allied would still have exercised due diligence (or due care).

The due diligence (or due care) standard is also unsatisfactory because it may not provide a defendant with clear notice of the conduct which is subject to criminal liability. In the case of Allied, the company might well have installed the waste treatment plant in good faith compliance with the industry-approved standard and yet be held criminally liable by a court which subsequently rejects that standard as too low.[40] To specify standards clearly in advance, however, is to give corporations and their well-paid advisors room to find loopholes.[41] Imagine a pollution compliance standard which required every chemical company manufacturing pesticides to have a prescribed form of backup waste treatment facility. Putting aside the possible evasive tactic of transferring the manufacturing process to a fly-by-night independent contractor,[42] the intention behind such a rule could be defeated when a company installs the prescribed backup facility but alters the throughput of waste material so as to cut the costs of operating the primary treatment plant and leave the previous level of pollution unabated.[43]

Another hazard is the risk that imposing minimum legal standards will depress moral expectations within society; although law can serve as a strong educative force for the good, it usually projects a low common denominator.[44] Thus, consider the message transmitted when, in our hypothetical illustration, Allied is acquitted after successfully pleading that installation and careful operation of an industry-approved treatment plan amounts to due diligence. The impression conveyed is that this level of compliance is entirely acceptable and that what counts legally and morally as "due diligence" is a mediocre performance rather than taking the high road. This impression, it should be added, is strongly reinforced by the enduring credo of private enterprise that business morality is governed only by the law-corrected signals transmitted by the market.[45] Yet the law, if locked within a proactive timeframe for standard-setting, has difficulty in signalling more uplifting standards. To return to our illustration, it would plainly be unjust to disallow the defense of due diligence on the ground that Allied should have anticipated the limitation of the waste treatment plant: that limitation emerged only in light of later experience.

A further source of concern in standard-setting is the incompatibility between legal pressures toward conformity and stability, on the one hand, and rapidly changing social and corporate conditions, on the other.[46] Take Allied's defense of due diligence under the circumstances described above. The gravitation of law toward conformity and stability pulls the standard of due diligence down to a customary level and exerts a field of minor incremental change. If this is allowed to happen, the law puts its power behind existing compliance technology and provides little or no incentive for corporations to develop more innovative solutions, or apply state-of-the-art techniques. Furthermore, if social assessments of the gravity of pollution undergo a marked change, as they have over the past two decades, adherence to preexisting standards of due diligence is at best an exercise in social irrelevance. Yet, if the law ties itself to a proactive timeframe for the assessment of liability, it can easily be faced with an invidious choice: to impose a demanding new standard and thereby take a defendant unfairly by surprise, or to retain a lax old standard and thereby deprive potential victims of more adequate protection.

In sizing up the significance of these problems of defining appropriate standards of corporate criminal liability, account should be taken of various ways in which they are now minimized. First, particularistic standards, tailored to individual corporations, can be imposed under an injunction or consent order, an approach not uncommon in the enforcement of antitrust laws, securities regulations, and corruption offenses.[47] Second, broad standards of liability can be made more precise by using an injunction or declaration to crystallize their meaning and application in particular situations.[48] Third, moral standards need not necessarily be depressed by the adoption of minimum standards of liability: In addition to mandated social impact-assessments and other means of enhancing the sensitivity of corporate decision-making,[49] the higher moral road can be followed in mitigation of sentence and signposted by expressly commending an exemplary response to the violation for which sentence is imposed.[50] As regards the static force of legal standards, some dynamic thrust is possible through the imaginative use of several propellants, notably negotiation and bargaining in enforcement,[51] prospective rulemaking in judicial decisions,[52] and administrative techniques for inducing technological and other change (e.g., forced-technology through offsets against penalties).[53] Though all of these methods are valuable, they fall short of providing rules of criminal liability which are particularistic rather than universalistic, focused rather than hazy or loopholed, morally uplifting rather than depressing, and dynamic rather than static or incremental. Herein lies the promise of standard-setting within a reactive timeframe.

One model for exploring the potential of a reactive approach is Enforced Self-Reaction; as indicated in the previous section, this is an extension of Braithwaite's model of Enforced Self-Regulation.[54] Under the model of Enforced Self-Regulation, each corporation in an industry would be required to formulate its own internal rules and, subject to official screening, those rules would serve as particularized obligations which would bind the company and, in the event of breach, enable the imposition of criminal liability. The timeframe for standard-setting is thus proactive, and the standards set, although tailored to the particular corporation, relate to types of situations, not a particular case.[55] By contrast, under the model of Enforced Self-Reaction, a corporation against which a violation is proven would be required to produce a compliance report setting out the steps it proposes to take in response and specifying the goals and standards it seeks to attain; in the event of an unsatisfactory reaction to this requirement, or in the event of non-compliance with a reactive program approved by the court, criminal liability could be imposed.[56] Accordingly, the timeframe for standard-setting would be reactive: standards would be set in response to an incident or pattern of harmcausing or risktaking rather than as a matter of routine prevention. Furthermore, the standards set would be tailored not only to the particular corporation but also to the facts of the particular case in relation to which a reaction is sought from the company. Given these differences, what advantages might Enforced Self-Reaction have as a standard-setting device?

At the outset, Enforced Self-Reaction would promote more effective regulation by enabling particularized standard-setting on a case-by-case basis. In an example previously given (Kepone revisited), a defense of proactive due diligence would have succeeded even if the company had made no effort to install the backup waste treatment facility which, in its particular circumstances, would have been a relatively inexpensive solution. The result would be the same under the model of Enforced Self-Regulation because the cause of the violation – a weakness discovered in the primary waste treatment plant – could not reasonably have been foreseen. Under the model of Enforced Self-Reaction, however, the company would be expected to learn from experience and to react by proposing a standard of due diligence tailored to its own circumstances; in the hypothetical case put, Allied would be expected to react by installing the backup treatment facility.

Enforced Self-Reaction could also help to focus and give fair notice of criminal prohibitions without introducing precise, loophole-prone rules. Taking the need for focus and fair notice, a company that installed a waste treatment plant in good faith compliance with an industry-approved standard would not necessarily fail to exercise due diligence (or due care) if that standard was subsequently held to be too low: The emphasis would be on the adequacy or inadequacy of the corporation's response to being put on notice that a higher standard of due diligence (or due care) was expected and to the guidance given by the court as to the nature of that higher standard.[57] With regard to the danger of creating loopholes if fair notice is given by defining precise rules in advance, the approach suggested would not attempt to provide fair notice by such a means, but would rely instead on guidance by a court as to what will be regarded as a satisfactory response to a violation. Thus, if a court indicated that a defendant should seriously consider responding to a pollution violation by installing a backup waste treatment plant, formalistic compliance with that suggestion would not be enough to constitute a satisfactory reactive program. What would matter would be the goal for which guidance was provided, namely, the minimization of pollution outflow from the defendant's premises.[58]

How might Enforced Self-Reaction enhance the level of moral expectation projected by legal standards? An initial point is that, by obviating the need for precise rules of criminal liability, it would become possible to rely on broader and more flexible proscriptions. This would have the advantage of allowing legal standards to be written in terms more coextensive with the general exhortations typical of morality.[59] Second, by making corporate reactive programs the subject of inquiry into criminal liability, Enforced Self-Reaction would bring exemplary reactions out into the open, and hence instill exemplars within an industry.

Third, and more fundamentally, Enforced Self-Reaction would embody a shame-based system of morality, a system geared to the encouragement of generally higher standards of behavior.[60] The moral foundation of Enforced Self-Reaction is not inflicting guilt for having occasioned harm or risk, but shaming those who, having been given ample opportunity, fail to react constructively and responsively. The difference between these two philosophies was pinpointed by Peter French in an earlier chapter:

> Guilt is a minimum maintenance notion. Guilt avoidance involves meeting very basic standards of behavior . . . the primary concern is to be in a state of nonviolation. . . .
>
> In contrast to a guilt-based morality, certain societies, and in part our own, emphasize development and maintenance of personal worth and image in comparison to exemplary models of behavior. In such moralities the central notion is shame rather than guilt.[61]

Finally, how might Enforced Self-Reaction help to reduce the incompatibility between stability-inducing rules of law and rapidly changing corporate and social conditions? The answer lies in the adaptive mechanism built into the model. Reconsider the example where Allied pleads a defense of due diligence on the strength of having installed an industry-approved waste treatment plant. It was argued that a defense of proactive due diligence imposes a relatively static and undemanding standard of care. In comparison, a defense of reactive due diligence lends itself to a more dynamic and demanding standard of care. Far from being confined to *ex ante* due diligence, the reactive due diligence standard would extend to the care that should be taken by a corporation to learn from and respond to a violation. Thus, in the case of Allied's defense, a reactive standard of due diligence might well have required the company to install a state-of-the-art backup treatment facility and not merely a treatment plant then accepted as customary within the industry. Provided that Allied received notice of the higher standard expected (as is contemplated under the model of Enforced Self-Reaction),[62] that higher standard could have been imposed without eliciting complaints of unfair retrospective application.[63]

Individual Accountability for Corporate Wrongdoing

A common worry with respect to corporate criminal liability is that it may be used as a fast and cheap substitute for individual criminal liability, thereby severely compromising the value traditionally placed on individual accountability as a means of social control.[64] A reactive perspective, however, opens up the possibility of using corporate criminal liability as a means of exploiting the capacity of internal disciplinary systems to promote individual accountability to an extent that no public system of justice could otherwise hope to achieve.

Although it is often claimed by enforcement agencies that their priority is to proceed against individuals,[65] this seems more a fond hope than an expression of practical reality. Certainly the claim is difficult to reconcile with the stream of cases in which a corporate defendant has been proceeded against either alone or together with merely two or three of its executives.[66] Few statistics have been reported, but any corporate crime-watcher's pile of newspaper clippings is likely to contain numerous reports of cases where a corporation is more obviously in the frontline of enforcement attack than in the rear. This is consistent with the piquant observation of one commentator that "in the West decision-making is presented as individualistic until adversity proves it collective."[67] At the same time, it is readily understandable why, as a matter of investigation and evidence-gathering, enforcement agencies often lean heavily on proceedings against a corporation. In the Ford Pinto reckless homicide trial,[68] for instance, only the Ford Motor Company was prosecuted because, as the prosecutor explained, "Ford Motor Co., the corporation itself, was all that Elkhart County could handle. To go further, and take the next step, which may be individuals, [would have to be taken by] somebody with far more resources than we have."[69] Mention may also be made of the dismal headline of a *New York Times* report describing the task of a special review committee which looked into the question of corrupt practices at one large company: "McDonnell Douglas: Interviews for 1½ Years."[70]

The diehard individualist's response to the risk of a slide away from individual criminal liability is simply to abolish corporate criminal liability.[71] However, this response to the problem is unpersuasive for two main reasons. First, there is no escaping the fact that corporate criminal liability has provided an expedient means of coping with the well-nigh impossible task of investigating individual accountability for offenses committed on behalf of large, sprawling corporate enterprises. By imposing liability at the corporate level it has at least been possible to exert some pressure on personnel within an organization. Weak as that pressure often is (e.g., a corporate defendant may write a check for a fine without bothering to go further and take disciplinary action),[72] nonetheless it behooves those who advocate the abolition of corporate criminal liability to suggest some better method of promoting individual accountability for corporate wrongdoing. Second, corporate harmdoing or risktaking is often accompanied by fault of an exclusively corporate nature. One of many illustrations is Air New Zealand's Mount Erebus crash.[73] The Royal Commission investigating the causes of the crash attributed blame, not to the personnel who programmed the flight path without advising the aircrew of the correct navigational coordinates, but to "the incompetent administrative airline procedures which made the mistake possible."[74] In a situation like this prosecution of a corporation for manslaughter by gross negligence may be appropriate, yet there would be no justification for proceeding against any personnel on such a charge.[75]

Rather than abolishing corporate criminal liability, the balance between individual and corporate criminal liability might be controlled through improved guidelines for the exercise of prosecutorial discretion. As Jed Rakoff's contribution to this anthology has revealed, much can be achieved at the level of prosecutorial discretion to refine the application of white-collar offenses.[76] Moreover, in so unmapped an area of liability, there is merit in administratively blazing a trail before dispatching any judicial settlers. In recognition of these considerations, the Law Reform Commission of Canada has recommended the formulation and publication of formal prosecutorial guidelines,[77] the animating goal being "to minimize the risk of abuse and reduce the apprehension of those concerned about the possibility of undue emphasis on corporate responsibility."[78] This recommendation is commendable as far as it goes, but the question which needs to be settled is the policy governing the content of the guidelines contemplated. Furthermore, once that policy is settled, it may prove possible to move beyond reliance on administrative discretion and to uphold the importance of individual accountability by means of judicial as well as administrative controls.

Given the ideal of settling and implementing some policy for preserving the due imposition of individual accountability, it has been proposed that resort to corporate criminal liability should be contingent upon a finding that it is "impossible, impractical, or unjust" to impose individual criminal liability.[79] Although this approach is not unprecedented,[80] it suffers from a number of significant difficulties. First, a far-reaching investigation, and one intruding deep into corporate internal affairs, would usually be necessary in order to ascertain whether or not reliance on individual criminal liability would be impossible, impractical, or unjust. Second, corporations are likely to build a wall of secrecy against such an investigation, not only because of invasion of privacy, but also because of the risk of throwing capable and respected executives into the whirlpool of prosecution. Third, to the extent that corporations would cooperate, there is a real danger that they would do so by producing scapegoats; the vice-president "responsible for going to jail" is not a figment of the imagination.[81]

If it is unworkable to make corporate criminal liability contingent on the impossibility, impracticality, or injustice of recourse to individual criminal liability, why not reform individual criminal liability so as substantially to lower the hurdles which now hinder enforcement against corporate officers and executives? An obvious possibility, as suggested by the Supreme Court decision in *United States* v *Park*,[82] is to impose strict liability on top-ranking personnel, subject to a defense of impossibility of supervision or the like. Unfortunately, this solution is also problematical. An inevitable objection is that the approach in *Park*, if applied not merely in the context of food and drugs legislation but generally across a broad spectrum of corporate regulation, would sweep aside the fundamental common law presumption that criminal liability requires proof of *mens rea*.[83] Furthermore, although the burden of investigation would be greatly eased, only a limited range of personnel would be subject to prosecution (in *Park* the chief executive officer was prosecuted, but the subordinates on whom he had relied were not) and, in singling out only a few corporate representatives for prosecution regardless of their lack of *mens rea*, the law could itself be accused of scapegoating.

Bearing in mind the above-described obstacles, it is worth considering the potential which a reactive model of corporate compliance might have for promoting individual accountability. Let us take the model of Enforced Self-Reaction, as previously outlined. Under this model, a corporation against which a violation is proven would be required to prepare a compliance report. A major item in this report would be the disciplinary action taken by the company, one policy aim of Enforced Self-Reaction being to promote individual accountability by exerting pressure on corporations to activate their internal disciplinary systems. The most obvious forebear of the model in this respect is the SEC's voluntary disclosure campaign in the wake of the foreign bribery crisis: faced by the impossibility of investigating hundreds of companies, the SEC induced the companies to conduct their own internal reviews and to report the results.[84] By and large this campaign appears to have been successful, with internal disciplinary repercussions being catalyzed in many corporations. In the case of Gulf Oil, the investigative review was even published as a paperback, thereby adding the impact of adverse publicity to the critical findings made in the report.[85]

Enforced Self-Reaction offers several potential advantages as a means of promoting individual accountability for corporate wrongdoing. First and foremost, much of the burden of investigation and enforcement would be transferred to corporate violators rather than left in the hands of the state; as the Law Reform Commission of Canada has indicated, this holds considerable promise:

> Rather than having the state monitor the activities of each person within the organization, which is costly and raises practical enforcement difficulties, it may be more efficient to force the corporation to do this, especially if sanctions imposed on the corporation can be translated into effective action at the individual level.[86]

Enforced Self-Reaction follows this suggested strategy, except that disciplinary action would be coerced in the first instance through the threat as opposed to the imposition of conviction and sanction.[87]

A second potential advantage is that Enforced Self-Reaction would pursue a policy of maximizing individual accountability, not only for the violation triggering a reactive compliance report, but also for unsatisfactory reactions to the violation. As mentioned above, a compliance report would be required to indicate the disciplinary steps taken in reaction to a violation. In the event of unsatisfactory compliance, whether at the stage of preparing a reactive program or at the time when a program is undertaken, managers and supervisors would be prime targets for enforcement, especially if the court were to pinpoint them by nomination in advance.[88]

Third, Enforced Self-Reaction would provide a framework for the administrative development of prosecutorial guidelines and for the judicial channeling of prosecutorial discretion. One guideline immediately prompted is that individual criminal liability be a top priority in enforcement where a corporate defendant fails either to provide a satisfactory compliance report or to make due effort to carry out an agreed reactive program. Regarding judicial constraints on prosecutorial discretion, corporate criminal liability could not be used by prosecutors as a fast lane for whipping through their caseload: Liability would be structured to make individual accountability within a defendant's organization a mandatory preliminary factor.

Finally, if more emphasis were placed on corporate internal discipline there would be less warrant for resorting to offenses of strict liability. In *Park*,[89] for example, it is questionable whether much was really achieved by subjecting the chief executive officer to conviction and a low fine. Conceivably, a great deal more pressure could have been brought to bear on Park and his subordinates had their employer, Acme Markets, been subjected to Enforced Self-Reaction rather than conviction and a paltry fine: Internal discipline might well have covered a wider range of personnel and, if sufficiently pressurized, could have resulted in severe monetary penalties and demotion. If so, it would seem preferable to retain *mens rea* as a requirement for criminal offenses and to confine strict liability to internal disciplinary codes.[90]

Notwithstanding these potential advantages, it must be wondered whether Enforced Self-Reaction could ever overcome the propensity of corporations for secrecy, evasion, and scapegoating. There is, of course, no entirely reassuring answer but, beyond the possibility of monitoring compliance by means of special masters or other court-appointed watchdogs, two points should be stressed. The first is that given the threat of criminal liability in the event of an unsatisfactory reaction, Enforced Self-Reaction seeks to make compliance the lesser of two evils; if the threat of criminal liability is backed by severe sanctions, as discussed in the next section, it could be expected to have some credibility.[91] The second point is that full and open compliance would be less of an evil for corporations if the law was to foster the shame-based morality system which underlies Enforced Self-Reaction. A major fear on the part of corporations is that if they admit to a violation, they and their personnel will be slaughtered by the courts and the media. This partly reflects the prevalent backward-looking, guilt-based morality system that is strongly influenced by the traditional command and sanction conception of legal rules. The prospect to be contemplated is that these orthodoxies might be displaced by a shame-based morality system and a complementary guide and impel conception of legal rules.[92] Corporations would then have less to fear because they would be judged on the quality of their reactions to earlier deviations rather than merely on these deviations themselves.[93]

Design and Application of Sanctions Against Corporations

The development of sanctions against corporations has proceeded on the basis that liability is imposed within a proactive timeframe rather than by reference to a corporation's reactions to a violation. At least partly as a result of this time-warp, three undue tendencies have crept into the law: a bias toward noninterventionist sanctions (notably the fine), a lean toward factually unsupported assessments of quantum of sentence, and a mind-set against developing a full range of parallel civil and criminal sanctions. As we shall see, these tendencies might be countered by devising and applying sanctions in accordance with the implications of a reactive model.

The first untoward tendency arises from the interdependence of rules of liability and principles of responsibility, on the one hand, and forms of sanction and sentencing principles, on the other. Liability rules for corporations have usually focused upon a violation in the past rather than on what a defendant has done about that violation for the future. Given this orientation, there has been an inevitable pressure to adopt a principle of vicarious corporate fault, and this in turn has biased the law toward reliance on fines and monetary penalties.

To take the pressure toward vicarious fault initially, it is usually impossible in practice to prove that a corporation committed the *actus reus* of an offense with personal *mens rea* (in the sense of a criminal corporate policy or gross corporate negligence); typically, corporations take the elementary precaution of installing compliance policies and procedures sufficient to show the absence of such *mens rea.*[94] By contrast, it is much easier to prove *mens rea* on the part of some representative acting on behalf of a corporation when it committed the *actus reus*, especially if it is immaterial whether that representative be a manager or a minion.[95] For this reason, among others, the general principle now applicable in most U.S. jurisdictions is that corporate fault requires merely fault on the part of an officer or employee acting on behalf of and with intent to benefit the company.[96] Granted this development, how has it biased the law toward noninterventionist sanctions against corporations? The primary source of bias is that vicarious responsibility projects a noninterventionist attitude toward corporate decisionmaking. The emphasis is on the state of mind of a single representative, rather than on the *corporate* decisionmaking process.[97] Thus, to impose a punitive injunction directed at compliance policies and procedures would be to enter a new arena and to abandon the coherence of an integrated noninterventionist theory of sanctions and responsibility.[98] Mention should also be made of another factor, namely, that vicarious responsibility is historically related to vicarious tortious liability, an area of liability heavily dependent on the remedy of damages and the mere monetary "internalization" of enterprise costs.[99]

A second time-spun bias in the sanctioning of corporations is the tendency to assess the quantum of sentence on the basis of inadequate facts. The focus of a trial under the present law is on the conduct of a defendant at or before the time of the alleged violation. One trouble with this approach is that it does not generate the facts needed if sentencing decisions are to be made on rational grounds rather than by guesswork. Consider the sentencing decision in a leading Australian case, *Trade Practices Commission* v *Pye Industries Sales Pty. Ltd.*[100] Pye was found to have committed resale price maintenance in violation of the Trade Practices Act, and the court adjourned the matter for sentence. At the sentencing hearing, the court was able to conclude that at the time of violation, "there was an almost total lack of supervision or interest by the board of directors in the conduct of their management and executives in relation to resale price maintenance."[101] However, the court was left in the dark as to the nature of the company's actions in response to the violation: The company itself had not come forward with relevant evidence, and the evidence that had emerged from the trial was largely confined to the issue of whether or not a violation had been committed. The court, after describing the violation as "ruthless," then imposed a penalty of $A120,000, the maximum being $A250,000. This split down the middle represents an optimistic feat of judicial divination because, for all the court knew, the company's reactions might have been so unresponsive as to warrant a much higher penalty. Admittedly, more adequate sentencing facts can be provided by means of presentence reports, but in the context of corporate offenders, presentence reports are still rare and given the expertise and resources demanded of an already overworked probation service, unfortunately seem destined to remain so.[102]

A third consequence of ill-timing is the failure of the law to develop a system of corporate regulation in which all sanctions have criminal and civil counterparts.[103] Under the timeframe which has prevailed, civil and criminal means of regulation have tended to be seen as alternative avenues of response to a violation; there has been no clear sense of a structured progression from civil means initially to criminal means, if necessary, at a later time. As a result, two substantially independent tracks of enforcement have developed, and one outcome of this today is that the sanctions available in civil regulation are not always matched by those available in corporate criminal law. Fines obviously provide a counterpart to civil monetary penalties (although not necessarily a more financially severe counterpart: The maxima for penalties are often higher than those for fines).[104] The civil injunction however, remains unparalleled in the criminal law, and as Coffee has pointed out, this is remarkable: "It is a curious paradox that the civil law is better equipped at present than the criminal law to authorize [disciplinary or structural] interventions."[105] In some jurisdictions an attempt has been made to resolve this paradox by using probation against corporate offenders,[106] but since corporate probation has yet to be used anywhere near as forcefully as institutional reform injunctions, the paradox survives.[107]

The practical significance of the above-described tendencies should be emphasized. First, noninterventionist sanctions (above all, fines and monetary penalties) have been fostered despite their serious limitations. As argued in a previous chapter, monetary sanctions against corporations have a relatively weak deterrent capacity, and can occasion unwanted overspills, such as higher consumer prices or worker layoffs.[108] By contrast, interventionist sanctions, notably the punitive injunction, are capable of pinching much harder on the nerves of corporate government and by reason of their emphasis on internal compliance policies and procedures, cannot as readily be spilled over to consumers or workers.[109] Second, to the extent that reliance should be placed on monetary sanctions, a backwards-oriented focus at trial means that the quantum of the fine or cash penalty imposed now often depends on uninformed guesswork rather than measured consideration of the nature and quality of a defendant's reactions to the violation committed. Plainly, the reactive performance of a defendant should be a prime factor in aggravation or mitigation of sentence yet the only reliable generator of facts relevant to that issue – the trial process – is preoccupied with a corporation's past conduct.

These problems would become more manageable if handled from within a reactive timeframe. To set the frame, consider the possibility of an integrated civil and criminal model of corporate liability.[110] Under such a model, civil and criminal means of regulation would be seen as alternatives not only at or before the time of the initial violation but also after a sufficient interval has been provided for corporate reactions to emerge. Within the first timeframe, civil liability would be the enforcement target in most situations (by reason mainly of the greater expediency of civil process).[111] The range of civil measures available would include monetary penalties, injunctions, community service orders, and publicity orders. Within the second timeframe, criminal liability would be the enforcement target in situations where the defendant's compliance efforts displayed reactive fault. The range of criminal sanctions available would include fines, punitive injunctions, punitive community service orders, and punitive publicity orders.

A conspicuous feature of such an integrated model is that the pivotal concept – the concept of reactive corporate fault – implies the need for interventionist as well as noninterventionist sanctions. To elaborate, it should first be stressed that the basis of reactive corporate fault would not be vicarious but personal: Intentional or negligent noncompliance would be required, and as explained in our introduction, this requirement would be workable because in a reactive setting, a corporation can be forced to indicate where it stands as a matter of corporate policy.[112] Given this understanding of reactive corporate fault, what types of sanction does the concept suggest? Unlike vicarious fault, reactive fault implies interventionist sanctions, especially the punitive injunction: Emphasis is placed on a corporation's reactive decisionmaking on compliance, and where the reaction is palpably unsound, punitive control over that decisionmaking process is a fitting response.[113] The implication, however, is not entirely interventionist since noninterventionist sanctions are also implied. The clearest example is the sanction of formally ordered adverse publicity.[114] As we have seen, reactive fault is underpinned by a shame-based morality system, and the Hester Prynne sanction would be essential as a means of reflecting that system in law.[115]

More straightforward is the advantage a reactive model of corporate criminal liability would have in generating reliable sentencing facts. Thus, in the *Pye* case discussed above, the focus of the trial would not be on the earlier illegal acts of resale price maintenance alone but on whether the company was reactively at fault. That issue would be the subject of detailed evidence, and the sentencing court would no longer be in the dark as to whether the company had reacted by thumbing its nose at the law.

Finally, the integration of civil and criminal corporate liability, if based on the pivotal concept of reactive fault, would foster the development of a parallel range of civil and criminal sanctions. The heuristic power of reactive fault helps to expose the need for sanctions capable of effecting a smooth transition between less and more drastic means of regulation. Thus, assume that a defendant has been subjected to an injunctive order stipulating that effective pollution control devices be installed. Efforts at compliance are made but are later wantonly abandoned as a result of competing cost pressures. The company is proceeded against criminally and held liable on the basis of reactive fault. In cases such as this, something should be done to ensure compliance. Imposing a fine would be an oblique and inadequate method of making the company comply. And, given the defendant's recalcitrance, issuing a further civil injunction would fail to capture the gravity of the reactive noncompliance. The sanction ideally equipped to cover both of these concerns would be a punitive injunction requiring the defendant not only to install the necessary device, but also to do so in some punitively demanding and constructive way (e.g., at accelerated speed, or by going beyond state-of-the-art technology).[116] This idea of progressive escalation is latent in the subtle difference between monetary penalties and fines[117] but has not been implemented systematically. If done so under the model outlined above, the effect would be to generate a wide range of parallel civil and criminal sanctions. More fundamentally, this would resolve a time-locked paradox – the paradox of a criminal law with fewer teeth than its civil counterpart.[118]

Conclusion

The thrust of this chapter has been that several key issues of corporate regulation – state intervention in corporate internal affairs, expected standards of corporate behavior, individual accountability for corporate wrongdoing, and design and application of sanctions against corporations – can usefully be approached by constructing a reactive timeframe of inquiry. Suggestive as this line of inquiry is, two general objections are bound to be raised. The first is that a reactive approach is too lenient, and the second that it is too inefficient. To these inevitable objections some parting response should be made.

A reactive approach, it may be argued, would result in excessive leniency toward corporations. Corporate violations would be treated too softly because offenders would be given the chance to undertake a satisfactory reactive program and thereby escape the imposition of criminal liability: Why should corporate offenders be given a free bite at the apple of crime?[119] This objection may be countered on several grounds. First, the objection does not stem from existing reality. It assumes a command and sanction model of regulation, whereas negotiated settlement is predominant in practice today.[120] Second, our suggestion is not that corporate criminal liability be imposed exclusively on the basis of reactive fault. Where blameworthy intentionality or negligence can be established in relation to a proven initial violation, criminal liability should be possible at the very outset.[121] Third, and above all, the bite at the apple of corporate crime would not be free under the reactive model proposed. For one thing, civil means of regulation, including mandatory injunctions and compensation orders would be used as measures of first resort.[122] For another, reactively demanded measures on the part of a corporate defendant would not be soft options but would be capable of exerting much more internal pressure than is possible by means of conviction and the mere imposition of fines or monetary penalties.[123]

Nonetheless, if a reactive approach were applied rigorously, would it suffer from excessive inefficiency? Increasing the extent of legal intervention in the internal decisionmaking processes of private enterprise would not be costless but would impose additional burdens of investigation, supervision, and, in extreme cases, state management. These burdens would be kept to a minimum under the model of Enforced Self-Reaction,[124] but even so there is no denying that enforcement costs would increase. How can this increase be justified given the much-proclaimed efficiency of noninterventionist control through monetary sanctions? An immediate reply to this question, and one already mentioned in an earlier chapter,[125] is to draw a parallel with the use of imprisonment against individual offenders. As Richard Posner has explained in his leading work, *Economic Analysis of Law*, monetary sanctions are unsuitable in the context of serious offenses because fines of sufficient deterrent weight are beyond the resources of most offenders; imprisonment is thus necessary despite the extreme relative inefficiency of this form of sanction.[126] Relatively inefficient interventionist means of controlling corporate crime can be justified on a similar ground: The level of fines required to satisfy the economic calculus for the deterrence of serious corporate offenses is so high as to be beyond the resources of most corporate offenders, and hence an alternative means of social control needs to be resorted to that, although regrettably more costly in terms of enforcement resources, is more likely to achieve the effective prevention of unwanted harms.[127] Beyond this reply, however, a deeper and more interesting answer can be found by challenging the assumptions about probability upon which the claim of inefficiency most fundamentally depends.

The superior efficiency claimed for monetary sanctions as a means of controlling corporate behavior depends on the application of an economic calculus. To apply that calculus, calculations of probability need to be made in relation to the likelihood of harm, the predicted extent and gravity of that harm, and the chances of detection, prosecution, and conviction. Yet, as John Byrne and Steven Hoffman have argued in their essay,[128] these calculations are impossible to make with any exactitude and, as far as their application to corporate calculations of risk is concerned, assume a unified managerial rationality which rarely exists in corporate practice. How should we cope with the impossibility of making the probabilistic calculations which govern the canon of efficiency?

Scepticism about the role of probability as a guide to life does not mean that we have nothing on which to go.[129] Frequently, we tend to be governed much more by rules of action than by assessments of probability. Probabilities are often swamped by other influences of many kinds. In some situations, there is simply no time to worry about probability. In others, we need to recognize that no probabilistic data is available. For instance, consider the application of a defense of corporate due diligence. As now applied, this defense usually is governed by standard industry practice than by any (hopelessly optimistic) attempt to calculate degrees of risk; in effect, the standard industry practice is often adopted as a pragmatic rule of action.[130]

If this pragmatic solution is applied to the more global problem of making the probabilistic calculations necessary to support an efficient system of corporate criminal liability, essentially two rules of action emerge. The first, for designers and engineers of the legal apparatus, is:

> Where the probabilities required for an efficient system of monetary liability are impossible to assess, create an alternative system of liability based on the down-to-earth ideas of
> (1) proscriptions based on considered assessments of the nature of unwanted harms;[131] and
> (2) fault-concepts and sanctions geared at impelling responsive corporate reactions to violations of those proscriptions.

The second, directed to corporations after the first rule has been acted on, is:

> Corporations are expected to comply with legal proscriptions and should not attempt evasion by engaging in probabilistic calculations of punishment costs; those calculations are impossible to make in practice and have been abandoned by your lawmakers. In the event of violation, stress will be placed on the adequacy of a corporation's attempts to prevent repetition and to facilitate or provide redress to victims. Should a corporation's reactions be inadequate, the punishment will be a fine only in relatively minor cases; in more serious cases, the defendant will be subject to a punitive injunction, court-ordered adverse publicity, and/or community service.

To conclude, law's target is not economic efficiency. Time's arrow, propelled by the concept of reactive corporate fault and the principle of responsive corporate adjustment,[132] heads in another direction, namely, the efforts made by errant corporations to redeem themselves.

NOTES

1. See generally Colin Howard, *Criminal Law*, 4th ed. (Sydney: Law Book Co., 1983), 12-15.
2. See Peter A. French, *Collective and Corporate Responsibility* (New York: Columbia University Press, 1984), Ch. 11; Brent Fisse, "Reconstructing Corporate Criminal Law: Deterrence, Retribution, Fault, and Sanctions," *Southern California Law Review* 56 (1983): 1183-1213; Brent Fisse, "Criminal Law and Consumer Protection," in A. J. Duggan and L. W. Darvall, eds., *Consumer Protection Law & Theory* (Sydney: Law Book Co., 1980): 186-90.
3. See Fisse, "Reconstructing Corporate Criminal Law," 1192-1213.
4. Ibid., 1202.
5. Ibid., 1192-96.
6. Ibid., 1197-1201.

7. Ibid., 1199-1200. See generally Lester R. Bittel, *Management by Exception* (New York: McGraw-Hill, 1964); Henry Mintzberg, *The Structuring of Organizations* (Englewood Cliffs, N.J.: Prentice-Hall, Inc., 1979), Ch. 21.
8. French, *Collective and Corporate Responsibility*, Ch. 11.
9. Ibid., 156-57.
10. See Fisse, "Reconstructing Corporate Criminal Law," 1183-92.
11. Peter A. French, "The Corporation as a Moral Person," *American Philosophical Quarterly* 16 (1979): 207-15. But see "Developments in the Law – Corporate Crime: Regulating Corporate Behavior Through Criminal Sanctions," *Harvard Law Review* 92 (1979): 1241, where it is contended that *mens rea* "has no meaning when applied to a corporate defendant, since an organization possesses no mental state." This proposition reflects the conventional but silly anthropomorphic assumption that one should in fact be looking for a humanoid mental state.
12. Fisse, "Reconstructing Corporate Criminal Law," 1191-92.
13. See generally "Developments in the Law," 1247-51.
14. Fisse, "Reconstructing Corporate Criminal Law," 1205.
15. See U.S. H.R. Committee on the Judiciary, Subcommittee on Crime, *Corporate Crime*, 96th Cong., 2d. Sess., 1980, 3-8.
16. See e.g., Christopher D. Stone, *Where the Law Ends: The Social Control of Corporate Behavior* (New York: Harper & Row, 1975); James A. Geraghty, "Structural Crime and Institutional Rehabilitation: A New Approach to Corporate Sentencing," *Yale Law Journal* 89 (1979): 353-75.
17. See e.g., Ralph K. Winter, *Government and the Corporation* (Washington, D.C.: American Enterprise Institute for Public Policy Research, 1978).
18. See e.g., Christopher D. Stone, "The Place of Enterprise Liability in the Control of Corporate Conduct," *Yale Law Journal* 90 (1980): 1-77; John Braithwaite, "Enforced Self-Regulation: A New Strategy for Corporate Crime Control," *Michigan Law Review* 80 (1982): 1466-1507.
19. Cf. Braithwaite, "Enforced Self-Regulation."
20. Stone, *Where the Law Ends*, 121.
21. Ch. 2.
22. Ibid.
23. American Bar Association, *Standards for Criminal Justice*, vol. 3 (Boston: Little, Brown, 1980), 18.162-163, 18.179-84.
24. Ibid., § 18-2.8(a)(v)(A).
25. See e.g., Hartnell v Sharp Corporation of Australia Pty. Ltd., 5 A.L.R. 493 (1975).
26. Andrew Hopkins, *The Impact of Prosecutions under the Trade Practices Act* (Canberra: Australian Institute of Criminology, 1978).
27. Consider American Bar Association, *Standards for Criminal Justice*, 18.180-81.
28. See Fisse, "Reconstructing Corporate Criminal Law," 1202-06.
29. Ibid., 1205.
30. Braithwaite, "Enforced Self-Regulation."
31. See further Stone, *Where the Law Ends*, 57.
32. Ch. 3.
33. Contrast American Bar Association, *Standards for Criminal Justice*, § 18-2.8(a)(v)(A).
34. Contrast ibid.

35. See Hopkins, *The Impact of Prosecutions under The Trade Practices Act.*
36. 420 F. Supp. 122 (1976).
37. See generally "Developments in the Law," 1257-58.
38. Cf. The T. J. Hooper, 60 F.2d 737, 740 (1932).
39. Ch. 3.
40. Cf. The T. J. Hooper, 60 F.2d 737, 740 (1932).
41. See generally M. Wessel, *Rule of Reason: A New Approach to Corporate Litigation* (Reading, Mass.: Addison-Wesley Pub. Co., 1976).
42. See Brent Fisse and John Braithwaite, *The Impact of Publicity on Corporate Offenders* (Albany: State University of New York Press, 1983), Ch. 6.
43. Cf. Bruce A. Ackerman & William T. Hassler, *Clean Coal/Dirty Air* (New Haven: Yale University Press, 1981).
44. See generally W. H. Walsh, "Pride, Shame and Responsibility," *Philosophical Quarterly* 20 (1970): 13; Judith N. Shklar, *Legalism* (Cambridge: Harvard University Press, 1964), 120-21; Franklin Zimring and Gordon Hawkins, "The Legal Threat as an Instrument of Social Change," *Journal of Social Issues* 27(2) (1971): 33-48.
45. See Ch. 2.
46. See generally Donald A. Schon, *Beyond the Stable State* (New York: W. W. Norton & Company, Inc., 1973); Richard B. Stewart, "Regulation, Innovation, and Administrative Law: A Conceptual Framework," *California Law Review* 69 (1981): 1256-1377; Braithwaite, "Enforced Self-Regulation."
47. See e.g., William J. Donovan and Breck P. McAllister, "Consent Decrees in the Enforcement of Federal Anti-Trust Law," *Harvard Law Review* 46 (1933): 885-932.
48. See Note, "Declaratory Relief in the Criminal Law," *Harvard Law Review* 80 (1967): 1490-1513; Note, "The Statutory Injunction as an Enforcement Weapon of Federal Agencies," *Yale Law Journal* 57 (1948): 1023-52.
49. Ch. 2.
50. See e.g., United States v Olin Corporation, Criminal No. 78-30, slip op. (D. Conn. June 1, 1978), as discussed in Fisse, "Reconstructing Corporate Criminal Law," 1195-96.
51. See e.g., Keith Hawkins, *Environment and Enforcement: Regulation and the Social Definition of Pollution* (Oxford: Clarendon Press, 1984).
52. See generally M. L. Friedland, "Prospective and Retrospective Judicial Lawmaking," *University of Toronto Law Journal* 24 (1974): 170-90.
53. See e.g., Stewart, "Regulation, Innovation, and Administrative Law"; Note, "Forcing Technology: The Clean Air Act Experience," *Yale Law Journal* 88 (1979): 1713-34.
54. Braithwaite, "Enforced Self-Regulation."
55. But cf. ibid., 1504-07 (corporate case-law approach).
56. See Fisse, "Reconstructing Corporate Criminal Law," 1202-06.
57. See ibid., 1205, 1246 n.512.
58. Cf. Ackerman and Hassler, *Clean Coal/Dirty Air.*
59. See Ch. 2.
60. See Ch. 8.
61. Ibid.
62. See Fisse, "Reconstructing Corporate Criminal Law," 1205.
63. See further ibid., 1209.
64. Fisse, "Criminal Law and Consumer Protection," 182-85.

65. See e.g., Australia, Trade Practices Commission, *Second Annual Report* (Canberra: Australian Government Publishing Service, 1976), para.2.67.

66. E.g., United States v Allied Chemical Corporation, 420 F. Supp. 122 (1976); United States v Olin Corporation, Criminal No. 78-30, slip op. (D. Conn. June 1, 1978); Marshall B. Clinard and Peter C. Yeager, *Corporate Crime* (New York: Free Press, 1980), 272; "Crime in the Suites," *Time* (10 June 1985), 52-53.

67. John Clark, *The Japanese Company* (New Haven: Yale University Press, 1979), 130.

68. See generally Fisse and Braithwaite, *The Impact of Publicty on Corporate Offenders*, Ch. 4.

69. *Los Angeles Times* (14 March 1980).

70. *New York Times* (31 July 1980), D2.

71. See e.g., Gerhard O. W. Mueller, "Mens Rea and the Corporation," *University of Pittsburgh Law Review* 19 (1957): 21-50.

72. Ch. 7.

73. See generally N.Z., *Report of the Royal Commission to Inquire into the Crash on Mount Erebus, Antarctica, of a DC-10 Aircraft Operated by Air New Zealand Limited* (Wellington: N.Z. Government Printer, 1981); Gordon Vette, *Impact Erebus* (Auckland: Hodder and Stoughton, 1983).

74. N.Z., *Report of Erebus Royal Commission*, para.393.

75. As it happens, under N.Z. law a company is not subject to liability for manslaughter: R v Murray Wright Ltd. [1970] N.Z.L.R. 476.

76. Ch. 9.

77. Canada, Law Reform Commission, *Working Paper 16, Criminal Reponsibility for Group Action* (Ottawa: Information Canada, 1976), 35.

78. Ibid.

79. Fisse, "Criminal Law and Consumer Protection," 184.

80. See e.g., Johannes Andenaes, *The General Part of the Criminal Law of Norway* (London: Sweet & Maxwell, 1965), 246.

81. John Braithwaite, *Corporate Crime in the Pharmaceutical Industry* (London: Routledge & Kegan Paul, 1984), 308.

82. 421 U.S. 685 (1975).

83. See generally Colin Howard, *Strict Responsibility* (London: Sweet & Maxwell, 1963).

84. See U.S. SEC, *Report of the Securities and Exchange Commission on Questionable and Illegal Foreign Payments Submitted to the Senate Committee on Banking, Housing and Urban Affairs*, 94th Cong., 2d Sess., 1976, 6-7. See generally Jacqueline C. Wolff, "Voluntary Disclosure Programs," *Fordham Law Review* 47 (1979): 1057-82.

85. John J. McCloy, *The Great Oil Spill: The Inside Report* (New York: Chelsea House, 1976).

86. Canada, Law Reform Commission, *Criminal Responsibility for Group Action*, 31.

87. See Fisse, "Reconstructing Corporate Criminal Law," 1202-06.

88. See Geraghty, "Structural Crime," 372.

89. 421 U.S. 685 (1975).

90. See generally Howard, *Strict Responsibility*; Fisse and Braithwaite, *The Impact of Publicity on Corporate Offenders*, 302-05.

91. See further Ch. 7.
92. See further Ch. 7; Walter Kaufmann, *Without Guilt and Justice* (New York: Delta, 1973).
93. As to the frequent lack of emphasis on corporate reactions to crises, see Fisse and Braithwaite, *The Impact of Publicity on Corporate Offenders*, 268-70.
94. The classic example is GE's Policy Directive 20.5. See ibid., Ch. 16.
95. See generally "Developments in the Law," 1247-57.
96. Ibid., 1247-50.
97. See e.g., R v Australasian Films Ltd., 29 C.L.R. 195 (1921). But see United States v T.I.M.E.-D.C., Inc., 381 F. Supp. 730 (1974).
98. An integrated theory of sanctions and responsibility is discernible in the *ut agitur* role of liability for contempt, but otherwise appears to have been neglected.
99. See generally Simeon M. Kriesberg, "Decisionmaking Models and the Control of Corporate Crime," *Yale Law Journal* 85 (1976): 1096.
100. A.T.P.R. § 40-089 (1978).
101. Ibid.
102. One possible solution is to rely on special court-appointed masters or monitors. See further Ch. 7.
103. See generally Fisse, "Reconstructing Corporate Criminal Law," 1213, 1234.
104. See e.g., Trade Practices Act, 1974-84 (Austl.), ss.76, 79.
105. John C. Coffee, Jr., " 'No Soul to Damn: No Body to Kick': An Unscandalized Inquiry into the Problem of Corporate Punishment," *Michigan Law Review* 79 (1981): 459.
106. See Geraghty, "Structural Crime."
107. See e.g., Owen Fiss, *The Civil Rights Injunction* (Bloomington: Indiana University Press, 1978).
108. Coffee, " 'No Soul to Damn: No Body to Kick' ": 401-02.
109. Ch. 7.
110. See generally Fisse, "Reconstructing Corporate Criminal Law," 1211-13.
111. See e.g., Sigmund Timberg, "The Case for Civil Antitrust Enforcement," *Ohio State Law Journal* 14 (1953): 315-28.
112. See text and reference at Note 15.
113. See further Ch. 7.
114. See Ch. 8.
115. Ibid.
116. See generally Stewart, "Regulation, Innovation, and Administrative Law."
117. See H. L. A. Hart, *Punishment and Responsibility: Essays in the Philosophy Of Law* (Oxford: Clarendon Press, 1968), 6, 239.
118. See text and references at Notes 105-07.
119. Cf. Note, "The Statutory Injunction," 1044-45.
120. See e.g., Clinard and Yeager, *Corporate Crime*, 87-89; Hawkins, *Environment and Enforcement*.
121. Consider e.g., the cases criticized in "Dealing with the Poisoners," *Washington Post* (20 August 1979), A20.
122. See Fisse, "Reconstructing Corporate Criminal Law," 1205.
123. See Ch. 7.
124. See text at Notes 28-35.

125. Ch. 7.
126. Richard Posner, *Economic Analysis of Law*, 2d ed. (Boston: Little Brown & Co., 1977), 168-69.
127. See further Ch. 7.
128. Ch. 6.
129. See generally Brent Fisse, "Probability and the Proudman v Dayman Defence of Reasonable Mistaken Belief," *Melbourne University Law Review* 9 (1974): 477-512.
130. See text and references at Notes 38-39.
131. See further Ch. 4; Ch. 5.
132. See text and references at Notes 3-9.

SELECTIVE BIBLIOGRAPHY

Ackerman, Bruce A. and William T. Hassler. *Clean Coal/Dirty Air* (New Haven: Yale University Press, 1981).

American Bar Association. *Standards for Criminal Justice,* vol 3 (Boston: Little, Brown, 1980).

_____ . *Standards Relating to the Prosecution and Defense Function* (New York: Institute of Judicial Administration, 1974).

Anonymous. "Developments in the Law – Corporate Crime: Regulating Corporate Criminal Behavior Through Criminal Sanctions," *Harvard Law Review* 92 (1979): 1227-375.

Beauchamp, Tom L. and Norman E. Bowie. *Ethical Theory and Business* (Englewood Cliffs, N.J.: Prentice-Hall, 1979).

Becker, Gary S. "Crime and Punishment: An Economic Approach," *Journal of Political Economy* 76 (1968): 169-217.

Braithwaite, John and Brent Fisse. "Varieties of Responsibility and Organizational Crime," *Law and Policy* 7 (1985): 315-43.

Braithwaite, John and Gilbert Geis. "On Theory and Action for Corporate Crime Control," *Crime and Delinquency* 28 (1982): 292-314.

Braithwaite, John. "Enforced Self-Regulation: A New Strategy for Corporate Crime Control," *Michigan Law Review* 80 (1982): 1466-507.

_____ . "Challenging Just Deserts: Punishing White-Collar Criminals," *Journal of Criminal Law and Criminology* 73 (1982): 723-63.

_____ . *Corporate Crime in the Pharmaceutical Industry* (London: Routledge & Kegan Paul, 1984).

_____ . *To Punish or Persuade* (Albany: State University of New York Press, 1985).

Buchanan, James. *Cost and Choice: An Inquiry into Economic Theory* (Chicago: Markham Publishing Co., 1969).

Carson, W.G. *The Other Price of Britain's Oil: Safety and Control in the North Sea* (Oxford: M. Robertson, 1982).

Clark, John. *The Japanese Company* (New Haven: Yale University Press, 1979).

Clinard, Marshall B. and Peter C. Yeager. *Corporate Crime* (New York: Free Press, 1980).

Clinard, Marshall B. *Corporate Ethics and Crime: The Role of Middle Management* (Beverly Hills: Sage, 1983).

Coffee, John C., Jr. "Beyond the Shut-Eyed Sentry: Towards a Theoretical View of Corporate Misconduct and an Effective Legal Response," *Virginia Law Review* 63 (1977): 1099-1278.

———. "Corporate Crime and Punishment: A Non-Chicago View of the Economics of Criminal Punishment," *American Criminal Law Review* 17 (1980): 419-76.

———. " 'No Soul To Damn; No Body to Kick:' An Unscandalized Inquiry into the Problem of Corporate Punishment," *Michigan Law Review* 79 (1981): 386-459.

Cullen, Francis T., Bruce G. Link and Craig W. Polanzi. "The Seriousness of Crime Revisited: Have Attitudes toward White-Collar Crime Changed?" *Criminology* 20 (1982): 83-102.

Davis, K. C. *Discretionary Justice: A Preliminary Inquiry* (Baton Rouge: Louisiana State University Press, 1969).

Dershowitz, Alan M. "Increasing Community Control over Corporate Crime: A Problem in the Law of Sanctions," *Yale Law Journal* 71 (1961): 280-306.

Elzinga, Kenneth G. and William Breit. *The Antitrust Penalties* (New Haven: Yale University Press, 1976).

Engel, David L. "An Approach to Corporate Social Responsibility," *Stanford Law Review* 32 (1979): 1-55.

Ermann, M. David and Richard J. Lundman. *Corporate Deviance* (New York: Holt, Rinehart and Winston, 1982).

Fisse, Brent and John Braithwaite. *The Impact of Publicity on Corporate Offenders* (Albany: State University of New York Press, 1983).

Fisse, Brent. "Reconstructing Corporate Criminal Law: Deterrence, Retribution, Fault, and Sanctions," *Southern California Law Review* 56 (1983): 1141-246.

———. "Community Service as a Sanction against Corporations," *Wisconsin Law Review* [1981]: 970-1017.

French, Peter. *Collective and Corporate Responsibility* (New York: Columbia University Press, 1984).

———. "The Corporation as a Moral Person," *American Philosophical Quarterly* 16 (1979): 207-15.

Friedman, Milton and Rose Friedman. *Free to Choose* (New York: Harcourt, Brace Jovanovich, 1980).

Fritschler, A. Lee and Bernard H. Ross. *Business Regulation and Government Decision-Making* (Cambridge: Winthrop, 1980).

Geis, Gilbert. *White-Collar Criminal* (New York: Atherton, 1968).

Geraghty, James A. "Structural Crime and Institutional Rehabilitation: A New Approach to Corporate Sentencing," *Yale Law Journal* 89 (1979): 353-75.

Goodin, Robert E. *Political Theory and Public Policy* (Chicago: University of Chicago Press, 1982).

Greenberg, Edward S. *Serving the Few: Capitalism and the Bias of Government Policy* (New York: John Wiley & Sons, Inc., 1974).

Hawkins, Keith and John M. Thomas, eds. *Enforcing Regulation* (Boston: Kluwer-Nijhoff, 1984).

Hawkins, Keith. *Environment and Enforcement: Regulation and the Social Definition of Pollution* (Oxford: Clarendon Press, 1984).

Heilbroner, Robert. *In the Name of Profit* (New York: Warner, 1973).

Hochstedler, Ellen, ed. *Corporations as Criminals* (Beverly Hills: Sage Publications, 1984).

Hopkins, Andrew. *The Impact of Prosecutions under the Trade Practices Act* (Canberra: Australian Institute of Criminology, 1978).

Kagan, R. and E. Bardach. *Going by the Book: The Problem of Regulatory Unreasonableness* (Philadelphia: Temple University Press, 1981).

Kaufman, Walter. *Without Guilt and Justice* (New York: Delta, 1973).

Kramer, Ronald C. "Corporate Criminality: The Development of an Idea," in Ellen Hochstedler, ed., *Corporations as Criminals* (Beverly Hills: Sage Publications, 1984): 13-37.

Kriesberg, Simeon M. "Decisionmaking Models and the Control of Corporate Crime," *Yale Law Journal* 85 (1976): 1091-129.

Leff, Arthur Allen. "Economic Analysis of Law: Some Realism about Nominalism," *Virginia Law Review* 60 (1974): 451-82.

Leibenstein, Harvey. "A Branch of Economics is Missing: Micro-Micro Theory," *Journal of Economic Literature* 17 (1979): 477-502.

Liebhafsky, H.H. "Price Theory as Jurisprudence: Law and Economics, Chicago Style," *Journal of Economic Issues* 10 (1976): 12-43.

McCloy, John J. *The Great Oil Spill: The Inside Report* (New York: Chelsea House Publishers, 1976).

McKean, Roland N. "Economics of Trust, Altruism, and Corporate Responsibility," in E. Phelps, ed., *Altruism, Morality, and Economic Theory* (New York: Russell Sage Foundation, 1975): 29-44.

Mintzberg, Henry. *The Structuring of Organizations* (Englewood Cliffs, N.J.: Prentice-Hall, Inc., 1979).

Murphy J. *Retribution, Justice, and Therapy* (Boston: D. Reidel Pub. Co., 1979).

Nader, Ralph and Mark Green, eds. *Corporate Power in America* (New York: Grossman, 1973).

Olins, Wally. *The Corporate Personality: An Inquiry into the Nature of Corporate Identity* (New York: Mayflower Books, 1981).

Olson, Mancur. *The Rise and Decline of Nations* (New Haven: Yale University Press, 1982).

Orland, Leonard. "Reflections on Corporate Crime: Law in Search of Theory and Scholarship," *American Criminal Law Review* 17 (1980): 501-20.

Parenti, Michael. *Power and the Powerless* (New York; St. Martin's Press, 1978).

Perlmutter, Amos. "The Tortuous Evolution of the Multinational Corporation," *Columbia Journal of World Business* 4 (January-February 1969): 9-18.

Posner, Richard. *Antitrust Law: An Economic Perspective* (Chicago: University of Chicago Press, 1976).

_____ . *Economic Analysis of Law,* 2d ed. (Boston: Little Brown and Company, 1977).

Schon, Donald A. *Beyond the Stable State* (New York: W.W. Norton & Company, Inc., 1973).

Schrager, Laura Shill and James F. Short, Jr. "Toward a Sociology of Organizational Crime," *Social Problems* 25 (1977): 407-19.

Shackle, G. L. S. *Epistemics and Economics: A Critique of Economic Doctrines* (Cambridge; Cambridge University Press, 1972).

_____ . *Imagination and the Nature of Choice* (Edinburgh: Edinburgh University Press, 1979).

Shapiro, Susan. *Wayward Capitalists* (New Haven: Yale University Press, 1984).

Simon, Herbert. "Theories of Decision Making in Economics and Behavioral Science," *American Economic Review* 49 (1959): 253-83.

Simon, J., C. Powers and J. Gunnemann. *The Ethical Investor: Universities and Corporate Responsibility* (New Haven: Yale University Press, 1972).

Solomon, Lewis D. "Restructuring the Board of Directors: Fond Hope – Faint Promise?" *Michigan Law Review* 76 (1978): 581-610.

Stewart, Richard B. "Regulation, Innovation, and Administrative Law: A Conceptual Framework," *California Law Review* 69 (1981): 1256-377.

Stone, Christopher D. *Where the Law Ends: The Social Control of Corporate Behavior* (New York: Harper, 1975).

_____ . "A Slap on the Wrist for the Kepone Mob," *Business and Society Review* 22 (1977): 4-11.

_____ . "The Place of Enterprise Liability in the Control of Corporate Conduct," *Yale Law Journal* 90 (1980): 1-77.

Stretton, Hugh. *The Political Sciences* (London: Routledge & Kegan Paul, 1969).

Sutherland, Edwin H. *White Collar Crime: The Uncut Version* (New Haven: Yale University Press, 1983).

United States, Justice Department. *United States Attorneys' Manual* (Washington, D.C.: Justice Department, 1980).

Vaughan, Diane. *Controlling Unlawful Organizational Behavior: Social Structure and Corporate Misconduct* (Chicago: University of Chicago Press, 1983).

Vorenberg, James. "Decent Restraint of Prosecutorial Power," *Harvard Law Review* 94 (1981): 1521-73.

Walsh, W. H. "Pride, Shame and Responsibility," *Philosophical Quarterly* 20 (1970): 1-13.

Williamson, Oliver E. *Markets and Hierarchies: Analysis and Antitrust Implications: A Study in the Economics of Internal Organization* (New York: Free Press, 1975).

Winter, Ralph K. *Government and the Corporation* (Washington, D.C.: American Enterprise Institute for Public Policy Research, 1978).

Wolff, Jacqueline C. "Voluntary Disclosure Programs," *Fordham Law Review* 47 (1979): 1057-82.

Yoder, Stephen A. "Criminal Sanctions for Corporate Illegality," *Journal of Criminal Law and Criminology* 69 (1978): 40-48.

INDEX